SONS OF CHINATOWN

ALSO BY WILLIAM WONG

Yellow Journalist: Dispatches from Asian America

Images of America: Oakland's Chinatown

Images of America: Angel Island (co-author)

SONS OF CHINATOWN

A Memoir Rooted in China and America

WILLIAM GEE WONG

TEMPLE UNIVERSITY PRESS
Philadelphia • Rome • Tokyo

TEMPLE UNIVERSITY PRESS
Philadelphia, Pennsylvania 19122
tupress.temple.edu

Copyright © 2024 by William Gee Wong
All rights reserved
Published 2024

Text design by Kate Nichols

Library of Congress Cataloging-in-Publication Data

Names: Wong, William Gee, 1941 July 7– author.
Title: Sons of Chinatown : a memoir rooted in China and America / William Gee Wong.
Description: Philadelphia : Temple University Press, 2024. | Includes index. | Summary: "In this memoir, pioneering journalist William Gee Wong chronicles a two-generation father-son story beginning from his father's experiences as an immigrant during the Chinese Exclusion Era through Wong's own journey from his beginnings in Oakland's Chinatown to acclaim on the national print stage"— Provided by publisher.
Identifiers: LCCN 2023025394 (print) | LCCN 2023025395 (ebook) | ISBN 9781439924877 (cloth) | ISBN 9781439924891 (pdf)
Subjects: LCSH: Wong, William Gee, 1941 July 7– | Gee, Ghee Gheng, 1896–1961. | Chinese American journalists—Biography. | Children of immigrants—Biography. | Chinese Americans—California—Oakland—Social conditions. | Immigrants—California—Oakland—Social conditions. | Chinatown (Oakland, Calif.)—Social conditions. | Taishan Shi (Guangdong Sheng, China)—Social conditions.
Classification: LCC PN4874.W69 A3 2024 (print) | LCC PN4874.W69 (ebook) | DDC 979.4/66004951073092 [B]—dc23/eng/20231031
LC record available at https://lccn.loc.gov/2023025394
LC ebook record available at https://lccn.loc.gov/2023025395

∞ The paper used in this publication meets the requirements of the American National Standard for Information Sciences—Permanence of Paper for Printed Library Materials, ANSI Z39.48-1992

Printed in the United States of America

9 8 7 6 5 4 3 2 1

For Pop, Mom,

and the Gee Wong clan,

especially Joyce,

Sam, Michelle, Milo, and Eva

CONTENTS

Author's Notes | ix

1 | Who Are We? | 1

2 | The Old Village | 10

3 | Paper Son | 19

4 | The New Village | 29

5 | Arranged Marriage | 41

6 | Chain Migration | 46

7 | The Lottery | 54

8 | Growing Family | 66

9 | Fateful Meeting | 72

10 | Shock and Awe | 78

11 | Finally, a Boy | 87

12 | The Great China | 93

13 | Moving Up | 105

14 | Assimilation | 117

15 | Chinese Lessons | 131

16 | Family Tensions | 137

17 | Bittersweet Summer | 143

18 | Wanderlust: The Peace Corps | 152

19 | Life Partner | 172

20 | Back to Chaos | 176

21 | Career Restart | 182

22 | Journalism Redux | 187

23 | Home, at Last | 192

24 | Roots Connection | 199

25 | Activism, Sort Of | 204

26 | Hometown Paper | 212

27 | Win Some, Lose Some | 228

28 | Lonely Downsize | 240

29 | Supportive Homefront | 249

Epilogue: Are We There Yet? | 252

Acknowledgments | 273

Glossary of Chinese Names | 277

Notes | 279

Index | 289

AUTHOR'S NOTES

CHINESE WORDS, ENGLISH SPELLING

Before we begin, I want to address the matter of spelling Chinese words in English. The subject is quite a thicket. No expert, I consulted Chinese American scholars who know about this language conundrum.

One complicating factor is that there is no one Chinese language. In written form, there are at least two, traditional and simplified. In spoken form, there are many dialects. Mandarin, the official government dialect, is the most ubiquitous. Another major dialect, Cantonese, is spoken in the southeastern province of Guangdong, where my parents were from. There is little, or no, understanding among the many spoken dialects in China and its vast diaspora. Chinese speakers must rely on written Chinese to communicate with one another. That also can be complicated because of the two principal written forms.

As for transcribing spoken Chinese dialects into English, the current system is called *pinyin*, phonetically spelling spoken Mandarin. In this book, I use pinyin and Cantonese with one major exception—phonetically spelling my father's dialect, which I am calling *Hoisan-wa*, Hoisan being the name of his county, and *wa* meaning "language." Phonetically, that is how I hear that dialect's sounds in English. *Hoisan* is usually spelled *Toisan* (Cantonese transliteration) or *Taishan* (Mandarin).

This issue is stubbornly personal for me, for I am honoring the integrity of Pop's dialect that is limited to his home area in Guangdong Province and to Chinatowns worldwide. In the grand sweep of China, Pop's area is small and obscure. But in the first hundred years of Chinese American history, most of the Chinese who came to America hailed from his region, also known as the Pearl River Delta or Greater Hong Kong.

This issue can get funkier. Consider how I spell *Hoisan*: It could be spelled *Hoy Saan*, or *Hoi Sahn*, and so on. See? My point is that for dialects like Pop's, there is no consensus standard English spelling.

In my Chinatown youth, we mixed *Hoisan-wa* and Cantonese because our Chinatown had people who spoke both. Toss in English words and phrases, and you have a spoken Chinglish trifecta.

When I went to Hong Kong for the first time in the mid-1960s, I spoke *Hoisan-wa* and got blank stares because Cantonese is dominant in Hong Kong. Much later, when visiting Shanghai and Beijing, I didn't even try to speak *Hoisan-wa*. No one whom I know of has ever said that the subject of Chinese language/dialects is easy to understand, speak, read, and comprehend.

AMERICAN COLOR PALETTE

Often, when we Americans refer to racial matters, we invoke a color or colors—white, Black, brown, and so forth. In this book, I occasionally do that, using *yellow* to broadly refer to people of Asian descent living in America. This use of that color is imperfect, for some Asians may object to *yellow* and prefer *brown*, or no color at all. Similarly, the use of other specific colors elicits disagreements and variations, as human skin tones range from relatively light to relatively dark. The use of specific colors is more political and metaphorical than it is precise.

I use *yellow* as a shorthand alternative to more usual labels, such as Chinese American, Korean American, Japanese American, or, more generically, Asian American. The colors *white* and *black* (now capitalized Black) are used most frequently to delineate America's long-standing racial issues. That invocation needs to be updated to reflect today's—and tomorrow's—America, a much more "colorful" populace thanks to the number of people from Latin America, Asia, the Middle East, and Africa.

SONS OF CHINATOWN

I

WHO ARE WE?

Wednesday, November 9, 1994, broke bright with sun, warmth, very little humidity, and no smog in Guangzhou, the southeastern Chinese city that used to be called Canton. Not nearly as well known in America as Beijing and Shanghai, Guangzhou was of central importance in the nineteenth century, it being practically the only Chinese city with which Europe and America had regular contact. It was essentially the entry point for international economic interests.

I wasn't there that day in 1994 to learn about the city's consequential history, nor were eight members of my extended family, all from California. For us, Guangzhou was the base camp for a much-anticipated "roots" visit to find the tiny rural village where our clan leader, my father, whom we called Pop, was from. I was fifty-three years old during my first visit to my ancestral homeland.[1] With me were three older sisters, two brothers-in-law, two nieces, a nephew, and the sister of one of the brothers-in-law. Since Pop's death thirty-three years earlier, in 1961, we siblings had often waxed nostalgic about him and wondered about his China life, of which most of us knew almost nothing.

I'm Pop's youngest child, his seventh, and his only son, giving me an elevated status over my sisters under the patriarchy of China and Chinatowns worldwide. Chinatown parents, like those in China and its diaspora, coveted sons, and many still do. Being his youngest, I spent the least amount of time with him, all in Oakland, California. I didn't know him all that well, in part because I was more into my own developing life in an America that was just beginning to allow the heretofore dammed-up narrow and scarce Chinatown tributaries into the roaring mostly white American mainstream. I was Chinese in a Chinatown sense, but when I began to wiggle my way into white America, I sometimes felt ashamed of Pop and Chinatown because they didn't meet the (white) American standards of status and achievement. Those standards, of course, were set by white men with impressive means and unchallenged power.

When some of my sisters started talking about a roots visit—or a homecoming for two, since they were born there—I was interested in a dispassionate, almost clinical way. It might have been my professional mind-set. During the 1980s and early 1990s, I was immersed in my newspaper journalism career, quite a psychological distance from my Chinatown youth, but, oddly, physically close since I was then working for the *Oakland Tribune*, whose iconic tower was an easy, six-block walk from Chinatown's commercial core, my childhood home. At the same time, I was in the middle of an internalized search for my racial-ethnic-cultural identities but wasn't ready to plunge into the deep waters of family-history research.

That fateful November morning, each of us had varying degrees of anticipation, anxiety, and hope regarding what we were about to experience. During our ride down to the village in a rented van, I enjoyed hearing my sisters reminisce about Pop and Mom. We were at once giddy and contemplative, loud and chatty, talking over one another at times, silent at others. I said little, as is my wont in the company of my often ebullient, talkative sisters.

I was most interested in observing Li Keng, Pop's second daughter, who was born in his village before she came with him to America as a seven-year-old. Now, she was in her late sixties and "going home" for the first time with her husband, Roger, who was from a village in the same vicinity as Pop's. What she might be thinking and feeling on this homecoming intrigued me more than whatever I was thinking and feeling. Another sister, Lai Wah, was also born in the village, but she was only two years old when she came to America, too young to remember much, if anything, of China.[2]

Our planning had significant gaps. We hadn't made prior arrangements with anyone in Pop's village, nor did we know exactly where it was. Brother-in-law Roger, whose *Hoisan-wa* and Cantonese were sharp since he came to America as a young adult, told the driver the name of the village and the market town near it. That hardly helped, as we got lost and stopped several times in the market town to ask for directions. One man idling his motor scooter said that he knew where the village, Goon Du Hahng,[3] was. With his two children, a boy about ten years old and a girl a few years younger, clinging on for dear life, he led us on an incredibly bumpy ride over dirt roads to a clearing in what seemed like the middle of nowhere. Here was your village, he said.

It was two o'clock in the afternoon. Li Keng was the first to stroll toward an opening in a bamboo thicket. Gripping my video camera, I trotted after her, sprinting ahead to record her reaction upon seeing the place of her childhood. At first, she didn't recognize anything, but once she cleared the bamboo, she saw a pond to her left. That's when she knew she was "home."

Our sudden and unexpected arrival caused a ruckus. People came out of their houses, wondering who these strangers were. We looked somewhat like them, dressed in more modern garb; some of us were softer and flabbier, and we spoke a foreign tongue. Were we look-alike aliens from another planet? A petite woman perhaps in her sixties and a slender, swarthy man maybe in his forties stepped forward, identifying themselves as mother and son. We exchanged rapid-fire bursts of *Hoisan-wa*. We told them that we were descendants of Gee Ghee Gheng, the name Pop was best known by in the village. They recognized it. We had hit paydirt, finding two people who knew of Pop. They told us that they were distant cousins, igniting even more excited chatter that was difficult to parse in the moment.

By now more relaxed, Li Keng showed us sights still familiar to her after all these years, such as the pond and the nearby banyan tree. Some of us stayed close to her; others wandered about aimlessly. I shot video, as did my sister Florence's husband, Ed, and son Brad, who also shot still photographs. Our newfound relatives told us to follow them along the only paved road next to the pond, past low-slung structures to an alleyway, and up some stone steps to a landing marked by a green plant of large, splayed leaves. We saw a small courtyard and there it was—Pop's house, which Li Keng immediately recognized.

Doorway of author's father's house in Hoisan (Toisan/Taishan) County, Guangdong Province, China, in 1994. (Author's Collection)

By now, I was in culture shock, steeped in an environment so different from what I was used to in America. Not that I hadn't seen poor villages before—I had seen plenty in the Philippines in the mid-1960s, when I was in the Peace Corps. Nonetheless, it was still a sensory quake to be in a place where residents dried rice pods and hung freshly harvested green-leaf vegetables on strings in front of their earthen houses, where three water buffalo rested in the pond, where some residents washed clothes by hand, where shirtless wiry and toned middle-aged men lugged long poles on which were tied bundles of rice stalks, two on each end. It was clear to me that Pop's village wasn't part of China's burgeoning middle class, a phenomenon that started to blossom in the late 1970s when farm people in remote villages like Pop's began to migrate to cities to get good-paying jobs rather than hunch over rice paddies all day long.

What I saw of Pop's house itself, a tiny mixed-clay and brick structure, deflated me. It was in shambles. There was no front door. Instead, a blue-and-white plastic sheet covered most of the door opening. One by one, we peeked in. Li Keng told us that it was the combined living room–dining room–kitchen. We saw a pile of dung, evidence a water buffalo now resided there. The other room, the bedroom, had no roof, and half of its sidewall was missing, with brush and weeds overgrowing where beds used to be. It was so small, I thought to myself, not much room for Pop, Mom, and my sisters Li Hong, Li Keng, and Lai Wah, all those decades ago in their childhoods.

We milled about for several more minutes, as our relatives and some village hangers-on peered at us in curiosity and wonder. I looked down at the dirt ground in the little courtyard and spotted a piece of what looked like a rice bowl and a bamboo sheath. I retrieved both as rustic souvenirs of no value other than sentimental, detritus from Pop's house. After about forty-five minutes—almost a blur—we were ready to leave because it was close to three o'clock, and we wanted to find Roger's house before sunset. We descended the stone steps toward the paved road. A few others and I turned right toward the banyan tree to spend a few minutes in the coolness of its shade. There, we saw three cute little girls, perhaps three to six years old, ogling us with giggles and active hand and body movements, almost tickling one another in unrestrained excitement at seeing these strangers in their midst. We smiled and tried to engage them in

Left to right: Flo Oy Wong, author, Felicia Wong (*background*), Li Keng Wong (*foreground*), and Lai Wah Chop Webster peering into the China village house of their father (or grandfather) in 1994. (Author's Collection)

whatever conversation we could and, of course, shot some photos. Their liveliness brought us fleeting joy. Now, it was time to find our way back to our van.

Instead of staying with the group, however, I trotted ahead to the alleyway that led to Pop's house. I bounded up the steps to get one last look at its dilapidated condition. I heard voices behind me. The nearest was that of nephew Brad, in his twenties, and, like me, a newspaper journalist. A few minutes later came his father, Ed, and his older sister Felicia.[4] We all had the same idea. Feeling that our visit was too brief, we needed to soak up as much as we could in this spot that began our China-Chinatown-America Gee-Wong clan.

Brad and I had similar thoughts: I'd go into Pop's house, and he'd take a video of me narrating what we had just seen and heard in less than an hour in the place where Pop had spent his youth and some of his adulthood. I didn't want to disturb the plastic covering at the front door opening, so I entered through the fallen-down bedroom wall to get to the all-purpose room. Standing outside, Brad aimed his video camera at me standing on the dirt floor. He started shooting. I started talking. A few phrases in, I lost it. I couldn't maintain the calm, professional composure of an objective news reporter describing the scene. Instead, I started a gentle sob.

I was overcome with emotions that I hadn't anticipated. Instead of being devoid of feelings, as journalistic observers are supposed to be, I was now flooded with thoughts about Pop and the unformed story of how he got to Oakland from this barebones space where I was standing. No longer dispassionate, I was now invested in the moment. I suddenly felt that I was on sacred ground. I felt that I, too, was "home," even though I had been born in Oakland and hadn't really felt "Chinese" in the sense that I "belonged" where Pop once lived. After a minute or two, I regained my composure, wiping away tears. Brad started shooting again, and I said a few more things, expressing myself in platitudes, unable to find the vocabulary to say how I really felt deep down beyond clichés. I didn't know how to express my feeling of spontaneous visceral connectedness. Looking around one last time, I muttered, "How lucky we are . . . ," reflecting on our materially more abundant life in Oakland than what I saw of Pop's half-standing house and rustic village itself.

We four outliers finally rejoined the rest of our departing family. As we piled into the van, our cousins thanked us for coming and asked us to return some day. In *Hoisan-wa*, they said that we *"you thlim"* (had heart), meaning that we were kind people to visit, or words to that effect. Without a word, I sat motionless as we drove away. My mind, however, was ricocheting with emotions. I couldn't calm them down even while others in our party fell into a loud silence, as though in shock at what we had just experienced.

That was the moment when big questions loomed large in my now overactive imagination: Who was Pop? Who was I, other than his seventh child and only son? How and why did our respective lives evolve so differently from our common beginning together in Oakland? What do our stories say about the broader American immigration story? My thoughts drifted to the concept of actual and metaphorical distances traveled by Pop and me—not just the 6,957 miles between Pop's village and Oakland, but the joint and then distinctive cultural journeys we each took, which I am still taking into my ninth decade of life.

Pop was a lightly educated farm-village immigrant teenager who didn't know a lick of English when he got to Oakland, with its cozy Chinatown across the bay from the much larger mother of all American Chinatowns in San Francisco. He eventually became a small business owner in Chinatown and his home village. He experienced hardships galore, but he also managed to grow a family in a land officially hostile to our kind. I am a relatively well-educated Chinatown-bred Chinese American middle-class professional, who has lost almost all of my first language, *Hoisan-wa*, and has used my second, English, to earn a living. Like everyone else, I've hit speed bumps, but nothing like Pop's violent, near-death experience, which pushed our family near poverty. This cultural distance was traversed in just one generation. *One.*

This tale might appear to be a familiar immigrant father–American son story, but the one I am about to tell, I believe, is from a rare vantage point, one that is not all that well known in the broad, deep, and complicated American cultural landscape. Pop came to America in the middle of the Chinese exclusion era, which spanned from 1882 to 1943. That period was when the policy of the United States was to ban almost all Chinese seeking entry and to bar ethnic Chinese already here from

U.S. citizenship. It was an overtly racist law and one of the first federal regulations of immigration. Pop had to engage in shady means to come here, first in 1912 and again in 1933, when he brought his family.

Growing up in Oakland, I knew nothing of the enormous barriers Pop had faced to be in America, nor did I care to learn about them. Chinatown's bamboo telegraph may have buzzed with audible whispers of the effects of the exclusion law, but I either didn't hear the gossip or chose not to listen. Shortly after he died, I began the sporadic, meandering search for who both of us were in the context of the Chinese exclusion law and America's contradictory expressions of love and hate for immigrants. The early arc of my life happened to coincide with the start of the Chinese exclusion law's repeal. That change enabled me to gradually integrate into the white-dominated American mainstream in ways that were impossible for Pop.

As singular as it is, our joint story is a vivid example proving that immigration works. This reality is so even though Asians were once officially pariahs and continue to be to many Americans well into the twenty-first century. It is also the case when America sends wildly confusing messages to non-Americans who want to come here to escape homeland misery. One message celebrates America as a land of unbridled opportunities for immigrants and refugees to achieve the American dream. An opposing message is more honest, truthful, and real. America has been and still is fraught with ugly racism, systemic and individualized, and violent white supremacy targeting many nonwhite newcomers and long-time residents and citizens.

Now, more than two decades into the twenty-first century, after impressive progress in the 1960s and 1970s for racial and ethnic minorities, women, people living with disabilities, and members of the LBGTQ communities, stubborn elements of the decreasing white majority resist that progress and wish for the days when white people, especially Christian men, were in a much larger majority and more fully in control. Our collective being, increasingly black, beige, brown, yellow, and shades in between, convulses sporadically and frighteningly from emotional, volatile, and sometimes violent arguments over who is an American, who should be an American, who belongs here, and who doesn't.

Pop and his Chinatown contemporaries managed to mostly duck and cover to survive the ignominy of racial hatred. Those were the days, from the mid-nineteenth through the mid-twentieth centuries, when the overwhelmingly white majority couldn't be bothered with immigrants of Asian descent living in America. Their descendants, like me, have learned to cope with more subtle forms of bigotry, while we have learned to love ourselves (maybe) after hating ourselves for not being white. Many of us of all different racial, ethnic, social, and cultural backgrounds still have distances to travel to coexist in peace and respect. For a time, some of us yellow folks could relax into the illusion that we were "accepted" or at least "tolerated," but the veritable tsunami of hatred of us during the coronavirus pandemic has given many of us renewed pause (and paranoia) about our place in America.

My sisters and I, our children, and our grandchildren are the beneficiaries of Pop's (and Mom's) struggles and sacrifices. Better positioned than Pop, we can't take for granted our freedom and liberties in a nation that is still trying to figure out what it means to be a democracy where everyone is treated with equality, justice, and dignity.

2

THE OLD VILLAGE

My epiphany on that November 1994 day in Pop's village was more of a slow simmer than an instant high-BTU wok blast of fire to explore identity questions and life-journey arcs. I had to address work and parenting responsibilities first. In February 2011, a few years after I had retired, just before my wife, Joyce, and I hosted our clan's annual Chinese New Year celebration, a thought popped up: The next year, 2012, would be the centennial of Pop's arrival in America. I wanted Pop's descendants—about forty of us—to know that. After we had feasted on our New Year's dinner, I announced Pop's American centennial year and expressed how important it was in our clan's history. I said that I wanted to tell Pop's immigration story to mark that date. My sisters knew the broad outlines, and a few of our children did, too, but most of the next two generations knew very little, if anything, since most of them weren't alive when Pop died. There was a murmur of excitement, which may have enticed me to assert that I would hand out Pop's story at our next Chinese New Year celebration in 2012. How silly of me.

I had nothing to hand out when the time came. I absorbed the shame, and from that point on, I took the first unsure steps in my search for who Pop was beyond what we knew of him through our lived experiences and individual and collective memories, enhanced by stories that Mom had told many times in the twelve years she was a widow. We didn't know basic things, such as Pop's true birthdate. Three of his children knew his China village since they were born there, but only one remembered it well. Most of us guessed why he came to America and under what circumstances and what he did in Oakland in his earliest years here. In other words, we were perhaps typical of any child—familiar with a parent but blissfully ignorant of the details of his or her earlier life prior to a common existence because we were, well, children, not historians, scholars, or activists . . . yet.

I needed more than our collective memories and family stories. I needed written materials that had information about Pop's village life and immigration process. Luckily, I had some. As the only son—a manifestation of old-school Chinese patriarchy—I inherited certain Pop-related papers, in Chinese and English. When I got the Chinese ones from Mom before she died, I paid no heed since my Chinese-language reading ability had all but vanished, and I was selfishly into my evolving American life. These documents included a Gee clan genealogy book[1] specific to Pop's lineage and two dozen pieces of flimsy, fraying rice paper. I also had some important English-language documents detailing his immigration process. Together, these papers paint a murky, contradictory, and incomplete picture of Pop's early years. The contrasts between the two are the essence of a Chinese immigrant man's dichotomous story during the exclusion era.

From oral and written sources, I was able to fill out some of Pop's earliest years, not a simple task, a consequence of the infamous Chinese exclusion law. He never said much, if anything, to us about his birthplace, parents, grandparents, childhood and early years, and his immigration experience. He kept silent, perhaps out of shame and to keep secrets that, if revealed, could jeopardize his iffy immigration status. He probably didn't think that it was important for his children to know about his past. Our parents and their Chinatown contemporaries often used the *Hoisan-wa* phrase *Imm gong wa* or its Cantonese equivalent, *Mo gong wa* ("Don't talk," "Can't talk").

What I learned in greater detail was that Pop had two origin stories—one that resided inside Chinatown, and the other for the outside world. The second of two sons, Pop was born in the mid-1890s in the village some of us descendants visited in 1994. The village name then was Jow Toon Goon Du Hahng.[2]

His exact date of birth is uncertain. I've seen three. One is November 15, 1894, a conversion from the lunar calendar date in his genealogy book. A second is May 26, 1896, found on his application for admission into the United States in 1912. This date is also a conversion from the Chinese calendar at that time. A third is April 14, 1895, which Pop wrote on a U.S. Selective Service Registration Card (military draft) in 1942 in Oakland. On his Oakland gravestone, Mom chose the 1896 date, most likely to preserve information he had given on his immigration application so as not to raise suspicions about his immigration history. Her choice says something significant about the internalized paranoia of Chinese immigrants during the exclusion period.

His surname was Gee.[3] He had several given names, a common practice for Chinese males of his day. At birth, his given name was Bing Du. One grown-up given name was Ghee Gheng, the one we cited to our distant cousins during our 1994 visit. His immigration name was Gee Seow Hong. Later, he wrote it as Seow Hong Gee, following the American practice of placing the surname last. Gee Foo Sam was another name on later immigration papers. To English-only speakers in Oakland, he was Sam Gee, the name used in Oakland telephone directories of the 1930s and 1940s (Gee, Sam, in phone directory–style).

The Chinese documents paint a bare outline of who his parents and other elders were. One is an orange sheet of paper, measuring thirteen inches wide by sixteen inches high and speckled with tiny black dabs. This paper lists his grandfather, grandmother, father, mother, older brother, sister-in-law, and his first wife. He commissioned its creation out of respect for his elders and their spouses. In its dark-brown wooden frame, Pop treated that single sheet as an altar-shrine in our Oakland homes. I also use it in that manner during our Chinese New Year clan dinners, when we light incense and offer food and drink out of respect. According to this document, Pop's paternal grandfather was Gee Yee Lo, his father was Gee Cheng Woon, and his older brother was Gee Bing Chew. The document lists only the surnames of the wives of each of these men, along with the word *Shee*.[4]

The fraying rice-paper Chinese documents are official local government records, personal promissory notes, other personal notes, and one investment stock (a local telephone company). They date from 1889 to 1943. They don't tell anything about what Pop's father and grandfather

Altar-shrine honoring author's deceased elders, as displayed during annual Chinese New Year celebrations. (Author's Collection)

did. There is a hint of the economic status of Pop's family in China, not dirt poor or obscenely rich, apparently wealthy enough to underwrite Pop's initial journey to America. The official documents are land deeds. The personal promissory notes tell of Pop's elders either borrowing or lending money and selling and buying parcels of land. The overall sense from these documents is that Pop's elders had resources, such as land.

Having visited the place twice, I can't believe that whatever assets my ancestors had were extraordinary.

What the village looked like in Pop's youth is impossible to know, since his children have never seen any photos, if indeed there were any, which I doubt. During our 1994 visit, Li Keng told us what she remembered from when she was a child. She said that it hadn't changed all that much, except for black-and-white TV sets in some houses—the small mud-clay abodes, perhaps thirty in all, packed into rows, one paved road, the pond, and banyan tree, all isolated from similar villages nearby and no commercial activity. Surrounding the village were rice fields, resplendently bright green stalks amid calm ponds, middle-aged and elderly men and women knee-deep in water, stooped over, tending to their lifeblood, tranquil in ways that cities can only dream of.

My feelings about the place were decidedly jumbled. Contrasting my emotionally connected moment inside his rundown house in 1994 was a disconnection. This place was Pop's, not mine. Oakland, California, America, was mine. During that visit, my California family provided me comfort in a place where I felt disoriented. That offbeat feeling returned when I went to Pop's village again twenty years later, in November 2014, with my thirty-something son Sam. I came away from that earlier visit discombobulated and reluctant to go again, but I knew that it was necessary to find out more about Pop's life there to enrich the story I'm telling now.

This second time, the village had far fewer people. I saw no children, only a handful of adults, and a few motor scooters; the only cars were those that drove us there and one belonging to officials from the county seat who had joined me, my son, and our translator. Through my aging eyes, the place looked even more desolate. The visit before, children gave the village a liveliness that was absent this time. In other words, on both visits twenty years apart, Pop's village was miniscule and simple with almost no modern resources. When Pop was there in his youth and periodically in his young adulthood, it was surely livelier, with more people and pets.

The dilapidated house we saw in 1994 was a duplex. Pop shared it with another family, according to Li Keng. Its footprint was only a few hundred square feet. This home was where Pop and his first wife raised their daughter, Li Hong. After his wife died, Pop married Mom and had two daughters, Li Keng and Lai Wah. The time span for these events was most of the 1920s and the early 1930s, when Pop split time between the village and Oakland.

The two families sharing the duplex worked the rice and vegetable fields but didn't socialize together. Pop's side had the two rooms we saw in 1994. Mom cooked at a corner stove, using twigs gathered by a maid-helper. The bedroom had three beds, two of which were boards on sawhorses, for up to six people (Pop, Mom, two daughters, a mother-in-law, and the maid-helper; Li Hong slept at a cousin's house but spent her days at Pop's house). The maid-helper tended to mundane household duties, such as washing the family's laundry in the village pond and hanging it to dry in the atrium. She bathed baby Lai Wah in a galvanized tub in the bedroom. Using wet towels, the rest of the family took "sponge" baths.

Because Pop regularly sent money home after he arrived in America, Mom didn't have to worry much about living expenses or about working too hard in the fields. In effect, she enjoyed an elevated status because she was married to a man who was in America, or *Ghim Saan* in *Hoisan-wa*, meaning "gold mountain." She was able to buy what food she didn't grow, such as pork and chicken. Under Mom's supervision, the maid-helper also cooked simple meals—breakfast, lunch, and dinner of "rice, rice, and rice," Li Keng said. "Usually, we had one stir-fry vegetable mixed with a few pieces of *lop cheng* (sausage). Sometimes, a meat vendor sold fresh pork." Mom was always around inside the house, Li Keng added. Not having to work in the fields as much as other village women, she took care of Lai Wah with the help of the maid, Li Keng added. For leisure, the family "sometimes sat outside of the entry door after the evening meal because it was cooler. When the sun went down, we came in and went to bed," Li Keng said.[5] Life in Goon Du Hahng was uncomplicated.

Who was this maid-helper? One Chinese document reveals who she was and how she became part of our family in Goon Du Hahng. According to a translation[6] of that document dated 1930, a married couple, Yin Gim and his wife, surnamed Gee, were from another Hoisan village. They had five children, all girls. "There is no money," the document says, to raise their fifth daughter, who was twelve years old. "The husband and wife discussed, and they want to give this fifth daughter . . . for someone else to raise."

They first asked some relatives to take her but were rejected. They asked a go-between, who went to Pop, who "bought her to be part of his household," the document says. "At the price of 250 yuan, the mother and father gave their daughter to Gee Ghee Gheng's household to raise. The money went to the husband and wife," the document continues, with this interesting disclaimer: "Everything is in order, this was not a shady dealing, nor was the girl kidnapped."

By purchasing her, Pop assumed great responsibility. "When the girl grows up, she will be Gee Ghee Gheng's responsibility. When she marries, her dowry will go to Gee Ghee Gheng," the document continues. "Even if she runs away and finds the Yin family home, she will still have to be returned to Gee Ghee Gheng. If she is kidnapped, the two families will have to go look for her together."

When Pop brought Mom and his three girls to Oakland in 1933, Mom married this fifteen-year-old girl off just before their departure. "The maid wanted to come with us. No way Pop could have done that," Li Keng said. "We never heard from her again. I really liked her. She was more of a mother to us three girls than Mom was."

China was in sad shape during Pop's childhood. The country's woes began earlier than that. In the eighteenth century, China, an imperial state, had some contact with America, a new democracy, through commercial shipping with wealthy U.S. merchants, mainly in New England. But it wasn't until the mid-nineteenth century that China really opened—against its will—to the West. It took an embarrassing defeat to Great Britain in the Opium War in the 1840s to shake China up. China lost Hong Kong, a desolate island at the time, to the British and had to give other European nations and the United States access to several other port cities.

The first and most important port city was Canton, now called Guangzhou, just north of Hong Kong, the place where members of my family and I gathered to start our 1994 visit. This region is known as the Pearl River Delta. More European and American ships entered China through Canton, resulting in more trade, commerce, business, and the need for workers, all relatively good news for nearby villages, such as in

Pop's Hoisan County. This Western incursion chipped away at China's sovereignty, beginning a century of humiliation for China until Mao Zedong's Communist revolution in 1949.

China's opening brought news from America and Europe more readily to the Pearl River Delta Chinese than to those in more distant places, such as Beijing (Peking then) and Shanghai. The typical Pearl River Delta villager wasn't so much interested in "big" news, like geopolitics or economics. They liked "small" news, like jobs and merchant opportunities. The discovery of gold in California in 1848 caught the attention of Pearl River Delta people. Merchant ships carried this news to Canton and Hong Kong (and around the world). Chinese from this region were among the most enthusiastic and desperate fortune seekers to join the famous Gold Rush.

Such was the start of Chinese America. Hoisan was one of eight Guangdong Province counties, out of more than ninety at the time, that sent almost all migrants to America from the 1849 Gold Rush through World War II.[7] In effect, the story of the first hundred years of Chinese America is almost exclusively the story of the people from these eight counties.[8] Why these eight counties, Hoisan being the most prominent? During this period, the largest plurality or, in some years, most Chinese migrants to America came from Hoisan.[9] It was a Chinese version of the "perfect storm"—the push of internal conditions and the pull of external forces. The internal conditions were overpopulation on not enough cultivatable land, violent interethnic conflicts, populist rebellions against a dying Qing dynasty, and natural disasters.[10] External forces were dreams of finding fortunes elsewhere and demand for cheap labor because of the industrialization boom abroad.

This backdrop was a perfect setup for Pop's biggest adventure of his young life. The exclusion law didn't dissuade his elders from sending him to America. Pop was a smart, obedient, and hard-working second son. Whether his parents wanted him to continue school is hard to know. They most likely wanted their second son to help them financially by finding a "fortune" in "gold mountain." Stories about other Pearl River Delta boys and men going to America to find fortunes no doubt inspired them.

Through a nearby store, Pop's father coordinated with an Oakland Chinatown herbalist shop owned by a Gee from the same region of

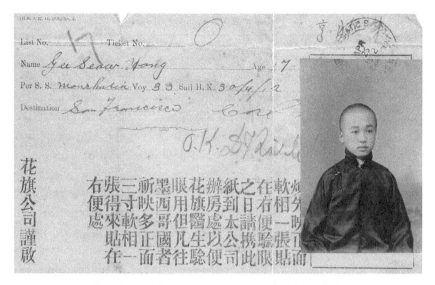

Official 1912 departure document of author's father.
(Author's Collection)

China. These stores were one-stop, all-purpose depots for immigration where one could buy transit tickets and travel goods, obtain documentation, and recruit laborers for work overseas.[11] On or about April 28, 1912, Pop and his father began the journey of his lifetime. The two likely walked, maybe an hour or more, to Hoisan City (Taicheng) to catch a ferry to Hong Kong, where the ocean liner SS *Manchuria* of the Pacific Mail Steamship Company was docked.

3

PAPER SON

Holding steerage ticket number 178, Pop boarded the *Manchuria*, a huge steel ship, on Tuesday, April 30, 1912. He was slight of build, scrawny even, barely taller than five feet. His black hair was cut short. Bushy eyebrows topped roundish brown eyes, which had a piercing quality to them. His longish nose and full lips made for a handsome face. He was in good shape—slender muscular arms and body—from working in the rice fields and hiking in the hills above the village. He wore a loose, high-collar black cotton tunic with toggles as buttons on the right shoulder, a white cotton collarless shirt underneath, plain black cotton trousers, and sturdy black slip-on fabric-covered shoes.

His parents told him what to expect on this journey, or as much as they could glean from stories they had heard from previous sojourners and what they had read in the local gazettes. The trip would take about a month. Space would be tight. He might get seasick. They also told him not to worry because Gees from Hoisan who had settled in Oakland would help him adjust. He studied a coaching book that detailed a story of his family and village life that wasn't exactly accurate. He needed to learn this partially made-up story to get around the restrictions of the Chinese exclusion law.

At the Hong Kong pier were scores of males, some about his age, others his father's age, some of them married. He was one of thirty-nine men

Bird's-eye view, looking south, of the Angel Island Immigration Station, in the foreground, around 1927. (Courtesy of the California Department of Parks and Recreation photographic archives. © 2023 California State Parks.)

and boys listed on one page of the *Manchuria*'s passenger list on that April 1912 departure.[1] Ten were teenagers, including Pop. Four were in their twenties; seven, their thirties; thirteen, their forties; and five, their fifties.

We don't know how much Pop's trip cost. When the Pacific Mail Steamship Company began its Hong Kong–San Francisco journey in 1867, steerage-class tickets, the cheapest, cost about $50. By 1912, the fee was surely higher. From Hong Kong, the *Manchuria* stopped in Shanghai on May 3, 1912; Nagasaki, Japan, on May 6; Kobe, Japan, on May 8; and Yokohama, Japan, on May 11. It docked in Honolulu, Hawaii, on May 21. Six days later, on May 27, it reached San Francisco, after a journey of twenty-seven days.[2]

Before he could get to Oakland, however, Pop had to go to the Angel Island Immigration Station in San Francisco Bay to get the U.S. government's approval to legally enter the country. That immigration station's main role was to enforce the Chinese Exclusion Act, a law that I knew nothing about during my Chinatown youth. We heard, however, the *Hoisan-wa* phrase *Hoo Gee Doy*, literally meaning "get paper boy/son," to describe someone who bought a paper entry slot to get into America under false circumstances to get around the exclusion law's restrictions. Years after Pop died, I began learning about the exclusion law and its ramifications, not from any classroom but from reading about it on my own and from scholars and activists.

Among the things I learned was the pervasiveness of white racism against people like Pop. When there weren't any Chinese or very few in America yet, many white Americans thought lowly of China and its people. Late-eighteenth-century sea traders, missionaries, and diplomats shaped those negative American perceptions. Historian Stuart Creighton Miller sums up well how these three groups of Americans perceived Chinese:

> The majority of Americans who journeyed to China before 1840 regarded the Chinese as ridiculously clad, superstitious ridden, dishonest, crafty, cruel, and marginal members of the human race who lacked courage, intelligence, skill, and the will to do anything about the oppressive despotism under which they lived or the stagnating social conditions that surrounded them.[3]

Once Chinese started coming to America in small but significant numbers during the California Gold Rush, face-to-face white racism and violence against Chinese newcomers began in earnest. Anti-Chinese actions heated up after completion in 1869 of the transcontinental railroad, which Chinese workers helped build. Too many workers competed for too few jobs, and the more powerful and organized white workers formed the Workingmen's Party in San Francisco in the 1870s with the slogan "The Chinese Must Go." That rallying cry landed in Washington, D.C., where an overwhelmingly white-male Congress (there were two Black representatives) passed the Chinese Exclusion Act in 1882.

The idea and reality of Chinese people wanting to migrate to America, whether temporarily or for good, greatly upset America's all-white political leadership in the final third of the nineteenth century. The exclusion act was but one manifestation of the prevailing anti-Chinese sentiments in America at that time. The 1882 act was preceded by the Page Act of 1875, the federal government's first law to exert control over immigration. Anti-Chinese Californians lobbied "to exclude Asian contract labor and women (mostly Chinese) suspected of entering the country for 'lewd or immoral purposes.'"[4] It was the first federal immigration regulation and set the stage for excluding most Chinese immigrants.

Until then, America had a pretty open-door immigration policy. The two major anti-Chinese pieces of immigration legislation were enacted even though few ethnic Chinese people lived in America. Chinese were less than 5 percent of total immigration to the United States in the 1870s. In the 1880 U.S. Census, Chinese accounted for only two-tenths of 1 percent of the U.S. population.[5]

Why did Congress pass such a blatantly racist law against such an infinitesimally small group of people? The congressional debates in the late nineteenth and early twentieth centuries over whether to exclude most Chinese immigrants were liberally littered with shamelessly open expressions of anti-Chinese hatred and fear. Two broad themes emerged from these debates: One was that Chinese were inferior, and the other was that Chinese were superior. Whatever the case, white Americans didn't want Chinese people in America.

Democratic senator George Turner of Washington State, who visited San Francisco's Chinatown in 1902, testified: "They burrowed in the ground like rats. They roosted in the air like crows. They were packed in every available space like sardines. . . . I should say that there were 500 Chinamen in this one building. The stench was something not to be forgotten. . . . The general impression left on one's mind is that of a seething, reeking, heaving mass of vermin, intermixed and intertwined, each striving with all its might to satisfy some animal need or craving, and having nothing in common with anything except an ugly, debased, and stunted human form."[6]

Massachusetts Republican senator Henry Cabot Lodge expressed the "superior" stereotype of the Chinese in 1902. Saying that they were not "a lot of simple, guileless savages," Lodge praised Chinese greatness in art, poetry, and literature. But he didn't like the superior attitude of the "highly educated and very astute" Chinese, referring to the leadership class, not the uneducated rural class seeking entry to America. "They are children of a civilization older, and they think, mightier than ours," he said. He believed that arriving Chinese held "contempt" for America.[7]

White supremacy was another popular debate theme—the "Caucasian race" was superior to the Chinese, even though Chinese civilization dated back more than four millennia, compared with America's then-paltry one century. Several federal lawmakers said that the founding fathers had envisioned only "Caucasians" as U.S. citizens. Indiana Republican senator Charles Fairbanks said during a 1902 debate, "I shall be glad to see the Chinese labor population diminish, and their places taken by Germans, by Dutch, by English, by Scandinavians, by other nationalities from whose blood we have sprung and have become the most puissant people on the face of the globe."[8]

Economic competition between politically weak Chinese and politically stronger white workers, as well as political exploitation—white lawmakers trashing Chinese workers for votes—was intricately interwoven into the racial narratives that drove Congress to exclude Chinese laborers for more than sixty years. Chinese organizations in America—principally, the Chinese Consulate and the Chinese Six Companies (Chinatown's city hall)—turned to U.S. federal courts to combat the discriminatory laws, but they had no success in overturning them.

The Chinese in America engaged inventive schemes to circumvent the exclusion law. For example, many Chinese claimed during deportation proceedings that they had been born in the United States. Such claims rose sharply after the exclusion law was enacted, and after the 1906 San Francisco earthquake and fires destroyed birth records at city hall. In the nineteenth and twentieth centuries, Chinatown leaders established overlapping networks of clan, regional, fraternal, and business organizations. These networks joined professional smugglers, corrupt white American officials, and Chinese government officials to devise ways to get around the law or carried out various extralegal strategies for legal entry. The intent was to outsmart the new U.S. immigration bureaucracy. The Chinese in America felt justified in these extralegal means because the exclusion law was unjust and discriminatory. These strategies were the Chinatown version of civil disobedience.

The most prominent defensive strategy was the so-called paper-son scheme alluded to earlier. This is how it worked: Some Chinese in America prior to the exclusion law claimed that they had been born in, say, San Francisco. When young, they had traveled to China, staying for years, during which time the exclusion law had been enacted. When these men returned to America, they asserted their American birthright, which would make them eligible for legal entry. Skeptical immigration

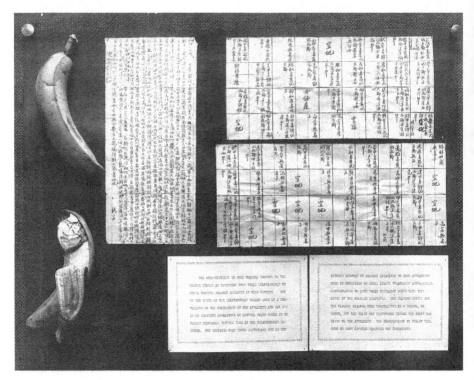

Typical "coaching" document, hidden in a banana, used by Chinese immigrants to prepare for interrogations at the Angel Island Immigration Station. (Courtesy of the National Archives and Records Administration.)

officials challenged these claims, blocking reentries, which precipitated many federal court cases. Surprisingly, federal judges ruled in favor of most reentering Chinese.[9]

On reentry, they told authorities that while in China, they had had children, mostly boys, a false or exaggerated claim in many cases. Hence, the paper-son scheme became fully formed. These "sons" represented available slots to sell to unrelated Chinese for future immigration. On the application for entry into America, the migrant who had bought such a slot claimed to be a "son (or in rarer cases, daughter) of a native," thus eligible for legal entry. The going rate in the 1930s was $100 per year of age of the boy or man (or girl or woman) using the slot.[10]

The paper-son scheme gave rise to partially false family and village histories that linked the paper son and his paper sponsor/father in ways that had to pass the scrutiny of skeptical immigration inspectors. Immigration-related companies or stores on both sides of the Pacific produced and distributed "coaching" books that helped the paper father and son tell the same family and village stories during immigration interrogations. These books were unique to each individual and his or her paper relatives. The detailed stories in those books discussed family history, village life, and even personal habits. Those using coaching books knew to destroy them before they landed in America. Chinese American scholars and U.S. immigration officials estimate that up to 90 percent of Chinese applicants for immigration during the exclusion era were most likely paper sons or daughters.[11]

Distributing these books in San Francisco and Angel Island required stealth and cunning. Friends, relatives, or corrupt immigration staff passed coaching books, among other things, through windows of the San Francisco wharf detention shed before the Angel Island station was operational. On Angel Island, notes were written on U.S. quarters and nickels. Peanut shells hid scraps of paper. Orange peels were wrapped around crumpled up pieces of paper; the peels were glued back to resemble an uneaten orange. Chinese pork buns were hollowed out to hold coaching papers. Couriers were visitors, Angel Island kitchen workers, many of them Chinese, and corrupt immigration guards.[12]

The exclusion law reduced, but didn't eliminate, a Chinese presence in America, which was tiny to begin with. In 1890, the Chinese percentage of the U.S. population was 0.0021. It dropped to 0.0005 in 1940. In 1880, Chinese made up almost 9 percent of California, the state with the most Chinese. By 1900, people like Pop and me were only 3 percent.[13] When considering the near invisibility of Chinese nationally, one wonders why such official animus toward Chinese people existed. The Chinese desire to come to America was inexorable, in part because of deep political and social instability in China in the late nineteenth and first half of the twentieth centuries. At the same time, the U.S. industrial revolution issued clarion calls for labor, whether domestic or foreign. Cantonese Chinese like Pop were eager to answer.

Starting in 1910, federal authorities switched enforcement of the exclusion law to the Angel Island Immigration Station. Angel Island, the largest outcropping in San Francisco Bay, was initially occupied by the Coast Miwok American Indians for at least a thousand years. The island was named by Spanish explorers in 1775. The Spanish, French, Russians, and British used Angel Island as a base in the late eighteenth through the early nineteenth centuries. From 1821 on, Mexico controlled the island but then lost it to America after a war. The U.S. made it a military base.[14] The first enforcement site, a San Francisco wharf shed, had problems with size, security, and sanitary conditions. In 1904, Congress appropriated $250,000 to build a dedicated immigration facility in San Francisco. New York's Ellis Island immigration station was the model, so Angel Island was a logical choice because it was relatively inaccessible to relatives and friends of detainees, and federal officials wanted detainees kept far away from the general population over health fears.

The immigration station on the northeast side of Angel Island officially opened on January 21, 1910. The campus had an administration building, barracks, a hospital, and, later, employee cottages. The facility housed between three hundred and four hundred men and boys and one hundred women and girls. Sleeping arrangements were quite tight. Beds for "Orientals" were three stacked metal bunks attached to poles in rows. There was no privacy and individual space.[15] Chinese detainees considered it a prison. Windows had iron bars. Barbed-wire fences surrounded the campus. Guards monitored and controlled movement of detainees. Many expressed their displeasure by scratching poems and feelings on the wooden walls. These writings, some in elegant Chinese calligraphy, were covered up by layers of paint, but were discovered by state park ranger Alexander Weiss in 1970 amid plans to tear down the station. Chinese American and Asian American activists mounted a successful campaign to preserve the station.

The Angel Island Immigration Station has frequently been called the "Ellis Island of the West," a misnomer because their core missions differed. Ellis was essentially a processing center to welcome new immigrants, primarily from Europe, but also others who crossed the Atlantic Ocean. Angel enforced the laws that excluded Chinese and later other Asian immigrants crossing the Pacific Ocean.[16] Ellis processed approximately twelve million immigrants from 1892 to 1954,[17] compared with Angel's three hundred thousand immigrants,[18] some one hundred seventy-five thousand of whom were Chinese.[19]

About 80 percent of Ellis immigrants were approved on the same day they arrived. Those detained, for legal or medical reasons, stayed only one night, in most cases. By contrast, some 60 percent of Angel immigrants were confined for an average of three days. Many Chinese detainees spent months and, in one case, one month shy of two years.[20] Even Chinese in the so-called exempt categories—merchants, students, travelers, and diplomats—underwent stiff scrutiny at Angel Island. Two non-Chinese witnesses generally had to testify on behalf of these exempted Chinese before they got in.

Pop claimed a status of "son of a native," one of the categories eligible for legal entry.[21] Pop's sponsor was Gee Bing Fong, his "father" on paper. Bing Fong said that he had been born in San Francisco in 1870—hence, his "native" status—and had gone to China with his parents in 1876. In 1890, he returned, but American officials, doubting that he was a U.S. citizen, blocked his reentry. By then, the Chinese Exclusion Act was in effect. Helped by a white lawyer, his case was adjudicated in U.S. District Court in San Francisco, and he won.[22] That victory cleared the way for the legal entry of his "children" as sons or daughter of a native. Bing Fong listed seven children born in China, six boys and one girl. Pop was listed as the second son, the slot his parents apparently bought.

Pop's Angel Island process spanned almost three weeks. The climax was the interrogations of him and two witnesses: Gee Bing Fong, his paper father, and Gee Seow King, his paper older brother. Those interrogations would determine his fate. On June 10, 1912, two weeks after Pop landed, authorities called him and his two witnesses, who ferried over from San Francisco. The interrogations focused on obscure details—for instance, of a village layout or a neighbor's family, such as who lived in the second house of the fourth row, and how many houses were in the third row? The government wanted to catch any discrepancies in the respective stories told by each person questioned. If their stories didn't match overwhelmingly, that suggested possible deception, which could lead to deportation.

C. E. Ebey, the chief interrogator, reported his findings to his superiors. "The testimony throughout is exceptionally consistent," with only one "discrepancy," which was Pop and Bing Fong identifying different families living in the first house, third row. The discrepancy, Ebey wrote, was "caused by a lapse of memory," whereas Bing Fong and Seow King's responses compared "favorably with that given at previous hearings." Ebey concluded that Pop "should be landed." Ebey's superiors concurred.

On June 15, 1912, Pop was admitted into the United States as a "son of a native."

Which documents tell the true story of Pop's early China years and immigration to America? Recall that the Chinese-language documents identify Pop as the youngest of two sons and his father as Gee Cheng Woon. The English-language documents identify Pop's father as Gee Bing Fong and Pop as the second son of six boys and one girl. (More later on who that girl was.) The Chinese documents are real, the English ones only partially so.

4

THE NEW VILLAGE

After departing the immigration station, Pop rode a Southern Pacific ferryboat to San Francisco, where a Gee clan member from Oakland greeted him at the pier. They took another ferryboat to Oakland. Finally, they rode the Southern Pacific Red Train, a local line, to Chinatown, the fifth of twenty-seven stops. The Gee clan member's help was part of the culture of the Cantonese networks established generations earlier. The highest network values were family obligations and clan solidarity. Clans were tight in the Pearl River Delta region of China. The honor and welfare of the clan were more important than individual happiness and fulfillment, whether in China or the diaspora. Pop's destination was the Sang Fat Chong Company on Webster Street, a two-block walk from the Broadway exit.

Pop arrived in Oakland at a fortuitous time, six years after the earthquake that had devastated San Francisco and, less so, Oakland and surrounding communities, and sixty years after it had become a city in 1852. Chinese were among Oakland's earliest residents. He had heard more about San Francisco than Oakland. San Francisco was called, in his dialect, *Aye Fow*, which means "big or first city," the place where immigrants landed. All he knew about Oakland[1] was that it would be his home for the foreseeable future.

Filled with immigrants and even American-born with China roots, Oakland's small Chinatown was beginning a growth spurt. In the decades following the 1906 earthquake, the number of families increased, thanks to some San Francisco Chinese staying after they had temporarily relocated to Oakland and to paper-son schemes. Oakland's Chinatown, a soft landing for Pop, was a socially segregated neighborhood about a half mile from city hall and the city's white-dominated commercial center. This area was where he began fulfilling some of the promise his elders had hoped for. The herbalist shop where Pop was to work and live was operated by Gee Ghim Gong, a Hoisan native like Pop and a distant relative, who taught Pop the basics of herbal medicine as well as how to use a hand scale to weigh herbal ingredients and an abacus to calculate prices.

Decades later, whenever one of us children felt a sore throat or a fever coming on, Pop wrote out prescriptions and sent us to the herbalist up the street to get them filled out.[2] Mom brewed the herbs into an acrid smelling bitter-tasting tea. We were so happy a packet of raisins accompanied the herbal package to offset the bitterness. That awful-tasting brew did its trick, as our pains and minor ailments went away. Yet for all the learning and camaraderie he felt at Sang Fat Chong, Pop didn't find a calling in herbal medicine, although it gave him a good start in Oakland.

In addition to work, Pop enrolled at Lincoln School, which started in 1865 when it had only two rooms. It has been the go-to school for Chinatown kids for many generations. There were hardly any Chinese school-age children in Oakland's earliest days. Those who were around were excluded from public schools. In the late 1870s, some Chinese children enrolled at Lincoln. In 1906, when a bigger school was built, more Chinese students enrolled.

We know almost nothing about Pop's six years there other than that was where he learned English. Pop started in the autumn of 1912 and graduated in 1918. His schoolmates were a mix of white European descendants and Asian immigrant children, mostly Chinese, with some Japanese, Filipinos, and Koreans. There were virtually no Latino or African American students. The staff was white, with mostly women teachers.

School photos provide a few superficial clues about his Lincoln years.[3] For the most part, Pop was in a class of other Chinese students of varying ages, he appearing to be one of the oldest. With more boys than girls,

Seow Hong Gee, Class of 1918: Top Row, 4th from the left
Father of Li Keng, Li Hong, Lai Wah, Nellie, Leslie, Florence, and William

Author's father (*top row, fourth from left*) in his elementary school class in Oakland, California. (Darlene Joe Lee and Janet Chan Lem, *Memories of Growing Up in Oakland, California, Lincoln School Alumni* [self-published, 2011], 47.)

his entering-year class had forty-eight students. There were two more all-Chinese/Asian classes in 1912. These classes were how the school dealt with Chinese immigrant children who didn't know English. In his graduating eighth-grade class in 1918, Pop was a racial minority; there were twelve Chinese boys and girls (and perhaps one Filipino American girl) in a group of about fifty-three students. The majority were white. The age range was from young teens to the twenties, including Pop, who was approximately twenty-three years old.

Learning English wasn't easy for Pop, a late teenager when he started the new language. He gradually learned to speak it with an accent and used it in his later business life, but *Hoisan-wa* and Cantonese were his default spoken languages. He learned how to read English, a skill he used to scan local English-language newspapers, although his preference remained reading Chinese newspapers.

Lincoln School's role in Americanizing Chinatown kids can't be overstated. Lincoln has a history of offering native and immigrant students numerous opportunities to be part of an American community. One clue as to how Lincoln socialized Chinese immigrant students is found in a 1931 school newsletter, which provides a glimpse of the school's activities that complemented classroom learning.[4] The nonacademic goings-on were mundane and quite creative. Most appear to have been generic child development activities, for American-born and immigrant children alike. Principal R. W. Snyder wrote, "We believe that boys and girls learn good citizenship by participation in government of the school. The Lincoln School pupils are given an opportunity for participating citizenship. Not only are the lessons they learn valuable to them, but the services they give are invaluable to the school."

Dated October 10, 1931, the newsletter is called "Du-U-No." It lists twenty-eight classrooms. Only one teacher was of Chinese descent, Effie Bailey Chew, a daughter of the Reverend Ng Poon Chew, a prominent San Francisco and Oakland Chinatown Presbyterian minister, Chinese newspaper publisher, public speaker (in English), and advocate for the Chinese American community. Effie Chew taught kindergarten and first grade from 1918 to the 1940s and was well regarded by students, staff, and community.

Lincoln had many clubs and activities, from leadership to arranging seating at assemblies, from office duties to hall monitoring. Chinese and Asian-named students are liberally mentioned in most activities. Among the little news items and student-written observations is a "Report from Room 14" by Lim Seung, an eighth grader: "There are several classes under the direction of Miss Booker for Oriental Boys and Girls. Most of their periods are spent in English and Social Studies. The English is the most important thing for them becuase [sic] when we came from other countries we did not understand much about English. So English is hard for us and is important for us to learn."

In 1924, William Greenwell, a Lincoln principal, wrote to the Survey of Race Relations, "I have never worked with a group of foreigners whom I would prefer to the Chinese." He called them "among our very best students" and said that they did the "best work" at the school. He cited their written English as "equal to if not superior to that which is done by the American children." He also noted their good behavior.[5]

This praise of ethnic Chinese students is an early indicator of a prevalent stereotype of Chinese American and other Asian American students—that we behave and perform well academically. This praise has led to Asian Americans being called a so-called model minority, a hated label by some segments of Asian America, but one quietly embraced by others.

Outside of work and school, what did Pop see of Chinatown and the immediate surrounding city? When Pop arrived, and in the decades after, Chinese were a concentrated presence in Oakland. The local telephone company created a dedicated exchange in the 1920s for Chinese Oaklanders called the Pekin Exchange. Phone books[6] from that decade list anywhere from 160 to 214 Chinese-named residents and businesses under the Pekin Exchange followed by five digits, the way phone numbers used to be presented (PE1-2345 and so on).

The Chinese presence was considerable in about two dozen square blocks that were part of almost one hundred square blocks that made up the vast majority of Oakland's core of business, industry, and some housing.[7] A few of those two dozen blocks were almost all Chinese. Others had Chinese and white businesses and housing about equally mixed. On other blocks that weren't part of the two dozen, Chinese businesses operated in a mostly white majority environment. In other words, Chinatown during Pop's earliest Oakland years was never exclusively Chinese.

Chinese-white interactions were primarily for business, legal and nefarious. White Oaklanders did, indeed, patronize Chinatown restaurants, meat markets, and herbalist shops. This level of interaction showed a noticeable increase in the 1920s.[8] The reverse was also true. White businesses, such as Hamburger Joe and Hamburger Gus, operated by Greek Americans in the heart of Chinatown, had a lot of Chinese customers. Chinatown kids loved the hamburgers and chunky French fries, while elders liked the nickel cups of coffee. Chinese lottery shops also did well with Japanese, Filipinos, and white and Black people. Chinese gambling bosses had cozy relationships with politicians, police officials, and beat cops (yes, bribes occurred). Chinatown gambling existed with virtual impunity. (More on this later.)

The Sherman Hotel was another indicator Chinatown wasn't a walled-off ghetto. In the late 1930s and into the 1940s, Black bandleaders who later gained worldwide fame stayed at the Sherman above the Chinese-owned Bowen Liquor Store in the heart of Chinatown. Diane

Lee Chin, whose family owned the liquor store, met Ella Fitzgerald, Fats Waller, Duke Ellington, Count Basie, Louis Armstrong, and Earl Hines before they became legends. They played gigs at the Sweet Ballroom a few blocks from Chinatown.[9] Major Black and white music stars performed at a Chinatown nightclub, Latin Quarters, in the 1940s. Morris D. Chin, a Lincoln alumnus who had a good voice, hung out there, meeting Billy Eckstein, Sammy Davis Jr., and Frankie Laine, among others.[10]

One street, Webster, was Pop's base in his early Oakland years, including the herbalist shop where he first worked and lived. Later, his storefront grocery-lottery on Webster was where his young family from China joined him when they arrived in 1933. In the mid-1940s, he took over a restaurant on that street too. Other Chinatown families had businesses on Webster, including a Gee who wasn't directly related to Pop who operated Man Sing Wo,[11] a popular hangout that sold Chinese newspapers, cigarettes, candy, sodas, Chinese pastries, and, for a time, lottery tickets. Another popular store, a step-up open-air stand, sold sodas, candies, and comic books, which kids loved to read without having to buy. Streets intersecting this one Webster block between 7th and 8th Streets were lined with restaurants, other retail outlets, and the Wong Family Association social hall. Charles Lee, the first Chinese licensed dentist in California, had his office in this area, as did some powerful organizations.

In the 1920s, Chinatown and Oakland also had a popular opera house near the waterfront. Chinese youth played organized sports, such as the semiprofessional Wa Sung baseball team, and the Young Chinese Athletic Club, which played basketball against other California Chinese and Asian teams. In the late 1920s, the city's first all-Chinese girls' basketball team, the Waku Auxiliary, played just before Chinese men's basketball games. The Waku[12] Auxiliary competed against Chinese girls' teams from other northern California cities and Japanese Buddhist teams too. Adventurous Chinatown boys found fishing holes near Lake Merritt, the city's beautiful man-made lake an easy walk from Chinatown. Some roller-skated along Webster through the Posey Tube that connected Oakland to the island city of Alameda, or they skated at a new rink near Chinatown.

In his teens and early twenties, Pop probably stuck mostly to Chinatown, walking everywhere he needed to go. At some point, he learned to drive, as one of his jobs in the 1920s was peddling produce from a truck. When he wandered outside, he likely took the 7th Street Red

Train to catch a ferry to San Francisco, or he'd stroll across Broadway to Swan's, Housewives, and Washington Markets. As he became used to life in his new village, Pop saw sharp contrasts in transportation modes. Livery stables and horse-carriage shops represented the old, while auto-repair shops and gasoline stations represented the future. Chinatown got its first gasoline station in the 1930s, when a young man named Arthur Tom and some friends opened one, responding to the needs of gambling bosses, who wanted to fuel up cars in Chinatown so they could sell lottery tickets outside Chinatown.[13]

Without a heavy load of cars, the main Chinatown streets of Webster and Franklin were paved with brick. Other streets were packed earth covered with boards. Streets had gas lamps that were lit each night by a man carrying a long taper.[14]

Another street, Harrison, one block east of Webster, was important to our family. After first renting living quarters on Webster and 7th Streets, Pop found a two-story Victorian-style house on Harrison between 7th and 8th Streets in early 1940. That place would be the site of tragedy and joy during our family's eight years there.

One Harrison neighbor was a Chinatown historical figure, Lon Yoke Wong, who later became known within Chinatown as Fong Get Moo,[15] a pioneering female barber. She was a rarity, an ethnic Chinese woman born in America in 1894. Her father—like Pop, a Hoisan native—had come to mine gold in far northern California. He and other Chinese miners formed a camp in Indian Creek, where Lon Yoke was born, the oldest of seven children. She married Fong Get Chong, a San Francisco barber who moved to Oakland after the 1906 earthquake. They settled at the southwest corner of 8th and Harrison Streets, a few doors from where our family lived.

Their shop and living quarters were on the street level of a two-story building that itself has Chinatown historical importance, the Oakland branch of the pioneering civil rights organization Chinese American Citizens Alliance (CACA). One of the branch's organizers, Charles Lee, the pioneering dentist, bought the building in part because of his devotion to the adjacent Methodist church.

First a homemaker raising two boys, Fong Get Moo was intrigued by her husband's work. One day, after dropping her boys at Lincoln School, she strolled by a barber college on busy Broadway near city hall

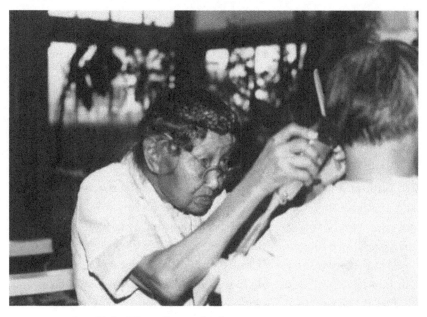

Lon Yoke Wong Fong, also known as Fong Get Moo.
(Courtesy of Clifton Fong.)

that caught her attention. She proceeded to get her license as one of the only female barbers, regardless of race. At first, she plied her new trade in the living quarters behind her husband's shop. When he passed away in 1949, she took over as the main barber. Over the next thirty-six years, she cut the hair of numerous Chinatown men and boys, including me. Her trademark was giving us candy after she cut our hair. (Ironically, her two sons later became dentists.) Her shop became a community place where families connected with one another during shopping or dining trips. She died in 1989 at the age of ninety-five.[16]

The informal western border of Chinatown was Broadway, Oakland's main street. From the 1930s to the 1950s, some of us Chinatown kids believed that Broadway wasn't to be crossed casually, if at all. It was as though the area on the other side of Chinatown was forbidden territory. The reason was murky, something to do with how "we didn't belong" because there were too many white or Black people. In fact, some Chinese in the earliest decades of the twentieth century lived west of

Broadway, which had a small, scattered Asian footprint (Chinese, Japanese, Filipino) long before our putative fears.

Some Chinese-run businesses were on that side, too, including two popular meat markets. Indeed, two prominent Chinese men had their businesses in West Oakland. One was Lew Hing, who with partners opened the Pacific Coast Canning Company in 1904 at 12th and Pine Streets, far from Chinatown. It thrived for about thirty years. In its best years, the cannery shipped its products widely in America and even to U.S. troops fighting in Europe during World War I. At its peak, it hired one thousand workers of all ethnicities. The other was Joe Shoong,[17] whose National Dollar Store chain had a branch just west of Chinatown. Shoong generously supported the Oakland Chinese Community Center, built in the 1950s, which consolidated several Chinese schools. Today, it bears his name.

One important China institution has long had a presence in American Chinatowns, including Oakland's.[18] That institution was—and is—the Kuomintang,[19] or KMT, the Chinese Nationalist Party. The Kuomintang's presence in Oakland encapsulates Chinese American history of the first half of the twentieth century. The KMT goes back to the Chinese Republic's founding by Sun Yat-sen and other revolutionaries, who overthrew the Qing dynasty in 1911. Later led by Generalissimo Chiang Kai-shek, the KMT fought the Mao Zedong–led Communist Party for control of China.

Since residents of American Chinatowns, including Oakland's, were mostly from the Pearl River Delta, they felt an affinity for Sun Yat-sen, a native of that region, and the cause that he and his associates fought for. Some local KMT leaders were also leaders of the most prominent Chinatown organizations, such as the Chinese Six Companies, family and district associations, and tongs.

Pop wasn't deeply political, but he believed in the KMT. He learned about tumultuous Chinese politics—the Qing dynasty's demise, the republic's rise, the May 4 movement, the KMT-Communist civil war, and the Japanese invasion of China in the 1930s—in San Francisco Chinese newspapers, from tong mates, and during his return trips to China. Even Mom, unschooled and also not overtly political, expressed disgust with the Mao Communists, who were brutal toward the Cantonese people, according to reports in the pro-KMT local Chinese newspapers and in letters from China relatives.

Intra-Chinese political divisions were much more pronounced in San Francisco than in Oakland. Chinese immigrants who came of age in the late nineteenth and early twentieth centuries overwhelmingly favored the KMT. Chinese Americans sympathetic to the Communists risked hostility, anger, and even danger. That was two to three generations ago. Today, even in San Francisco, the KMT-versus-Communist narrative is no longer as intense. Later generations of the exclusion-era Chinese Americans aren't nearly as invested in that still simmering, sometimes boiling China-versus-Taiwan conflict as are more recent immigrants, who are much more attuned to ongoing political happenings in their former homelands. My guess is that many older-generation Chinese Americans (my cohort) have relatively little interest in the geopolitics of China, Taiwan, Hong Kong, or Asia in general.

In addition to old-country politics continuing in the new-country Chinatowns, other, more subtle forms of regional rivalries existed before and during Pop's time in Oakland. One had to do with class divisions. In general, people from Pop's region, once called the Four Counties,[20] generally were of a lower class, speaking *Hoisan-wa* and other Cantonese offshoots and coming from more rural areas of the Pearl River Delta. People from the Three Counties[21] area, closest to Guangzhou, were more urbanized and relatively wealthier. They spoke Cantonese and were more of the merchant class, which led big Chinatown organizations. Even among Four Counties people, there were fault lines, such as the more numerous Hoisan people against Hoiping, Enping, or Sunwui people, from the other contiguous counties. In the case of Pop and others in Oakland's Chinatown, Four Counties people were merchants, too, not ceding that calling to the Three Counties people. They learned to speak Cantonese, while the reverse, Cantonese speaking *Hoisan-wa*, was less frequent.

In addition to political and socioeconomic matters, Chinatown also had religious and social concerns. Christian churches have been in Oakland's Chinatown since the late nineteenth century. In Pop's early Oakland years, at least four Protestant missions taught English to children and adults and tried to convert as many Chinese as possible. The Baptist, Methodist, Presbyterian, and Episcopal churches provided their Oakland Chinese followers (not Pop or Mom) with social and religious sustenance.

Some also housed male members without local families. A small Chinese Buddhist temple also existed, also unattended by Pop or Mom.

From the white establishment perspective, Christian missions were successfully Americanizing Chinese children. In 1912, Chinese children at the Baptist mission school delighted their mothers by singing American songs. A mission-school teacher said, "The Chinese children are very bright in their work and take readily to the dancing, which they enjoy. They are rapidly becoming Americanized. The families are interested in all the modern methods of education and many are trying to adopt the American mode of living."[22]

A house in residential Chinatown, Ming Quong Home for Girls, at 9th and Fallon Streets, reflected Christianity's influence. Ming Quong opened in 1915, when San Francisco Presbyterian missionary Donaldina Cameron and two sisters known as Misses Tooker opened a home in Oakland for Chinese immigrant, Chinese American, and Chinese biracial girls ranging from toddlers to late teens whose parents weren't able or didn't want to care for them. Named Tooker Memorial House, it moved in 1926 to the Mills College campus, five miles south of Chinatown, and then established its Chinatown home in 1935 and another facility in Los Gatos on the San Francisco peninsula at about the same time.[23]

One example of the communitarian spirit of Christianity in Chinatown occurred toward the end of World War II. Dorothy Eng and other Chinatown Protestant teenage girls went to a statewide conference in Lake Tahoe in 1944, where they learned that Chinese Christians from other California communities had hospitality clubs for Chinese American soldiers headed for service overseas. These soldiers weren't welcome at regular U.S.O. organizations that served only white soldiers. Dorothy and her friends started the Chinese Young Women's Society in 1944. The society held glamorous social events (dances, performances) for Chinese American soldiers, who came from all over. After the war, the society gave college scholarships to Chinese American women.[24]

Just outside the Chinatown bubble, the world beyond was different than anything Pop had seen before. Big and small retail businesses, banks, hotels, newspapers, and light industrial businesses were near Chinatown, as were heavier industrial businesses at or near the waterfront. Various cultural institutions were close to Chinatown, too, such as houses of worship, movie and drama theaters, dance pavilions, social halls, vaudeville stages, and gymnasiums. Local government offices, such as the new city hall at 14th and Washington Streets, were on the same block as Capwell Sullivan and Furth Department Store. Alameda County offices (jail, superior court, and courthouse) were clustered together only a few blocks from Chinatown.[25]

More than a half century after its founding, Oakland was moving forward in full throttle. In the first two decades of the twentieth century—the time of Pop's arrival—Mayor Frank K. Mott led Oakland to progressive changes: new parks, civil service system, enhanced fire and police departments, new museum, modern street lighting, lower water rates, and improved storm and sewer systems. Many new buildings went up, including city hall, the auditorium by Lake Merritt, schools, and Hotel Oakland. Among the expanding industries were port development, shipyards, automobiles, food production, and cotton mills. Growth and progress continued into the 1920s (port, harbor, airport, a tunnel to the island city of Alameda, better water management, and a regional park system).[26] Pop's timing in coming to Oakland in 1912 turned out to be fortuitous.

5

ARRANGED MARRIAGE

Slowly but surely, Pop was getting comfortable in his new village. Chinatown mentors advised him to shed his Chinese clothing for Western men's wear, such as light wool suits, some with vests; long-sleeved white shirts; and neckties. This formal Western attire was a status symbol for men who had left China to seek an American fortune. These men were called *Ghim Saan Haak* (*Hoisan-wa* for "Gold Mountain Guests"), a prestigious appellation back home, where envy and admiration were in equal residence. One scholar said of some Chinese sojourners, "To come back to one's native soil, beautifully robed and loaded with honors, is the best thing in life."[1] Pop's mentors taught him basic things, such as how to use flush toilets and a telephone, and more complicated things, such as how to drive a car and how Chinatown businesses operated.

At first, Pop's goal was to return to China after he had made his "fortune," a typical sojourner's tale, one successfully told by some *Ghim Saan Haak*. Pop's remittances were most likely modest. Nonetheless, his mother appreciated whatever he was able to send home. (His father had passed away already.) Pop's elders knew that sending him to Oakland was a long-term investment, or gamble. They were betting on him making enough money in Oakland to eventually return home to live a higher lifestyle.

Most of what he was learning was well within his Chinese heritage: herbal medicine and how things were done in Oakland by the Gee clan and Hoisan regional associations. He was learning other Chinatown businesses, such as peddling vegetables, running restaurants, and selling lottery tickets. On a personal level, as his late teenage self evolved into young adulthood, he developed a taste for whisky, regularly imbibed at clan and association functions. Early on, he smoked cigarettes, which he gave up, either before I was born or shortly thereafter. He didn't smoke or otherwise imbibe opium, thank goodness. After finishing the eighth grade at Lincoln, he didn't go to high school, which would have been Oakland Technical, the go-to high school for Chinatown youth. As for relations with the opposite sex—well, they were difficult. A few Chinese girls his age attended Lincoln. Dating as we know it, however, wasn't in the cards, given his work, studies, and a socially conservative Chinatown. Getting to know teenage white girls was well-nigh impossible—too many cultural and language obstacles.

Overall, I surmise that he must have felt good about his new village. Life, however, was nowhere nearly as easy as the stories told by those returning home, who often embellished stories of life in America to save face, keeping private distressful times, loneliness, and isolation. As for his post-Lincoln future, he continued working at the herbalist for another year, because he and his mother had a plan: He would return to his village four times for personal and vocational reasons, spanning 1919 to 1933. The first was from December 1919 to October 1921; the second, June 1924 to June 1926; the third, January 1929 to May 1930; and the last, September to November 1933.[2] He needed the U.S. government's approval to make these trips.

The primary reason for his 1919 return trip was to marry. A go-between helped his mother find a young woman in a nearby Yee clan village. Pop married her in January 1921, according to what he told American officials upon his return to Oakland. He departed China before the early 1922 birth of his first daughter, Li Hong. After giving birth, his first wife died. On his next trip, he married another Yee woman from the same village, another arranged union. This second wife was Mom, someone with whom he would spend the next thirty-seven years and have six children.

Mom was Yee Suey Ting,[3] born on October 2, 1903, in Aye Leng village, not far from Goon Du Hahng. She had four sisters and one brother. How she ranked in that order isn't known. Her father died when she was

Immigration photo of author's mother, Gee Yee Suey Ting, 1933. (Author's Collection)

fourteen.[4] Her mother died in an accident in 1933, after she had escorted Mom part way when Mom departed Goon Du Hahng with her daughters for America. Her siblings stayed in China or Hong Kong, and she didn't maintain much, if any, contact. She was happy to be a *Ghim Saan Poo*,[5] a wife of a man who went to America, a high-status title because she got money and food from her husband abroad. Sharing the food with villagers made her popular.

Pop's returns home excited her, but those visits were somewhat fleeting because of their vocational purpose. From his early Oakland experience, he decided to start a little business in the village area, which required him to spend a lot of time away from Mom. He spent enough time with her, however, to father two daughters: Li Keng, in 1926, and Lai Wah, in 1931.

What's fascinating is what he told U.S. immigration authorities on each of his returns to Oakland in 1921, 1926, and 1930. In addition to the three daughters, he said that he had also fathered three sons—quite a revelation to his children in Oakland many years after he died. Those false claims indicate that Pop was deep into his own paper-son scheme, selling those claims to nonfamily members to get boys and young men into America later.

It was almost accidental that I learned of his little enterprise. On November 5, 2014, I went to the village with my son Sam and our translator, Professor Selia Tan of Wuyi University, Jiangmen, Guangdong Province, China. We met Gee Fook Ying, the distant cousin I had met on my first trip in 1994. This time, a second villager, whose name I didn't get, was with Fook Ying at Pop's no-longer-standing house. The two men were talkative, conjuring up this story about Pop's agent business. These men weren't alive when Pop was around, but, apparently, Pop's legend as a *Ghim Saan Haak* lives on in his village.

Author (*right*) learning more about his father from village man Gee Fook Ying (*left*) and another unidentified village man in 2014. The back of the head of the author's translator, Selia Tan, of Wuyi University, is in the foreground. The unidentified crouching man in the background was with the county's administrative office. (Author's Collection)

Details the two villagers related to us about Pop's business were fascinating. One said, "I heard Ghee Gheng [Pop] was very successful in the home village at that time." They said that Pop had a boat to transport migrants from Hoisan City (Taicheng) to Hong Kong, where they boarded steamships to America. "He usually gathered a few kids here and sent them in a boat at one time," one man said, as translated by Professor Tan. "This was the way he earned quite a bit of money." Pop had credibility to offer his services since he knew the ropes of getting around exclusion restrictions and had up-to-date knowledge about life in America, or at least in Oakland.

I was frankly stunned by this story of Pop's China life, as neither my sisters nor I had ever heard it before. I had wondered why his return visits were so lengthy and what he did when he was back in his home village. About two months were needed for the round-trip ship travel, but what about the many other months away from Oakland? This story told by twenty-first-century villagers about twentieth-century Pop—if true, and I have little evidence to impeach their credibility—gives Pop's ignorant descendants like me a fuzzy picture of how he spent his time, even if aspects of that story are upsetting.

6

CHAIN MIGRATION

Pop's fourth return visit, in 1933, was the briefest and the most significant. He had decided to bring his young family to live in Oakland permanently. Exactly why he did that remains a mystery to his children. Despite its many problems, Pop loved China, according to what he told his daughters in Oakland years later. He thought that the landscape was more beautiful and the fruits sweeter than those in America. He seemed torn emotionally, exacerbated perhaps subconsciously by the segregation engendered by the exclusion law. His feelings were stretched between the country that had given him some opportunities and the one he cherished because of birthright and elders but that didn't have much of a future for him.

One possible reason for him to leave China for good has a dark undertone. Remember those two village men who told me in 2014 about Pop's agent business? They relayed a stunning denouement: After they gave details of Pop's business, they said that Pop was known to beat children he had taken on as clients. They also implied that Pop had cheated a young man he had promised to transport to Hong Kong. But this young man, confined, heard noises from outside that told him he was still in or near his village. That alleged incident sullied Pop's reputation, effectively ending his business. "He [Pop] had to escape to the U.S. and never came back," one of the men said.

Should I believe this disturbing account? I know one should be wary, if not outright skeptical, of reports from two men who weren't even alive when Pop was running his business. But why would they lie to me? As his only son, I am, of course, disturbed by those distressing allegations. My sisters and I remember Pop fondly. Yes, he had a temper, but that didn't define him. This portrait of him as a mean cheat muddies our affectionate memory of him, but it doesn't fundamentally change what we think of him because of our own lived experiences. But if these old village tales are true and he was forced to permanently flee China, however, the result for our family in Oakland was positive in the sense that he and Mom—for all the challenges and barriers they faced in their own relationship and in the place they had settled—grew us into a tight-knit family.

Pop departed for China on September 8, 1933, to prepare his wife and three daughters to leave with him for America. As with much that happened during the exclusion era, there were interesting twists. Besides asking for permission to travel to China, he applied for Certificates of Identity, required of Chinese seeking entry, for his three daughters. That was a clear signal he planned to bring his family over. He also told authorities another tall tale—that his second wife had died on February 25, 1933. That would be Mom, who was very much alive. That lie was another signal he was going to bring his family over. U.S. laws at that time forbade Chinese men living in America from bringing in their China-born wives. A sister, however, would be all right. To get around the fact he was married to Mom in China, he declared her "dead" and changed Mom's status to "sister."

We must return to Pop's paper father, Gee Bing Fong, for a moment. In a statement on board the SS *Siberia* on June 1, 1901, Bing Fong claimed that his seventh child after six boys was a girl named Shew Gwee, four years old. That "girl" turned out to be the slot that Pop bought for Mom to accompany him to America in 1933, as his sister. Her immigration name was Theo Quee, close to Shew Gwee. Mom's case tells us that paper schemes weren't exclusively for boys. Bing Fong's listing of a girl was either ingenious or a matter of broadening opportunities. For Pop to take advantage of that quirk was either plain luck or opportunism writ large. Whatever the motives, it was a perfect plan for Pop to get Mom to Oakland with their three daughters without revealing the truth.

On landing in America on November 27, 1933, he said that his three "sons" were still in China, whereas his three daughters and his "sister" were with him. Did this declaration raise eyebrows among immigration authorities? Apparently not. One wonders about the acuity of immigration officials in 1933. Were they not aware that China was (and still is) a patriarchy, favoring sons, not daughters? Why would a returning Chinese American bring in his daughters and not more favored sons? Pop bringing in Mom and their three daughters was bold, courageous, and humane, showing his love of family. Even though he and Mom would have preferred having boys, they took good care of their girls.

In the spring of 1933, Pop wrote his family that he'd be back in Goon Du Hahng in five months to move them to America. The news hit like a bombshell, but in the best of ways. Pop hired a tutor to teach Mom how to read Chinese and sent coaching papers to prepare her and the girls for Angel Island interrogations. Mom told the girls that Pop instructed them to call her *yee*, the appellation for "aunt," not *ma* for "mother."

The coaching papers were detailed, filled with possible questions U.S. immigration inspectors might ask around two false points. One was that Pop had five brothers and one sister and that his father was Gee Bing Fong. The other was that Pop and Mom were siblings, not husband and wife. Pop, Mom, and the three girls had to learn the same story, truth and lies mixed together. It was hard enough for the two adults to learn this convoluted story, but for their three daughters, especially two-year-old Lai Wah, the task was monumental.

With a flair for the spectacular, Pop, wearing a Western suit and tie, arrived at the village in a sedan chair. "I stared at this stranger," Li Keng writes in her memoir. "He was short, like most of the people in our village. His big, dark brown eyes sparkled and his round, pale face contrasted with the dark-skinned villagers. He looked well fed, unlike the wiry men of our village. His suit was made of fine material. . . . Baba seemed like a good person. At home he ate and played with us. His laughter echoed loudly, and we reacted with big smiles. He grinned whenever he caught my eyes. I was so happy."[1]

In reminiscing about Pop decades later, Li Keng told me, "He was very proud of the fact that he was *Ghim Saan Haak* ['Gold Mountain Guest']. Mama was overjoyed because her husband had come back." Pop slept at a cousin's house, which gave him cover for the sibling-not-spouse

Author's father, all dressed up, in an undated photo, perhaps in the 1930s. (Author's Collection)

lie. During the days, he watched over Mom and the girls, studying the coaching papers: "He [Pop] was very concerned about the fact that we may forget the fact that Mama was supposed to be called 'auntie.' Baba and Mama were very cordial toward each other when he was back in the village because you have to remember, he was almost like a stranger to Mom too. And Mom didn't really know exactly what kind of temperament he had."

On the early morning of their departure in early November, Pop, Mom, and the three girls rode in sedan chairs carried by villagers, a status symbol to further impress their neighbors. By then, more than twenty years removed from his initial departure, Pop had developed a taste for showing off his elevated status to the villagers. With the accompaniment of Mom's mother and four men, Pop walked his family to the nearby market town. The men carried shovels and other tools for protection, in case bandits threatened them, a common occurrence in the Pearl River Delta.

In the market town, Pop hired a sampan to take them to Canton (Guangzhou), where they boarded a train to Hong Kong. The family stayed at a hotel, a new mind-blowing experience for them. Wanting his family to look "American," Pop bought Mom and the girls new clothing, including winter wear, something they had never owned before. Now, he thought, they were ready for their new home. They took rickshaws to the pier, where they boarded the *President Hoover*.

The sea voyage was rocky for all but Lai Wah, the youngest. "Everybody was sick but me," she related decades later. "Oh, they were seasick. Mom was sicker than a dog, and I was the only one traipsing all over the deck."[2] With Pop in a men's passenger area, Mom and the three girls shared a third-class cabin, where they learned how to use flush toilets and had milk and butter for the first time. Li Keng didn't take well to those new foods—they upset her already queasy stomach—whereas Li Hong and Lai Wah were unfazed.

The nineteen-day ocean voyage stopped in Shanghai, Japan, and Hawaii before arriving in San Francisco Bay on November 27, 1933. Once off the *Hoover*, Pop went to Oakland, and Mom and the three girls went to Angel Island. Before leaving them, Pop again reminded the girls to tell authorities that Mom was their aunt, not their mother. The immigration station felt like a prison—chicken-wired windows, locked doors, and guards standing outside.

The four were called to a hearing two days after their arrival. The session was brief. All were asked their names and the dialect they would use in the interrogation, which would begin the next day. Mom gave her name as Gee Theo Quee to match the name of paper father Gee Bing Fong's seventh child. All said that they would use *Hoisan-wa*. Their interpreter was Edwar Lee, or Lee Park Lim, the first American-born Chinese to become a Methodist minister. He was from Oakland's Chinatown, their destination.

Pop ferried over from Oakland, as the only witness to speak on their behalf. His interrogation spanned two days, with 227 questions in all. Questions and his responses about his village were almost the same as those he gave in 1912 and on his subsequent returns from China. New questions discussed sleeping arrangements of his family and those of his alleged "brothers" in the village house and his "sons." More questions covered his "sister" (Mom), where she slept, and her education. Asked what his "sister" would be doing in America, Pop said that she would attend school, but he didn't yet know where she'd live. He also said that his "sister" had asked him via a letter to bring her to the United States after their "parents" had died.

Mom was asked 279 questions, among them the purpose of her trip. She said that her "brother" (Pop) had asked her to "come over to do whatever I could find here because my parents had died and I was lonesome at home." One of many interesting tidbits she offered was this: Her "father," Gee Bing Fong, "told me when I was born he had me reported in Oakland." What she meant by that isn't certain, but it's true that as early as 1901, as noted earlier, Bing Fong told U.S. immigration officials that he had a daughter, allegedly his seventh child.

Other than three minor discrepancies, Mom's answers matched those of Pop's. At one point, the interrogator hinted at suspicions that Mom wasn't who she said she was: "You are advised that it will be in your best interests in this matter to tell the whole truth, regardless of any instructions you may have had to the contrary. Do you understand that?" Mom said that she understood. The official didn't further pursue this line of questioning. It was remarkable how well Mom did. For a mostly uneducated woman, confronted with numerous questions in an intimidating setting, her performance excelled.

Oldest daughter Li Hong, eleven years old, faced 169 questions spanning two days. Asked, "Of what country are you a citizen or subject?" she responded, "The United States." "Why do you consider yourself a citizen of the U.S.?" "Because my paternal grandfather [Gee Bing Fong] was born in this country." Several other questions about Pop and Mom were crucial. "Are you sure the woman at this Station with you is your father's sister?" "Yes." "Isn't she your stepmother?" "No." "Is your aunt who is here with you married?" "No." "While you were in Hong Kong did your father and your aunt occupy the same room with you at the place where you stopped?" "No, my father had a room by himself just next to us."

Many questions for Li Hong tested her responses against those of Pop and Mom, on such matters as space between houses, where the school was, who some neighbors were, what kinds of flooring were in the house, whether windows had glass panes or shutters, a partition in the parlor, other furnishings, kinds of beds, and where her family and her "uncles" ate. That Li Hong got through the interrogation with correct answers in almost all cases was especially noteworthy because of her learning disabilities.

Second daughter Li Keng, seven years old, was asked sixty-four questions. Three times, Li Keng corrected Li Hong. Li Keng said that her older sister had a "poor memory. She is playful all the time." On the important question of who Mom was, Li Keng told the same lie: Mom was her unmarried "aunt."

The interrogation transcript[3] shows only a description of youngest daughter Lai Wah, not any questions and answers. In her memoir, Li Keng relates an amusing anecdote about Lai Wah's interrogation:

> Lai Wah, almost three years old, was bright, friendly, and outgoing. She responded to the interpreter with a big smile and sparkling eyes.
>
> He looked at Lai Wah and asked pleasantly, "Little girl, what is your name, please?"
>
> Lai Wah retorted, "If you don't tell me your name, why should I tell you my name?"

Mama gasped. Li Hong and I exchanged glances. Lai Wah's reply had been honest and natural. She was just a little girl. But would the officials think she was very rude?

The interpreter translated Lai Wah's reply into English for the inspector and stenographer. Both men roared like lions with their loud laughter. The interpreter joined in, "Ha, ha, ha!"

Mama, Li Hong and I smiled. We felt wonderful. The tension we had felt a few moments earlier disappeared.

Little sister Lai Wah's quip had cinched the decision for the officials to allow us to stay in the United States. Hooray!

We watched the inspector, a big smile still on his face, stamp our papers.[4]

According to Li Keng, the interpreter told Mom and the three girls that they were being released immediately and that they would be ferried to San Francisco.

Before they left, M. A. Moore, chair of the Board of Special Inquiry, summarized the board's interrogations of Pop, Mom, and the three girls. He concluded that their statements "are in substantial agreement, and, while there are a number of discrepancies, I do not consider them of sufficient materiality to raise any serious doubt regarding the bona fides of these cases. There are certain features in the statement of applicant 9–6 [Li Hong] which indicate that the adult witnesses may have deviated from the truth in a few details, but this child does not appear to be overly bright and I believe we cannot hold her strictly accountable for everything she says. I was rather favorably impressed by the demeanor of the witnesses under examination." Moore further said that the evidence established that Mom was the "daughter" of Gee Bing Fong, a U.S. citizen, and that the girls were the daughters of Pop, also a U.S. citizen. He said that they should be admitted into the United States. The other two board members concurred.[5]

Mom and the three girls boarded a boat to San Francisco, where Pop greeted them and took them in a taxicab that drove them, via a big ferryboat, to Oakland, for a whole new life. This was on December 2, 1933, six days after their arrival in U.S. territory.

7

THE LOTTERY

As anxiety ridden as they might have been, upon arrival at a Chinatown storefront where Pop was now based, Mom and the girls felt somewhat at home. Several families who knew that Pop was bringing his family warmly greeted them in *Hoisan-wa*. That had to have soothed their nerves.

To celebrate their arrival, Pop ordered dinner to be delivered: beef with string beans, chicken with cashew nuts and snow peas, steamed ground-pork patty, and white rice.[1] Although modest, this meal was like an imperial banquet. After dinner, Pop escorted Mom and Lai Wah to a house three blocks away because he was paranoid that immigration agents would find him and Mom sleeping in the same bed. That's where the Gee family who had purchased his produce truck a few years earlier lived and where Mom and Lai Wah would stay for a short time.

He, Li Hong, and Li Keng, meanwhile, lived at his place on Webster Street. After a few weeks, when no immigration agents had shown up, the family reunited there. The morning after their arrival, Pop fed Li Hong and Li Keng *jook* (rice porridge) for breakfast and then walked them around Chinatown. The girls felt comforted seeing and hearing people who looked like Pop and Mom and who spoke *Hoisan-wa* and Cantonese.

For Pop, this experience was entirely new. He had split his last twenty-one years between Oakland and China. In Oakland, he was a "bachelor." In China, he was with his family some of the time, while tending to his agent business at other times. He had grown from an unsophisticated rural teenager with no English skills to an experienced transnational small businessman. Once scrawny, he had put on considerable weight. His hairline was beginning to recede. His accented English helped him navigate many American ways, while he remained a hardcore Chinatown denizen, firmly attached to social and business organizations that provided sustenance, protection, and a true sense of belonging against sometimes-unfriendly outside forces.

He proved himself to be a good family man, even though his two wives had not yet given him what he craved: a son. The extraordinary effort he had made since his first return trip to his village in 1919 was ample evidence that he was a faithful Confucianist, cherishing family. His work life in Oakland and, later, in the Pearl River Delta was aimed at providing for his family. Little else mattered. His possibly controversial business practice that may have prompted his decision to settle for good in Oakland was well in the past.

Now, in early December 1933, in his Chinatown store and living quarters, he was happy to no longer be separated from a family he barely knew. He wanted his family to grow together in one place without having to cross the Pacific Ocean again. He still loved China, but he knew how troubled his homeland was. The switch from imperial to republican governance was by no means smooth. Warlords still held regional sway. Two major political parties, the Kuomintang (Nationalists) and the Communists, battled violently for ultimate power, and, in the 1930s, archenemy Japan had begun a menacing invasion.

Pop couldn't dwell on China's woes. He now had a family to take care of. Inside his store, the shelves were almost bare, with only a few rolls of toilet paper and some cooking utensils.[2] On the well-worn, scruffy wood-plank floor were empty or partially filled orange crates. His was one of four storefronts in a two-story building on the west side of Webster. Upstairs were apartments and business spaces, including a lottery company.

With his family now with him, it was time for Pop to tell Mom exactly what he did for a living—selling lottery tickets, an illegal business, not groceries. That news surprised her since in all the years they had been married, she had never known what he did. Pop explained how hard it was to find work during the Great Depression, especially for the segregated Chinese. "So, I created a job for myself for us to survive. I really don't want to break the law, but what choice do I have?" Li Keng remembered him saying.

The lottery and the broader gambling industry had been major economic forces in California Chinatowns for decades before Pop's arrival. The gambling business, especially lottery, was highly lucrative for Chinatown bosses. Moreover, these pursuits were largely recreational and not thought of as criminal activities, except by the all-powerful, often corruptible white establishment. Up to the 1940s, when the exclusion law was still in effect, the wealthiest Chinese Americans ran gambling operations.[3]

By sheer coincidence, during Pop's first twenty years in America, Oakland gained a reputation as being *the* place for the big Chinese lotteries in northern California,[4] although San Francisco had lottery companies, too, dating back to the Gold Rush era. Oakland's lottery reached six neighboring counties: Alameda, San Francisco, Contra Costa, Solano, San Mateo, and San Joaquin.[5] Chinatown had other forms of gambling, such as *pai gow*, fan-tan, and mah-jong, more for Chinese and other Asians (Japanese, Filipinos) than for non-Asians.

Lottery's reach was broader, attracting non-Asian people from Oakland and surrounding communities. It generated the most revenue and employed a large percentage of Chinatown and West Oakland Chinese.[6] Chinese lottery was the precursor of lotto and keno, games played legally and widely all over America today. In ancient China, going back two centuries, the lottery was called, in Cantonese, *pak kop piu* ("white pigeon ticket") because pigeons allegedly carried tickets and winning numbers between bettors and game operators.

Chinese lottery tickets had eighty Chinese words, the start of "The Thousand Character Classic," a poem children learned for basic literacy. The beauty of using the first eighty words was that none of the words repeat, perfect for a game in which bettors chose favorite words, often nine ("nine-spot") or ten ("ten-spot"). To win money, a bettor had to "hit" a certain number of his or her chosen words—say, five or more of a nine-spot bet—of the twenty winning words drawn twice daily. The more hits, the higher the winnings. For example, if a bettor "hit" all ten words (extremely rare), he or she would have won four thousand times the bet amount.[7] Chances of winning much, if anything, were slim.

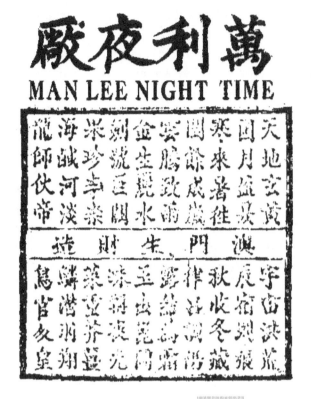

A typical Oakland Chinatown lottery ticket in the 1930s. (Author's Collection)

Pop began selling lottery tickets before he brought his family over, but we don't know exactly when. He had worked an apprenticeship of sorts in Reno, Nevada, as a lottery ticket marker. By 1933, that had become his main line of work. Pop sold two brands, *Mon Lee* and *Soon Lee*, of as many as seventeen brands controlled by five companies in Oakland's Chinatown, according to several descendants of lottery dealers. His shop opened every day at nine o'clock in the morning and closed about ten in the evening, except for Chinese New Year, the only day off.

Bettors strode past the grocery-store goods up front and headed straight for the lottery room. That's where Pop, Mom, and a Gee male cousin marked bettors' choices and gave them duplicate tickets. The most common bets were nickels and dimes; quarter, fifty-cent, or dollar bets were rare. Shortly after two o'clock, Pop stopped selling tickets to sort by brand those that had been sold. Just before three o'clock, with marked tickets in hand, he or his cousin dashed a block away to the second-floor hall of the company that controlled the tickets he sold.

The twice-daily routine of drawing the winning words, first at three o'clock in the afternoon, then at nine o'clock at night, occurred in these halls, which were a bevy of intense activity, excitement, and anticipation. Brokers like Pop handed over the marked tickets and collected their commission, 15 percent of sales, then waited for the labor-intensive drawing process. Each company had similar routines for picking the winning words. They involved randomly picking each word written on scraps of paper, a dice-roll winnowing down the twenty winning words, the flash duplication of those words onto sheets that brokers like Pop grabbed so they could produce results tickets at their shops to distribute to bettors. For lotteries outside Oakland's Chinatown, in such places as San Francisco, Emeryville, Stockton, and Marysville, company men made telephone calls to report the winning words. The San Francisco Chinatown phone exchanges were extremely busy during these times.[8]

Back at his shop, Pop plunged into action with Mom, his cousin, and Li Keng to produce results sheets. Li Keng organized these sheets into folded packets that a helper distributed to bettors and the non-betting curious. Of greatest interest to each bettor, of course, was whether he or she had won any money. Most often, they hadn't.

How did brokers like Pop make money when most bets were only a nickel or dime? Lottery brokers commonly used three strategies to make money. One was to pass the entire bet to the company that issued the tickets and get the 15 percent commission. If a bettor won, the company, not the broker, paid. A second strategy was the opposite: Instead of selling the bet to the company, Pop kept it. Doing so was a gamble, an element of excitement and intrigue—and the possibility of earning more money or losing a lot. Pop did this by a gut feeling. If he believed that a bettor had chosen words that wouldn't "hit" or if the bet were relatively high—say, one dollar—Pop kept the bet to himself. If Pop's tactic was wrong, and the bettor "hit" enough words to win some money, Pop had to pay up.

A third strategy was in the middle, with brokers and companies sharing the risk. Brokers occasionally "rewrote" a bet this way: Pass along a percentage (a third, a half) of the bet to the company, keep the rest, and earn the 15 percent commission for the amount sold. If such a bet lost, Pop pocketed the percentage of the bet he decided to keep plus a 15 percent commission on the amount he sold to the company; the company would keep the portion of that bet it got from Pop. That was a win-win for broker and company. If such a bet won, however, both broker and company paid off the winnings proportionately. But the broker would also get a 10 percent fee from the company for selling a winning ticket. Pop never got wealthy from his lottery business, but he managed to support his growing family until one of his gambles lost.

For our family and others in Chinatown, the lottery meant surviving the Great Depression. Some operated similarly to Pop's, while others went to their customers, in their homes or at a public place. Manley Wu's father and uncle did the latter from West Oakland, not Chinatown. The Wu lottery sent runners door-to-door to sell tickets and inform bettors of results. Manley was a runner when he was a teenager in the 1940s. With marked tickets, he drove to Chinatown with his father to five different lottery companies. The two split up the task of waiting for the results at each before driving back to West Oakland to process the tickets, which his elders did. He then drove to bettors' homes to deliver the results.

Manley and his father knew my Pop. When they went to Chinatown twice a day for the drawings, they sometimes killed time at our restaurant, enjoying coffee and pie. That's how Manley met my sisters, Li Keng, Lai Wah, and Nellie. "Your father was a friendly person; he would talk to us," Manley told me. "Sometimes, our family would eat dinner upstairs. He even roasted a turkey for us on Thanksgiving."[9]

Yung-Chu Chinn's lottery shop in a cigar store a few doors from Pop's did what the West Oakland Wus did. Chinn's lottery business in the late 1930s through the 1940s supported his family of seven children, all of whom pitched in to help, but only after finishing schoolwork. He and one of the youngest sons, Victor, sold and settled tickets outside Chinatown. For the early afternoon shift, Yung-Chu Chinn went to Jack London Square less than a mile away and set up temporary quarters at the First and Last Chance Saloon, made famous by the legendary writer Jack London. Not yet ten years old, Victor went along. "I watched him mark many brands of tickets at that saloon. He'd be sitting in a booth, and customers came around with tickets that they had already marked," Victor said. Bettors were primarily white shipyard workers during World War II. For the night shift, father and son went to West Oakland to sell tickets, mostly to African Americans. "They were addicted to playing every day. We also had white customers in West Oakland. Word of mouth got us new customers," Victor said.[10]

Tickets sold outside Chinatown were processed in the same manner as those sold in Chinatown. The Chinn lottery operated on a larger scale than Pop's, with more people involved since it sold as many as fifteen brands. The major difference between the Chinn lottery and Pop's, other than the scale, was how Victor handled the winning tickets, which were a thicker packet. Victor rolled each stack like a cigar and then bent it like a boomerang, which he tossed at customers' houses. He did that twice a day.

Calvin Wong's father and uncles ran a lottery around the corner from Pop's and the Chinn shop, in the 1930s through the early 1950s. The Wong operation, dating back to the 1880s, was behind a candy store and laundry. It sold many brands to customers who visited the store and those in neighboring Alameda. Calvin's task was to run tickets out to Alameda and to deliver the results.[11]

With all this illegal gambling going on in Chinatown, what was local law enforcement doing? Not a lot, really. Sure, Oakland police raided Chinatown gambling joints. But how serious were those raids? Calvin Wong said that police went to his father's lottery store monthly. Beforehand, a uniformed cop would tell his father when a raid was scheduled. "The raids were planned; they even needed a few customers. The sellers would put up old doors, and the police would hack those down. We didn't want to replace a new door," Calvin told me. "It was a big game. The officer would get the cash and distribute it to higher-level police officials or lower-level cops."

Police raided Pop's shop too. Li Keng remembered that in anticipation of police action on his backroom lottery, Pop hired an electrician to install a light switch on a front counter. If cops rushed in, someone flicked the light, giving bettors an alert to leave and Pop a chance to hide tickets and money. Nonetheless, Pop and a helper (not Li Keng) were arrested and hauled away in a police van. They made bail and were released a few hours later. Another time, Pop knew that a raid was imminent, so he closed the lottery room and crawled into bed, pretending he was napping. One cop checked the inactive lottery room and saw Pop in bed—no arrest that day. At other times, Pop got no warning. Once, cops rushed in, demolished the lottery-room table, and arrested Pop and his adult helper. Again, they were quickly released.[12]

Oakland police raids of Chinatown lottery shops were routine, dating back to the late nineteenth century and continuing into the mid-twentieth century. Oakland newspapers carried many stories about such raids. In the earliest decades of the twentieth century, graft and corruption were endemic in Oakland's political and police cultures. Some politicians wanted Chinatown gambling to continue because the city got bonus revenue from the consequences of raids (bail, fines, and forfeitures), to say nothing of outright bribes.

A banner year for public exposure of high police corruption was 1919. Local newspapers published sensational front-page corruption stories about successive police chiefs and other high-ranking city officials. The most explosive story that year was the trial of police chief John F. Nedderman on graft charges—specifically, receiving bribes from as many as seventy-five Chinese gambling operators. A former chief, Walter J. Petersen, was one of those who identified him. Among the prosecution witnesses who testified against Nedderman were Chinatown lottery bosses Gee Sam Kee, described as the "king of the Chinese lotteries," and "Little Ernest" Lun (or Lum). In the end, nothing much was resolved. The trial of Nedderman et al. ended in a jury deadlock.[13]

Money was one way to pay off dirty cops, but there were other methods. A descendant of one of Oakland's Chinatown's gambling bosses told me that at Thanksgiving or Christmas, his "father would put his name stamp on a card and give them to Oakland police officials, who then went to the fish store on 8th near Franklin, and they'd pick up free turkeys and other free food."

Ironically, the illegal gambling industry helped bond some Chinatown men with white leaders. Otherwise, given the legal discrimination against Chinese people living in America until after World War II, white-Chinese socializing was rare. In our family, a few connections were forged. Li Keng said that a white couple who bought lottery tickets from Pop liked her and sisters Li Hong and Lai Wah so much that the couple had dresses made for them. Another time, a white bettor took the three girls to the World's Fair on Treasure Island in San Francisco Bay in 1939, a big treat for otherwise Chinatown-bound children.

The *Oakland Tribune* published a fascinating story of a rare white-Chinese "friendship" in 1901 based on the lottery. A major lottery boss named Gee Nom, or Gee Mun, threw a huge party in Chinatown to celebrate his wedding to an eighteen-year-old woman. Here, in part, is how the *Tribune* described the gala function:

> There was plenty of music of a type that would put the orchestra chosen for "The First Born" to shame, and the tables were heavy with a repast which Gee Nom modestly admitted had cost him $20 a plate. . . . The menu . . . was as follows: Sauterne, Oysters on the Half Shell, Bouillon, Cream Sweet Breads, Burgundy, Roast Squab and Fresh Mushrooms, Cold Roast, Cold Roast Turkey and Chicken, Ox Tongue and Boiled Ham, Shrimp Salad a la Mayonnaise, Champagne, Neapolitan Brick Ice Cream, Cakes, Salt Nuts, Candies, Glace Fruits, Ice Cream. . . . [M]any of his friends, good and true, of the white population, were present to offer congratulations and participate in the merry festivities, which will long be remembered by those fortunate enough to count the genial Oriental their friend.[14]

The article listed by name Oakland political and law-enforcement leaders, including the mayor, city councilmen, district attorney, judges, police chiefs, and police officers and detectives. That impressive list of white leaders suggests Gee Nom's political acumen and keen business sensibilities. His inclusion of these powerful luminaries at this major personal social event was more an expression of his appreciation for their tolerance of his illegal business than it was a manifestation of genuine friendships.

Long before he became chief justice of the United States, Earl Warren served as Alameda County's district attorney from the mid-1920s to the late 1930s. (Oakland is the county seat of Alameda County.) As the county's top law enforcement official, Warren oversaw police raids of Chinese lotteries. He saw rampant corruption among local law enforcement officials. At least two county sheriffs were cozy with criminal elements, including Chinese lotteries, so Warren ordered certain illegal activities shut down. Given his power, it's unsurprising he was a bribery target. Warren recalls:

The first day after our return to Oakland [from a honeymoon trip], I came home from the office to see my wife admiring some beautiful Chinese jade jewelry. I asked her who had sent it, and she said it must have come from a friend of mine because she did not recognize the name. The card showed it was from a Mr. L. Ben. I recognized immediately that this must be Lim Ben, the biggest Chinese lottery operator in the county. Nina's possession of the gift was short-lived, for the next day I notified the foreman of the county grand jury, and, with one of its members accompanying them, two of my men located L. Ben, returned the jewelry to him, and brought back a written receipt.[15]

After a long run, Oakland's Chinatown's lottery and other gambling activities ended abruptly, or so it seemed. In 1951, Congress passed two laws taxing gambling.[16] One imposed a 10 percent excise tax on lottery wagers, among other gambling activities. The other was a $50-a-year "occupational stamp tax" on persons engaged in the gambling trade. This law required such persons to register certain information (place of gambling business, names and residence of people who wagered) with the federal government. If someone involved in the gambling trade didn't pay those taxes and register, that person could be fined $10,000 and sentenced to five years in prison. Those two laws, in effect, put the kibosh on Chinatown gambling, including the once-lucrative lottery trade.

By this time, the early 1950s, Pop had long severed his ties to the lottery. But the demise of the Oakland Chinese lottery industry hurt Chinatown businesses, and many people lost their jobs. Former employees moved out of Oakland, contributing to the decline of Chinatown during that decade.

Despite the oppressive gambling taxes, some illegal gambling continued in Oakland well into that decade. An April 1953 *Oakland Tribune* article noted that at least twenty Chinese lottery houses operated openly in Oakland, but not in Chinatown itself, and they were busy. Many of those houses bribed two Oakland police sergeants $60 a week each, the article said. In late January 1959, police arrested sixteen men playing *pai gow* in the rear of a Chinatown laundry, the *Tribune* reported. They were all released after posting bail. Two months later, an Alameda County grand jury indicted six Chinese men for attempting to bribe police officials up to $18,000 a month. They had wanted to set up *pai gow* and *fan tan* card games in Oakland's Chinatown.

One Oakland Chinese gambling boss made headlines in the local newspaper in the 1950s. He was Chin Bok Hing, also known as Chan Bock Hing, who owned a lot of property in the Bay Area and elsewhere through his gambling fortune. He made news because of his legal problems—evading income-tax convictions, allegedly violating the Trading with the Enemy Act, and fleeing the country for Hong Kong.[17] However, in California Chinatowns and in Hoisan County, Guangdong Province, China, where he was born (Pop's birthplace, too), his philanthropy and business acumen made him a hero.

One can't talk about the lottery and other gambling businesses in American Chinatowns like Oakland's without discussing certain organizations. Their mere mention can yield a cloudy mist of intrigue, secrecy, mystery, and stereotyping. Three types of organizations were prevalent: family/clan associations, district/regional associations, and tongs. All played inordinately important roles in the lives of men like Pop during the exclusion era because they were the social safety net, the essential human infrastructure, for Chinese immigrants excluded from white America.

The Chinese Six Companies, also known as the Chinese Consolidated Benevolent Association, was the master organization in many Chinatowns. Its leaders were from the biggest and most powerful family and/or district associations. Formed shortly after the Gold Rush for self-protection, the Six Companies was a combination city hall and chamber of commerce, helping new immigrants get jobs, housing, and legal help.

Many Chinatown men belonged to all three types of organizations. Because of crossover memberships and common goals, the relationships between and among the organizations and their members were complicated and not well understood from the outside. Competition and rivalries between and among tongs and the associations developed early. Underlying the rivalries were power dynamics, class and root regional differences, money, and territorial disputes over various businesses, legal and illegal.

Tongs[18] have the sketchiest reputation, inside and outside Chinatown. They conjure up images of violence, especially in the late nineteenth century through the early twentieth century. The phrase *tong wars* popped up in American newspapers during that time in cities that had

Chinatowns. In their heyday, tongs were a fraternal association of Chinatown men of various clans. Some of these men were outcasts or members of small clans. The tongs maintained a cadre of fighters—"hatchet men"[19] or "highbinders"—to protect their criminal enterprises (gambling, drugs, and prostitution). Wealthy merchants and leaders of district associations and the Six Companies hired these fighters. Some tongs used youth gangs as enforcers.

Tongs go back several hundred years to southeastern China, including Guangdong Province, where most Chinatown residents were from. Secret societies, known as "triads," or the Heaven and Earth Society, emerged from the social and economic upheavals in south China in the nineteenth century.[20]

As a business necessity, Pop joined a tong, and their bond was mutually strong and contentious. His tong gave him financial support to start several businesses, a gesture that engendered his loyalty. Getting such help from white banks was all but impossible. Out of loyalty, he was part of whatever the tong was up to. When tong rivalries teetered toward armed conflicts, Pop and other members fled town for such places as Stockton, Marysville, Sacramento, and Reno, stay-aways that lasted weeks.[21] That happened before and after he had brought his family from China.

It's difficult to know what his tong was like in Pop's days. Its secret nature hid its inner workings from those who weren't members. Members didn't, and don't, say anything about the tong to nonmembers. As a child, I got a glimpse of tong life. During a Chinese New Year celebration, Pop took me to his tong across the street from his business. His tong was above a restaurant operated by the parents of Ben Fong-Torres, who later gained fame as, among other accomplishments, a *Rolling Stone* editor and writer. The large social hall was alive with *Hoisan-wa* and Cantonese chatter, clacking mah-jong games, Chinese opera music, sweet and savory snacks, and cigarette smoke. Lacquered wooden chairs lined the room's perimeter. An altar sat high above the double door of the back room. You could feel the camaraderie in the smoke-filled room.

8

GROWING FAMILY

Mom and the three daughters learned to live with Pop's lottery business. Literally fresh off the boat, they had little other choice. They knew nothing else, and they had no leverage to question his choices. Mom had little time to think about much other than helping Pop sell lottery tickets while maintaining mothering and household tasks. With no schooling or exposure to life outside a rice-growing village, she knew nothing of the social and economic circumstances into which Pop had put her.

Her elevated status in Pop's village as the wife of a man who went to America was deflated in Oakland by the rugged reality of everyday life in a segregated American Chinatown during hard economic times, surrounded by an alien and modern society. The longer Mom lived in her real world and not in the fantasy of a high-status wife, the more disillusioned and angrier she got. She once expressed her deep disappointment to her youngest daughter, Florence, in *Hoisan-wa*: *Loy Mee Gwok yew heck foo*, meaning "You come to America, you 'eat bitter.'"[1]

Pop tutored Mom on selling lottery tickets. She learned a little conversational English. Fortunately for her, other Chinatown women about her age, mothers too, all from the same Chinese region, were in similar circumstances. Their bonding eased her early adjustment.

Within a month of her arrival, Mom became pregnant. That posed a

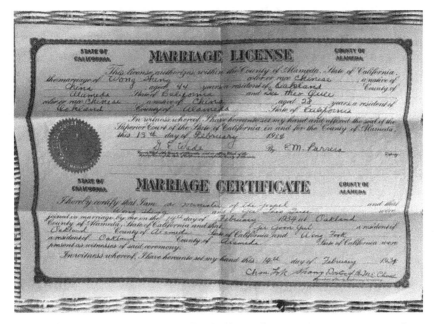

Official marriage certificate of author's mother to a man commissioned to be her "paper" husband in 1934. (Author's Collection)

potential legal issue because she was a single woman, Pop's "sister," according to her official immigration status. It would indeed be scandalous for an unmarried woman in Chinatown to be pregnant, but Chinatown insiders knew the truth. For the outside white world, Pop and Mom had to concoct another falsehood to legitimize her pregnancy. That strategy was a doozy: A Chinatown minister found a man named Wong Sheng, who was paid to "marry" Mom, a marriage on paper only. Wong Sheng and Mom never consummated the marriage, nor did they live together. That "marriage" in early 1934, however, legitimized the September birth of Nellie, yet another girl.

Mom's sham marriage explains why the four children born in Oakland, from 1934 to 1941, all carry the Wong surname, and not Pop's Gee surname. To the world outside Chinatown, four of us were Gees (Pop and the three China-born daughters), and five of us were Wongs (Mom, three Oakland-born daughters, and me). Inside Chinatown, however, we were all Gees. That dual-name conundrum was common in our Chinatown and probably in others.

Given chronic worries over their legal status and their unfamiliarity with one another, Pop and Mom had major adjustments to make. This was the first time they lived together without him leaving for business or living overseas. Pop was in his late thirties, Mom in her early thirties. They were about the same height, his five feet four inches to her five feet two inches. Both were attractive, with his full head of hair over a round face that broke easily into a smile, and occasionally growled as his temper flared, and her smooth pretty face at first reserved and reticent, but soon she learned to smile at customers and speak up at home, without smiles, with displeasures and disappointments.

America was still so new to her and unlike anything she had imagined it would be, given the fantasy existence she had thought that she'd have. Instead, her new life in Oakland shocked her system. The unrealistic dream of an easy life was quickly disabused when she saw the simple family living quarters and Chinatown itself, with its rows of undistinguished buildings packed with stores, restaurants, herb shops—and no gold in the streets. Compared with rural life in China, the Chinatown family quarters were relatively luxurious, with indoor plumbing, flush toilets, and reliable electricity. Yet it dawned on her that Chinatown was a place of hard work, noisy city life, no-nonsense business, and avoidance of contact, as much as possible, with the nearby white world.

Then there was the matter of a continuing quest for a son. That wasn't to be, at least not at first. Barely sixteen months after Nellie's birth came Leslie, yet another girl. Then came Florence more than two years later. Mom cried; Pop wasn't happy. Another girl, another mouth to feed. Where was the son? The three new daughters added to the financial pressures. The lottery income was unpredictable and never abundant, a situation that stressed Pop and Mom. Pop had to occasionally borrow money from Gee cousins and get credit from grocery stories. Our family got help from Mom's brother-in-law, a San Francisco laundryman who generously brought over food and gave us money. Learning to cope with a tight budget, Mom waited for sales at department stores, grabbing multiple sets of socks, underwear, and other clothes until her money ran out.

By now, Mom had taken on a somber, even unhappy persona. It didn't help her disposition to have to move three times in a little more than six years. The Webster Street space lasted about two years, as the landlord started rebuilding the old wooden structure and reconfigured the interior space to six units from four. Pop found a Victorian house around the corner on 7th Street, where he continued his lottery business. Unoccupied for years, the house was musty, so the family moved again shortly thereafter to another rental house a block away, also on 7th Street.

The address was 333 7th Street and is notorious in our family's early Oakland history. Florence, Pop's sixth daughter and Mom's fifth, was born in this house. The live-in *amah* (nanny) whom Mom hired to help take care of the new baby swore that the house was haunted with ghosts. The next-door neighbor, the Tom family, who ran a grocery store, believed similarly. This claim spooked Mom, who thought that the place had bad karma, compounding her unhappiness with having yet another girl. Adding to the bad vibes was an incident with oldest daughter Li Hong, in her mid-teens, looking out the front window and seeing a Red Train run violently into a man our family knew, killing him. She went into shock. It took some time for her to return to a semblance of herself, who was usually smiling, cheerful, singing. After two months of intermittent crying and agony, Mom pleaded with Pop to move yet again, which our family did to another rental, on Harrison Street, one block east of Webster.

Among the many vociferous arguments Pop and Mom had, my sisters remembered one that stood out as particularly scary. (I wasn't born yet.) It occurred at our Harrison Street house sometime in early 1940. Pop and Mom shouting at one another stunned my sisters; some started crying. Pop screamed at Mom that if she hated him so much, she should shoot him with his gun. Memories differ slightly among my sisters: Florence remembered frantically trying to open the big free-standing safe where the gun was kept, after pleading with a sister who knew the safe's code. Li Keng recalled Pop wielding the pistol and threatening to shoot himself. Leslie said that someone pulled Pop away from the safe he was trying to open to get the gun.

Whatever the case, no one shot anyone that day, but the argument's intensity was so fierce that the incident is emblazoned in the memories of my sisters. None of them knew when Pop acquired the gun. Given Pop's sometimes-dicey lottery trade and the threat of tong wars, it's no surprise he owned a pistol, for self-protection, if nothing else. I remember the gun. I once held it, examining its features, feeling curious, somewhat macho but also frightened. It was a shiny black revolver with a long barrel. After Pop and Mom died, someone—we don't know who—broke into the safe and stole the gun.

Somehow, parental arguments and housing instability didn't deter Pop's growing family from fitting in nicely with other growing families with similar backgrounds. On Webster, the Chan family had a barbershop and children about the same age as Pop's. My sisters and I played with kids from the Louie, Tom, Chan, and other Gee families who ran various small businesses. Before I came along, my sisters had fun when they could, going to the Lincoln Square clubhouse for dances or to Harrison Railroad Park. They playfully shot lima beans through straws at one another and pretended to have sidewalk wars, carving up pieces in front of our parents' businesses. They loved the storefront at 7th and Webster, which sold comic books, candies, and sodas.

White Oakland was very close by, and we Chinatown kids ventured out of our fenceless Chinese enclave into the "real" world, to movie theaters, such as the T&D ("the tough and dirty"), the Roxie, the Fox Oakland, and Paramount. We were thrilled to walk up Broadway, enjoying hamburgers and French fries sold at a storefront opening at the T&D Theater or a Kasper's hot dog. Some of us went to the main library, at that time on 14th Street, a few blocks west of "forbidden" Broadway.

From the perspective of Chinatown families in the 1930s and 1940s, it truly was a village transformed from the tranquil rice fields of Hoisan to the modern hustle and bustle of a *Ghim Saan* ("Gold Mountain") city where we felt insulated and isolated. And, yes, there were also Chinatown versions of Peyton Place, whereby some men had second families unbeknownst to the first, left behind in China, and a woman or two had children from different men. These circumstances made for juicy bamboo-telegraph gossip.

In the late 1930s, Pop worked a hodge-podge of jobs in addition to or in place of the lottery. For a time, after Prohibition (1920–1933), he and Mom distilled a liquor called *bok dieu*, "white whisky" or "white lightning," out of one of the 7th Street houses, bootlegging it for Chinatown consumption at $5 a gallon. *Bok dieu* was an ingredient in a postbirth chicken whisky soup[2] for new mothers that purportedly replenished blood lost during childbirth. The strong liquor smell permeated the house and attracted cops. "The smell was so strong, one day police came and took Pop to jail. He got bailed out," Lai Wah recalled.

Pop also got into two restaurant partnerships. The first was Sam & Harry's Café with Harry Louie on Webster Street. This café featured American food and operated for a couple of years before shutting down over business differences. The second involved a $500 investment in a partnership with five other Chinatown men. While this restaurant was being built, Pop couldn't be active. This place lasted about a year, however, as potential workers preferred better-paying wartime jobs.

In 1939, a year before the second restaurant deal, Pop abandoned his sole-proprietorship lottery and got into a new lottery partnership with five other men, all from the same region in China, but now living in California Chinatowns. The shop was on Franklin, only a couple of blocks from our family's other homes and places of business. Each man invested $250. Pop was the designated operator.

9

FATEFUL MEETING

The new lottery partnership showed a more ambitious Pop. Having had a sixth child in late 1938 motivated him to try to increase his income. That's also probably what prompted him to take more risks when selling lottery tickets, especially the strategy of keeping a bet all to himself on the chance it wouldn't win so that he could keep the amount bet.

Sometime in the late winter or early spring of 1940, Pop decided to take the riskiest lottery path. Alas, that decision was disastrous. The bettor won big, and Pop and his partners lost big. We don't know the amount Pop and his partners lost, but it drained the partnership and our family's coffers. The big loss devastated him and Mom, already stressed over money issues. Realizing his mistake, Pop chose not to say anything to his partners. He figured that they didn't need to know, as he thought that he could make up the loss, betting, so to speak, on the incremental accumulation of revenue from future tickets sold that didn't win.

One of his partners, Gee Bing Fook, who lived in Marysville, heard the bad news through the well-connected northern California Chinatown networks. Marysville, in the north central valley above Sacramento, had an active Chinatown of residents with similar China roots as Pop's. Complicating matters for Pop were rumors flying around Chinatown that, as treasurer of his tong, he had embezzled several hundred dollars to support his family after the big loss. Tong leaders noticed something funny with the books, suspecting that Pop had taken out unauthorized funds.

On April 23, 1940, Pop got a phone call at the Harrison Street house that he had hoped he'd never get. The caller was Gee Bing Fook, his business partner and paper brother. Although several years younger than Pop (both in their mid-forties), Bing Fook had entered the United States in 1910, two years before Pop did. The two men had known one another for about thirty years but weren't close personal friends in the modern Westernized sense of sharing common feelings, interests, tastes, personalities, opinions, and politics. Among their cohort, a sense of obligation—to a clan or a place—governed relationships, not friendship.

This version is what I imagine occurred during that call and events following it the next day, based on local government and newspaper accounts and family stories. After exchanging pleasantries about each other's families, Bing Fook got to the point: Would Pop help him fill out an immigration application for Bing Fook to bring over a son from China? That request surprised Pop because he had figured that if he were to hear from Bing Fook at all, it would be about the lottery debacle. After a pause, Pop said that he'd help since he had experience with these applications, not only for himself and his family but also in his former agent business. Bing Fook told Pop that he'd be driving down to Oakland from Marysville the next day. Pretending conviviality, Pop invited him to come for dinner then.

After hanging up, Pop's mind likely was swirling with doubts about Bing Fook's intentions. Was his immigration request genuine? Why didn't he ask about the lottery loss? Pop sensed instinctively that this meeting might not be just about an immigration matter. He couldn't shake a feeling of foreboding. But rather than directly challenge Bing Fook, Pop fell back on a culturally ingrained mind-set, an obligation to help his paper brother. Yet another stress point arose: He dreaded asking Mom to prepare a special dinner because, with little money, Mom had to shop for food on credit, an embarrassing loss of face.

The next day, Wednesday, April 24, 1940, at 725 Harrison Street, Pop was fidgety, more so than he had been lately. Not one to sit quietly, he paced hesitatingly, between the kitchen in the back and the hallway leading to the front of the house. It was close to six o'clock. Mom was in the kitchen, preparing a chicken dinner. The aromas were intoxicating—rice cooking, chicken bubbling in hot water infused with herbs and vegetables. The tension between Pop and Mom was palpable. They said nothing to one another, as each went about his or her own chores.

With a slightly trembling hand, Pop pulled out his pocket watch to check the time, almost six o'clock. He checked his shirt pocket to verify that he also had his little address book that had information about Bing Fook's family. Back and forth, he strolled from room to hallway to room. He paid no attention to his three youngest daughters, who were somewhere else in the house.

A little after six o'clock, the doorbell rang. Breathing more quickly than usual, Pop opened the door. Standing there was Gee Bing Fook, holding a big envelope and wearing a gray fedora, gray wool overcoat, and a dark suit. The two men greeted one another cordially, as though this visit were another casual social call.[1]

"*Nee ho la ma?* [How are you?]" Bing Fook asked with a hearty, if strained, smile in guttural *Hoisan-wa*, as he stepped inside.

"*Ho, ho* [Good, good]," Pop said, gritting his teeth in an equally strained smile.

He undoubtedly felt unnerved by Bing Fook's actual presence, although he tried his best not to show it. Mom stood behind Pop with a thin half-smile, exchanging a muted greeting. After an awkward silence, Mom retreated to the kitchen. Pop wheeled around, gesturing to Bing Fook to follow. They walked through the narrow center hallway that separated the banister and staircase on the left and living room and bedrooms on the right.

They stepped into the warm kitchen filled with delicious smells. Li Hong, the oldest daughter at eighteen years, was washing clothes in the bathtub. Florence, the youngest daughter at eighteen months, toddled around barefoot, looking up with big eyes at the adults. Two other daughters, Nellie, five, and Leslie, four, came out of their bedroom to politely greet the visitor and then departed while Florence stayed close to Mom, who had water boiling for tea. She offered Bing Fook a cup, but he said that he didn't want any. Instead, he got right to the point, asking for Pop's help. Pop said, "*Huey koy ga fong la* [Let's go to the other room]," meaning the dining area just outside the kitchen.

Pop sat down at the round table, clearing space so he could write. Bing Fook gave Pop the big envelope with an immigration application form inside. Reaching for a fountain pen on a side table, Pop asked Bing Fook a few questions about his family in China and began writing down what he heard. Completing the application took almost thirty minutes. In addition to Bing Fook's on-the-spot information, Pop looked at the small address book that had other information. Bing Fook stood silently, only a yard away. When he finished, Pop put the address book back into his shirt pocket and handed the form to Bing Fook.

No longer interested in his family in China, Bing Fook curtly brought up the sore subject that had hovered over the faux-polite banter: Pop's recent lottery loss and the embezzlement allegations.

"Why didn't you let us know?" Bing Fook asked Pop. Pop stared at Bing Fook without saying a word. "How are you going to recover the money?" Bing Fook persisted, his voice now straining.

"I hope to make up the loss in the future," Pop answered, lamely.

"That's not good enough!" Bing Fook retorted, in a rising, seething tone. "And why did you take $300 from the tong?"

Again, silence from Pop. Pop's fragile demeanor grew tense. He didn't quite know how to respond to Bing Fook's hectoring. Still wearing his overcoat and fedora, Bing Fook looked fiercely at Pop. He demanded an accounting and asked for his $250 investment back.

With a hint of anger, Pop said that he didn't have the money. Without another word, a livid Bing Fook reached into his right coat pocket, pulled out a pistol, and shot Pop four times—*bang! bang! bang! bang!*—first in the left shoulder, twice in the lower stomach, and last in the upper left chest. The four shots rang out in quick succession and were heard throughout the house.

"We were standing at the table facing one another," approximately a yard away from one another, Pop later recalled in court testimony at his shooter's arraignment and preliminary hearing. "After I got through writing, I put a little memorandum book back into my pocket, then he took a gun and shot me. . . . [H]e drew a gun right from his back pocket. I don't know exactly what pocket. I am writing at that time when he shot me right in the shoulder, when I got up, he shot me in the abdomen. . . . The blood was running when he shot me. I was kind of dizzy. . . . After that, I fainted."[2]

From the kitchen, Mom could hear muffled voices but nothing substantive of the conversation of the two men. When the shots rang out—

what she later said sounded like firecrackers—she bolted into the dining area. Mouth agape, eyes bulging, her heart pounding, and beginning to breathe heavily, she saw Pop slumped on the floor, his white shirt turning bloody red in the chest and left arm, and blood sprayed on the wall and the velvet curtain near the bedroom doors. Moaning in pain, he muttered "murder" to her.

"Then I ran face to face with Sam [Pop], running toward Sam face to face and he says, 'I am shot. They are killing me.' Then, all of a sudden, another bullet whizzed right by the wall," Mom testified later in court.[3] The pistol still in his right hand, Bing Fook looked at Mom with stern, angry eyes and threatened her in *Hoisan-wa*: "If you follow me, I will shoot you too." He ran down the hallway and out the front door. Instead of collapsing or attending to Pop, and despite the threat, Mom bolted after Bing Fook. She bounded down the five front steps and pursued the man who had just shot her husband.

From their bedroom, Nellie and Leslie heard the shots. Startled by the loud bursts, they smelled the gunpowder residue as they cautiously peeked out to see what had happened. Seeing Mom run down the hallway, Nellie and Leslie instinctively followed her with fright in their eyes, not knowing what else to do.

Keeping her eyes on a fleeing Bing Fook, Mom headed up Harrison Street toward 8th Street past Fong Get Chong's barbershop, crossed over 8th, turned left toward Webster Street, and passed the Wing On Teng grocery store where she had gotten provisions for the ill-fated Bing Fook dinner. She turned right, past the Bowen Liquor Store at the corner of Webster and 8th, and headed up Webster toward 9th. At some point along the way, she either kicked off her well-worn silk-brocade stiff-soled Chinese slippers or they slipped off her feet as she ran after Bing Fook.

As she ran, she yelled at the top of her lungs in *Hoisan-wa*: "*Gew meng ah, gew meng ah! Bing Fook ah thlee uh Ghee Gheng!*" ("[Help] save a life! [Help] save a life! Bing Fook killed Ghee Gheng!"—referring to Pop by his inside-Chinatown name).

Lee Ming and Wing Siew happened to be inside the Bowen Liquor Store. They heard Mom's screams and saw Bing Fook and her run by outside. Lee Ming knew Mom, so he and Wing Siew bolted out and gave chase after Bing Fook,[4] who continued running up Webster toward 9th Street, past Yuen Hop, a bean sprouts and noodle store. The two male pursuers, having overtaken Mom, leapt to tackle Bing Fook, subduing him, as a barefoot Mom closed in fast. Confronting him directly, Mom screamed, "If you killed him, you might as well kill me too."[5]

Oakland Police Officer Joseph B. Jackson happened to be on foot patrol in Chinatown at the time. He saw a man later identified as Show Lee Gee (a version of Bing Fook's immigration name of Gee Seow Lee) "first running west on 8th Street between Harrison and Webster at about 7:10 P.M." He said that "several other persons" were chasing him too. Officer Jackson joined the pursuit. "He went west on 8th Street, north on Webster to 9th Street[,] where he was apprehended and arrested."[6]

The officer searched the suspect and found a "black revolver, automatic pistol, caliber 7.65 millimeters" in his right-hand overcoat pocket. The gun was later identified as a Deutsche Werke-Werkerfurt, caliber 7.65 millimeters, black metal with a wooden handle. After Officer Jackson arrested Bing Fook, a heavy-breathing Mom ran back to the house with daughters Nellie and Leslie in tow to check on her husband, who was prostrate, bleeding profusely.

10

SHOCK AND AWE

The shooting of Pop shocked our family, friends, and Chinatown. "'Why is this happening to our own people?'" Li Keng, who was fourteen at the time, recalled people asking. Chinatown people were angry. "'They should take him to jail and let him rot.' 'Shoot him and kill him.' That's what I remember people saying."[1]

Richard Gee, whose herbalist father employed Pop in 1912, told me that he remembered hearing about Pop's shooting, with some inaccurate details: "I heard it was his nephew that had a little argument, and he had his gun in a paper bag, and when things did not go right, he lost his temper and just pulled it out and shot your dad. But your dad survived. It was mostly about money problems; that's what I heard."[2]

Betty Chew, a friend of Li Hong and Li Keng, told me that her father asked her, "'Do you know that your friends' father got shot? I heard it was over money problems.' The next day I went to see how your family was. I was concerned about Li Hong and Li Keng.... The whole town knew about it. There was a lot of shock in Chinatown."[3]

Victor Chinn, whose father's lottery shop was near Pop's, recalled the shooting "quite well.... Your mother was a good friend of my mother. She told us the whole story.... It was the talk of Chinatown—the heroics of your mother, how she chased the guy."[4]

The shooting made news in the *Oakland Tribune* and the *Oakland Post Enquirer*. The *Tribune* story carried the headline "Shooting Stirs Tong

Local newspaper story of the shooting of the author's father in 1940. (*Post Enquirer*, April 25, 1940. Accessed via https://newspaperarchive.com.)

War Fear," with a sub-headline, "Police Act to Prevent Vengeance After Chinese Wounds Kin." The first paragraph said, "Rumblings of tong war spread through the Chinese quarters of San Francisco and Oakland today as an aftermath of the shooting last night of Su Hung Gee [sic], 46 [sic], by his relative, Shon Lee Gee [sic], of Marysville."[5] The *Post Enquirer* story's headline read, "CHINESE SHOT/BY BROTHER/IN ROW."[6]

At least one Chinese newspaper reported the shooting. The *Chinese World*, under the headline "Attempted Killing of Oakland Chinese," identified Pop as Gee Ghee Gheng, a native of Goon Du Hahng in Hoisan County, and his shooter as Gee Bing Fook.[7] This story used the inside-Chinatown names, whereas the English-language papers used their immigration names, misspelled at that. The *Chinese World* followed up with another story[8] that said that the two men were partners in a business at 827 Franklin Street. The partnership included eight men,[9] each of whom had invested $250. The first *Chinese World* story had the same basic facts that the English-language newspaper stories did, with no extra reporting. The fact that it used Pop's and Bing Fook's Chinatown names suggests that someone in Chinatown told the *Chinese World* their "real" names.

Who was Gee Bing Fook, also known as Gee Seow (Show) Lee, other than being Pop's younger paper brother, a Gee clan member from the same area of China as Pop, and a fellow tong member? Several sisters remember him as Bing Fook. Li Keng said, "He was not blood related to us. His name came up once in a while. He drifted in once in a blue moon to visit us." She and Lai Wah had heard that he was a so-called *boo how doy*[10] ("hatchet man," a tong enforcer).[11] Lai Wah also said that Mom babysat his children.[12]

According to his immigration papers, he had arrived in America through the Angel Island Immigration Station on September 19, 1910, approximately twenty months before Pop came. He was fourteen years old. He listed his father as Gee Bing Fong and Pop as a brother just older than he. He stayed somewhere in California for seven years. In the summer of 1917, he traveled back to China. At the time, he was a twenty-year-old student at San Rafael Grammar School in Marin County, north of San Francisco. While in China, he married a Yee woman, who gave birth to a boy, Gee Hung Yin. He came back to America in July 1919, leaving his wife and son behind. From 1921 to 1931, he made two more trips to China, claiming in the end to have had six children, four boys and two girls. His American jobs during that span were a cigar-store clerk in Los Angeles and a gambling-house worker in Reno, Nevada. When he came back in July 1931, he gave a new Americanized name, Chester Gee.

There is no more documentation in his immigration file, suggesting that he stayed put, presumably in California and perhaps in Nevada.

The next time his name appeared publicly, in Oakland English-language newspapers, was on April 25, 1940, the day after he shot Pop. Twenty years later, when the U.S. government had a "confession" program for Chinese immigrants who had entered America illegally during the exclusion years, the name Show Lee Gee, a version of his immigration name, resurfaced.

In 1960, his first-born "son," Gee Hong (Hung) Yin, confessed his illegal status to the Immigration and Naturalization Service. He said that his alleged father was "Gee Shew Lee," who claimed to have been born in "Gwoon Doo Hong," Pop's village. The "son" said that he didn't know the real birthplace of his alleged father. He also said that he saw this man in San Francisco after he himself had been admitted in 1935.[13] He gave his real parents' names and his real birthplace in another Hoisan County village, not Pop's. He also said that his real birth year was 1918, not 1915, as his paper father had said. The U.S. immigration investigator, Harry H. Savage, asked Gee Hong Yin, "Is your paper father, GEE SHEW LEE, related to you in any way?" Gee Hong Yin responded, "In Chinese style we are only clan cousins. Actually, we are related to the same family clan—the GEE clan."[14]

The most fascinating question, of course, was why Bing Fook shot Pop. There are at least two possible answers, based on official testimony and unofficial family stories. In his court testimony, Joseph B. Jackson, the Oakland police officer who arrested the shooter, said:

> The defendant stated that he had contacted his brother Sam Gee [Pop] for the purpose of collecting some money that his brother owed him. In other words, according to his statement, his brother had borrowed $250.00 from this defendant in 1929[15] to go into business in the Chinese district and that the defendant had made several requests from the complainant [Pop] endeavoring to collect this money or a portion of it.
>
> He said that when he went to contact the complainant the day of the shooting, he said he was broke, he was hungry, had no place to go, and that during the conversation, the brother ordered him out of the house and had threatened him and had [told] him to leave town and not bother him anymore.

An argument ensued and the defendant stated that he could readily see that he wasn't going to get any money from him. He says "I just became angered and took the gun out of my pocket and shot him."

He further stated that he went to the address (725 Harrison Street) with the automatic on his person and intended to use it if he did not collect the money. That was the extent of the conversation.[16]

The *Oakland Tribune* and the *Oakland Post Enquirer* reported what the police concluded was Bing Fook's motive for shooting Pop, a business deal gone bad. Both stories about the shooting said, in the *Tribune*'s version, that Pop and his "brother" and "seven other Chinese had gone into business together at 827 Franklin Street a year and a half ago." Each partner had put in $250 to establish "China Trading Post" and sold merchandise in the front, while selling lottery tickets in the back. When police had raided the lottery several months earlier and closed the store, Bing Fook said, he had demanded an accounting. He said that he had gotten no satisfaction from Pop, so he had come from Marysville to collect. Then, he said that he had argued with Pop, and Pop had lunged at him. Then, Bing Fook said, he had drawn a pistol and shot Pop four times.[17]

This "official" narrative doesn't square with what my sisters heard from Mom, either immediately after the shooting or in subsequent decades, in her recurring retelling of the most traumatic—and dramatic—incident in our family's Chinatown experiences. My sisters have different versions about why Bing Fook shot Pop. Their stories hint at internal Chinatown conflicts, jealousies, and resentments related to Pop's lottery business, his misfortune in losing a lot of money, and his desperation to feed his family when his business collapsed.

One such divergent story is trivial. Lai Wah, Nellie, Leslie, and Florence remembered Mom saying that the meeting between Pop and Bing Fook was a "special dinner," topped off, for the men, with cigars. Li Keng didn't believe that Mom cooked a meal for Bing Fook.[18] More substantively, the lottery business's nosedive could very well have precipitated the shooting. But given the incomplete, vague, and imprecise official explanation at the time, and the divergent and equally murky memories of my sisters, the exact reason why Bing Fook shot Pop remains elusive.

The essence of what Mom told my sisters is that the shooter believed that Pop had cheated him, the tong suspected Pop of embezzling funds to cover his lottery loss, and the tong dispatched the shooter to try to get the money back. As a side note, my sisters speculated on who started rumors about Pop embezzling tong funds, a Chinatown family who had befriended Mom upon her arrival in Oakland in 1933. Lai Wah said that some in Chinatown "were always jealous of Pop. . . . It's like a power play between cousins and brothers." Nellie added, "There were rivalries among the Gee clan [in Oakland]," perhaps because Pop was doing well before his lottery business went bust.

As to the press reports about a possible "tong war" erupting because of the shooting, several sisters dismissed that speculation. Lai Wah said, "It was a family thing, it had nothing to do with the tongs." Leslie, however, wasn't so quick to dismiss the possibility of tongs going to war: "It's hard for us to really say it wasn't related to tong rivalries. We don't know that. We don't know the politics behind the tongs."[19]

In court, Pop limited his testimony to Bing Fook's request for immigration help. Pop, however, also used the word *accounting*, suggesting that Bing Fook wanted to know about the lottery loss or missing tong funds. He said nothing specifically about the latter, however. It wouldn't have been in Pop's best interest to spill the beans about having an illegal lottery business or anything about internal tong business. Another clue to Pop's disingenuousness is the fact that he and Mom, in their court testimonies, maintained the fiction that they were siblings. Telling the truth about their relationship could have jeopardized their legal status in America.

Another intriguing wrinkle in Mom's court testimony was her reference to another man coming to the door of 725 Harrison just before Bing Fook shot Pop. Prosecutor Freeman asked Mom whether anybody else was in the house other than Pop, Mom, the children, and Bing Fook. Mom said, "Yes. . . . There was another man there that time." Just before the shooting, she testified, the doorbell rang. "Another man by the name of Gee came to the door and rang the bell and came in just as the shot happened," Mom said. This other man, whom Mom said was named Gee Jim Art, asked her whether Pop was busy. She said that he was.[20]

This testimony contradicts other versions of how things unfolded. If Mom went to the front door just before Bing Fook shot Pop, that meant that she wasn't in the kitchen but between the shooter and the front door when he fled the house, not behind him. If, however, this Gee Jim Art was at the door just before the shooting, a mystery remains as to who he was, what he did, and where he went afterward. Never once in the many times my sisters have talked about the shooting has another man been mentioned.

In her testimony, Mom added, intriguingly, "I will tell everything about relations of mine, I will tell everything. There was another man rang the bell. Another man by the name of Gee came to the door and rang the bell and came in just as the shot happened. I thought my testimony was enough but if you want me to tell everything, I'll just tell everything. And that man was there at that time."

What did she mean by "I will tell everything"? One can infer that she wasn't going to hold anything back about intra-Gee clan or intra-Chinatown relationships. No further explanation, however, appeared in Mom's court testimony, or in family stories. In the end, her invocation of another man in the house during Pop's shooting raised more questions that are without plausible answers decades later.

On October 30, 1940, after a trial[21] that started on September 23, an Alameda County Superior Court jury found Show Lee Gee[22] guilty of attempted murder of Pop, a felony. He served three years in San Quentin state prison and was paroled on November 10, 1943. Where Bing Fook went after that isn't known. He reportedly died in 1960 in Los Angeles.[23]

Miraculously, Pop survived the four gunshot wounds but lost a kidney. Henry B. Woo examined Pop at the Alameda County Hospital about an hour after the shooting: "At that time the man was in profound shock and he had several wounds in his left shoulder and arm. . . . They were punctured wounds in his abdomen in front and in back." Dr. Woo added in court testimony that Pop had four wounds in his left shoulder and left arm, "and one in his abdomen, one in his back on the right side." Woo further said that those wounds could have killed Pop.[24]

In Pop's small address book, Woo wrote, "April 24, 1940 Patient shot through the abdomen, left shoulder and left arm. Alameda County Hospital, Oakland, California. For emergency treatment. Patient was shot, and an exploratory laparotomy, revealed perfection of the gall-bladder, laceration of the liver, abrasion of the mesentery, and ruptured right kidney which was removed. Left radial palsy was present for which an operation was performed on June 27, 1940 (neurolysis of left radial nerve). . . . Partial paralysis left hand. Alameda County Hospital, Oak, California, [signed] Henry B. Woo, MD."[25]

Pop talked openly to family members about the shooting. Nellie said, "After Pop had his surgery, and then after he was healed, I remember how he liked to show his scar. It was on his stomach. It looked like a big flower. He did that to show what happened to him and how serious it was. I remember hearing about how the gold watch he was wearing saved him."

As though the shooting weren't enough of a family trauma, that April 1940 incident might have been the *second* time Pop was a target. A man once close to our family[26] told me of a previous shooting of Pop in the late 1930s or early in 1940, something my sisters had not heard of previously. This man heard shots fired on the 700 block of Webster Street, where Pop's lottery business was. This man, at that time quite young, had been dropped off by his businessman father in the early afternoon at the open-air store at 7th and Webster Streets.

"I was sitting on a chair reading a comic book," he said. "It happened so fast. Suddenly we heard two shots—*bang! bang!* The storeowner grabbed me and pulled me down. We both ducked down. I heard two shots; I remember that very distinctly. Then, I saw this man run down the street. I didn't know who he was. I didn't find out until later your father was the target." After this shooting, my informant said, there was "very quiet gossip around Chinatown because they wanted to keep it quiet and because it was related to gambling. They didn't want to scare people off."

Pop wasn't hit. "The guy was shooting up [from the street level up a staircase]. The speculation was that it was over some gambling dispute." The shooter "might have been the same guy" who shot Pop later. "Maybe he took his time again to try to get your father. Maybe he had revenge in mind. He might have been another [tong] member. Your father was more accessible [the second time]."

The shooting on April 24, 1940, has been a family legend. Hearing about an earlier attempt on Pop's life deepened my feeling of despair. How could my beloved Pop have been a target of possible murder twice, within months of one another? After many blood transfusions, it took Pop months to recover, first in the hospital, then at home. Fortunately, an insurance policy provided $50 a month to cover his disability. Li Hong and Li Keng gave Mom their earnings from doing household chores for white families to help our family too.[27]

This time was tough and embarrassing for Mom. Without Pop working and him needing her attention, household management was even more challenging. She peeled shrimp with help from the girls, earning up to $5 a day. Yet quietly and almost miraculously, something was stirring inside Mom that brought the possibilities of better times, or at least more optimism. She became pregnant with me.

11

FINALLY, A BOY

By mid-1941, Pop was in his mid-forties. Since he came to Oakland twenty-nine years earlier, he had had business successes and failures in Oakland as well as in China. Most of 1940 was miserable for him and Mom. His lottery business collapsed. He almost died after getting shot multiple times. His prospects for doing better were gloomy.

Shortly after the autumnal equinox of 1940, things began to turn for the better based on what had to be unbelievable determination of Pop and Mom. As practitioners of China's deeply ingrained culture that favored males over females, they still had a burning desire to have a son, all their problems be damned. Six daughters, as worthy as each was, weren't enough. It didn't matter to Pop and Mom that he was still in recovery. In early October, like a lottery winner, they "hit." It was her sixth pregnancy in fifteen years.

That news apparently energized Pop, who borrowed money from clan cousins to buy a little grocery store in Berkeley, just north of Oakland. He knew that he had to do something to rejuvenate our family's finances. He had eight mouths to feed, with another in the offing. Although pregnant, Mom helped at the store until she couldn't. The store sold fresh fruit, vegetables, and other standard American food items. To boost a modest customer flow, Pop offered simple Chinese food to go, noodle and rice dishes. It was a big hit, at 50¢ a box. At first, Mom did the cooking while Pop tended to customers. When Mom wasn't there, he cooked. Pop called on Li Keng, in her mid-teens, and ten-year-old Lai Wah to help.

The big moment Pop and Mom had longed for came in the summer of 1941, my birth, a roly-poly boy of ten pounds plus. I was born in the rented Harrison Street house where Pop had been shot the previous April. I, of course, didn't know it at the time, but my birth was a very big deal. A super-excited Pop called lots of relatives and friends, and all of Chinatown soon knew that I had arrived. During the ensuing month, Chinatown folks flooded into our house to see precious little me. My red-egg-and-ginger party, a traditional event that usually occurs a month after a birth, brought in a lot of money stuffed into red envelopes. With that money, Pop started a bank account for me, the only child to get such a benefit, male privilege in action.

Pop named me William, pronounced Weeyim in *Hoisan-wa*, after a British king—who knows why?—and Wah Keng[1] in Chinese, meaning "strong country," referring to China, yet another indicator of Pop's love of his birthplace.

My older sisters were probably relieved and resentful about my joining their world. Pop and Mom hadn't cheered with joy at their births the way they did at mine. Chinatown didn't welcome them the way it did me. Some of my sisters told me that Pop thought my birth brought him good luck after so much bad luck. Family legend has it that Florence, the sister born thirty-two months before me, resented me so much that she pushed me out of a highchair when I was either an infant or toddler. I, obviously, survived, and her childishly wanton act of jealousy didn't permanently wreck our future relationship.

By sheer coincidence, the world shook during my birth year. Five months after I was born, we in Chinatown, like all other Americans, felt the ripples from Japanese warplanes bombing Pearl Harbor in Hawaii on December 7, 1941. Pop had no love for Japan, which had invaded China in the 1930s, a feeling shared in other American Chinatowns. His anti-Japan feelings, however, didn't transfer to Oakland's Japanese Americans, who worked and lived in or near Chinatown.

Whatever historic animosities existed between China and Japan, there's a historic link between Chinese and Japanese immigrants to America, starting in the late nineteenth century. When the exclusion

Author as a toddler, perhaps in 1942 or 1943, in front of the family's rental house in Oakland's Chinatown. (Author's Collection)

law eliminated Chinese laborers, American employers hired Japanese immigrant workers, who came in significant numbers to Oakland, starting in the 1880s. By 1910, approximately 1,500 lived in the city. By 1940, approximately 1,800 lived in Oakland, mostly in West Oakland and Chinatown. Together, the footprint of Chinese and Japanese residents was tiny, making up only about 2 percent of the city's three hundred thousand people that year.

Pearl Harbor had a disparate effect on Oakland's Chinese and Japanese residents. For some of us Chinese, it was the start of a major uptick in economic fortunes. For the Japanese, it was devastating. In February 1942, three months after Pearl Harbor, President Franklin D. Roosevelt ordered the evacuation of ethnic Japanese living on the West Coast, regardless of whether they were U.S. citizens, to desolate areas in California, other western states, and even Arkansas, where the federal government put up internment camps that were like prisons. About 110,000 to 120,000 Japanese Americans and legal Japanese immigrants lost their homes and businesses and were locked away without cause other than the fact they were of Japanese descent. The U.S. government never found a case of espionage among Japanese Americans. Instead, some Japanese American men joined the U.S. Army and fought valiantly in Europe for America.

Some Chinatown children felt the need to tell white Oaklanders that we weren't the enemy, wearing labels that said, "I am an American" or "I am not Japanese." Chinese youngsters, including my sisters, however, felt bad for their Japanese American friends, who were school buddies and otherwise kindred souls. I was still too young to experience these communal woes. In general, Chinese Americans and Japanese Americans at Lincoln School got along fine. I wasn't aware of any open hostility between our parents and those of Japanese descent. I've heard stories, however, of ill feelings and even fights between the two adult (and perhaps youth) groups in other California cities in the 1930s and early 1940s.

When I heard stories years later about what a big deal my birth was, I didn't feel especially privileged. That's easy for me to say because, to Pop and Mom, my perch was higher than that of my sisters. Sure, I felt protected and nurtured in the peculiar Chinatown style of the 1940s and 1950s, but no more so than my sisters. My so-called privilege was cocooned within this "village" bubble. Whether Chinatown boys fully realized that we were more privileged than our sisters wasn't a central issue in our collective lives. There was the almost natural gender segregation, but there was always gender integration during school recesses and street play time.

I spent most of the 1940s on five somewhat contiguous square blocks: a house where we slept, a restaurant where we worked and ate, Chinese school, Lincoln School, and Lincoln Square, where we played. In that closed-in space, I was surrounded by family and folks who looked and sounded like my nuclear family. I'd play with other Chinatown kids on the streets. The adults we saw knew who we were, and if any of us did something mischievous, our parents would hear about it quickly. Chinatown was our village, and its grown-ups were our guardians, whether we liked it or not.

Feeling better physically and spiritually, Pop continued to run the Berkeley grocery store for a little while after I was born. Shortly after Pearl Harbor, though, he sold it because, suddenly, good-paying work

Official U.S. Selective Service registration card of author's father, on which he declares, among other things, his date of birth and his employer. (Author's Collection)

came begging for anyone not joining the military. All around the San Francisco Bay Area, old and newly established or expanded military bases and shipyards needed all the workers they could find, including previously excluded racial and ethnic minorities and women.

Pop seized the opportunity. He got good-paying war-related jobs for himself and Li Hong at an area shipyard in early 1942. My sisters remember them putting on flannel shirts, heavy jackets, fire-resistant gloves, sturdy boots, safety goggles, and hard hats and carrying lunch pails in the afternoons to their night shift somewhere. That somewhere was Richmond Shipyard No. 2, a fact I discovered on a copy of a Selective Service card Pop had to fill out in 1942, when he was in his late forties. On the employer line of that card, he wrote, "Richmond Shipyard No. 2," which was in the wartime boomtown twelve miles north of Oakland.

Richmond's main attributes were a deep harbor and lots of unused land. Oakland, Alameda, and Richmond were the East Bay cities that had the most war-related shipyard employment in the early 1940s. The four Richmond shipyards were an enterprise of Oakland industrialist

Henry J. Kaiser, whose companies before the war paved highways and built bridges and dams throughout the western United States. Kaiser had shipyards in other states, almost all building Liberty merchant ships that were essential for the U.S. war effort in Europe and Asia.

Pop was a welder, a new skill for which he and Li Hong were trained. Pop heard that the pay was good, and he thought that Li Hong, who was twenty years old, had dropped out of high school, and worked as domestic help, could also earn good money welding and performing other chores, like sweeping and cleanup. He preferred the swing shift, starting in the late afternoon, because he and Li Hong could earn ten cents more an hour. They worked seven days a week, but the good pay salved the agony of the heavy workload. They spent perhaps a year or more working at the shipyard. Their earnings helped our family's finances enormously, finally a sign of good fortune after nearly two years of hardship.

Having me as her coveted new baby didn't stop Mom from working outside the home. With neighbors and my sisters looking after me, she found work in a parachute factory a half block from our house. She also worked at a canning factory in East Oakland.

12

THE GREAT CHINA

As grueling as the shipyard work was, Pop wasn't looking to change jobs. In the spring of 1943, however, someone approached him with an interesting idea: Quit your shipyard job and open a restaurant. The solicitor was Gee Cheng Yet, whom our family called Cheng Yet Goong,[1] Pop's cousin from his region of China. He told Pop that a restaurant on Webster Street was for sale and that he should take it over. His reasoning: As well paid as shipyard work was, the war would someday end, and now that Pop had seven children, he needed to think about the future of caring for us.

Intrigued, Pop said that he couldn't afford to buy a restaurant, to which Cheng Yet Goong said that he'd lend him the money. With that reassurance, Pop bid for the restaurant and won. His benefactor brought him a paper bag filled with $3,000 in cash. Humbled and appreciative, Pop promised to repay the loan with interest. Cheng Yet Goong told Pop not to worry about paying it back, but there was a catch: Would Pop store some boxes of his at our house? Sure, Pop said. What was in those boxes? Opium. Cheng Yet Goong was a prominent drug dealer looking for a way to launder drug money. Pop knew this and told no one other than Mom. Li Keng, seventeen years old at the time, was home alone one day when a man was sent by Cheng Yet Goong to retrieve one of the boxes,

Author's family in 1944. *Standing, left to right:* Nellie, Li Keng, Li Hong, Henry (Li Hong's new husband), Lai Wah, Florence (*foreground*), and Leslie. *Sitting, left to right:* author's mother, author, and author's father.
(Author's Collection)

which were hidden in Pop and Mom's bedroom closet. When Li Keng found out what was in it, Pop and Mom swore her to secrecy.[2]

Pop and Li Hong quit their shipyard jobs, and he opened the restaurant in the summer of 1943, as World War II raged on. The timing was good, as nearby military-base and shipyard workers needed to eat. Pop called the restaurant the Great China,[3] yet another sign of his love for his home country. Li Keng designed the big sign that protruded out from the wall above the awning. The Great China name appeared over a coffee cup and saucer, which were over the words *chop suey*.[4] The pairing of a Western coffee cup and the words *chop suey* perfectly captured the restaurant's hybrid cuisine.

The Great China became our family's universe for the next eighteen years, or 90 percent of my life by the time it closed. Our rental house a block away was almost irrelevant: We only slept and washed up there. Otherwise, our waking hours were mostly spent at the Great China (and,

Sign over author's family's restaurant, the Great China, in Oakland's Chinatown, with the Oakland Tribune Tower in the background, in 1958. (Photo by the Downtown Property Owners Association. Courtesy Oakland Public Library, Oakland History Center.)

for the children, school). We ate there. We celebrated holidays and family birthdays there. We met friends there. Our collective identities were at the restaurant. Pop's longest-lasting business, it yanked us from the edge of the poverty cliff and pulled us to more stable ground near the start of American middle class.

Pop was inspired by a popular San Francisco Chinatown restaurant called Jackson Café, which featured a hybrid Chinese American cuisine, meaning chow mein and chop suey were served alongside beef prime rib and beef stew. Other San Francisco Chinatown eateries had similar hybrid identities.[5] The Great China's Chinese food was dumbed-down Cantonese fare that wouldn't offend non-Chinese tastes but wouldn't excite today's more demanding, worldly, and sophisticated diners. At the time, there weren't enough Oakland Chinese people who ate out to support a place that offered authentic, unadulterated Cantonese cuisine, so the Great China and a few other Chinatown eateries offered simplified Cantonese food that wouldn't turn off non-Chinese customers. The American stuff was an eclectic mix: pancakes, waffles, bacon, ham, eggs, and toast for breakfast; for lunch and dinner, things like fried halibut, spaghetti and meatballs, veal cutlets, liver and onions, beef stew, lamb curry, chicken-fried steak, tripe in tomato sauce, roast pork, and beef prime rib.

The Great China's inside space was long and narrow, with a two-section counter on the right and booths and a large common table on the left. An upstairs dining space was serviced by a dumbwaiter, an open-faced box attached to a pulley that carried food up from the kitchen. A refrigerator near the kitchen held butter, eggs, and milk. I was scrawny when I was maybe seven years old. Not happy with my skinny physique and seeking to fatten me up, Mom frequently grabbed a pad of butter and stuffed it into my mouth. It worked. And, you know what? I still like butter, but not that way.

One of my favorite spaces was the small pastry room in the back. I'd linger there, watching the pastry chef, Chel Goong, make cakes, pies, rolls, and biscuits, all while nursing a lit cigarette whose ashes kept growing. I worried that the ashes would drop onto a cake or into the whipped-cream bowl. Miraculously, I never saw that happen. I loved to lick the whipped cream off the beater's spindle.

Pop had a small, step-in office in the main dining area. Inside, he kept a ledger, a big-binder checkbook, an abacus, a safe, a chair, and a typewriter. My sisters and I used the latter to type out the daily American menu specials dictated by Mom. The typed original sheet was in purple ink. Pop took the sheet and pressed it onto a pan of gelatin to imprint the menu. He pressed blank sheets onto the gelatin to make copies, which were clipped onto the permanent stiff yellow menu that listed Americanized Cantonese food.

The Great China could feed about fifty people, more or less, at one time. In its first two or three years, every seat was filled for lunch and dinner, thanks to those wartime workers. Sometimes, a customer or two waited in line behind someone eating at a counter seat. The place was hopping. One reason was its food was affordable. Full-course American meals, including soup, salad, entrée with rice or mashed potatoes and vegetables, rolls with butter, and dessert, ranged from only 50¢ (fried halibut) to $1 (beef prime rib). Coffee or tea cost an extra dime. Many

Chinese dishes were in the same price range. In its eighteen years, the restaurant hardly ever raised prices. In the early postwar years, it conformed to the Fair-Trade price rules, which in effect held prices steady. The fact that this was an eighteen-year range and that prices stayed pretty much the same says something about Pop as a businessman—not so good or a good guy?

The low prices didn't hurt the bottom line at first. The restaurant's best years were 1944 and 1945, the war years. Pop didn't document 1944, but in 1945, according to a ledger in his beautiful cursive handwriting, the Great China had sales of $81,671.70 and a profit of $4,931.07 before taxes and after all expenses (cost of goods, salaries, utilities, and so forth). That sales figure would be about $1,361,798 in 2023 dollars.[6] Business was so robust that Pop was able to repay the $3,000 loan in a matter of months. World War II ended in August 1945, foreshadowing a drop in business. Over the next fifteen years, the highest sales figure was $47,503 in 1946, while the lowest was $19,402 in 1948, quite a drop from 1945's $81,671. The final ledger entry was for four months of 1961, when the restaurant closed, with sales on pace for $20,000 if it had stayed open that year.

The Great China had a small paid staff, from four to eight people. Pop never listed himself as being paid. Mom started getting paid in 1950, at $1,200 a year, to a high of $2,160 in 1959 and 1960. We children weren't paid. The highest annual pay was $2,520 in 1945 to Kim Gee, the head chef. Pop was the boss, but Mom was right there with him. He hired workers; bought the produce, meats, and other supplies; kept the books; and paid employees. Pop's most important hire was Kim Gee, or Gee Yuey Yung, whom we children called Yuey Yung Goong or How Chuey Goong, meaning "Mr. Head Chef," or simply Goong. He was a kind, soft-spoken man of about Pop's age, from the same area in China.

Like Pop, he had come to America when young. Unlike Pop, he didn't later bring his family over. He lived his entire adult life separated from his China family and became part of our family by default. He was skilled in cooking Cantonese and American food, having learned the latter when he was a chef at a University of California fraternity, which is where Pop met him when Pop peddled produce from a truck. We children loved him because he sneaked us tastes of his yummy cooking. My favorite was beef stir-fried with *bok toy* (the *Hoisan-wa* term for *bok choy*, a leafy green,

Author's mother preparing food at the family's restaurant, in the 1940s or 1950s. (Author's Collection)

white-stalked vegetable) in a brown gravy over white rice, sometimes topped with a fried egg.

Another cook was Chel Goong (real name: Chew Gee), an opium addict who had to be awakened at his single-room-occupancy apartment building to come to work. Florence often was the one to do that deed. When not working as the pastry chef, he filled in as a sous chef. Pop tolerated Chel Goong's flaws and accommodated his request for pay in advance so he could buy opium.

Pop and Mom were complementary all-purpose workhorses. Mom, in her crisply ironed blue uniform dress with white front buttons, was a central player everywhere, in the kitchen and with customers. She also shopped for food at Swan's or Housewives Market near Chinatown. The hours they worked daily were staggering. At first, the Great China opened at eleven o'clock in the morning, but both started working much earlier than that. It didn't take long, however, for the Great China to open for breakfast at seven o'clock because of the demand from shipyard and military-base workers. That's when Mom made her yummy pancakes, priced at 15¢.

Both worked at least twelve-hour days, seven days a week in the go-go war years. Mom didn't take a break. She was on her feet most of the time; her stamina was unbelievable. Pop took a few hours off after lunch, going home for a nap or, when we moved from Chinatown to a white neighborhood two miles away, tending to the garden. He returned for the dinner trade and closed with the help of at least one of us children.

At first, the Great China stayed open until eleven o'clock at night. As business slid in the 1950s, it closed at nine o'clock, then at eight o'clock.

Added up, the work life of Pop and Mom was prodigious. They had no time, really, to nurture my sisters and me in the conventional "American" way. They were still very much traditional rural Cantonese Chinatown Chinese parents who demanded that we children listen to them, do what we were told, and absolutely not talk back, a rule we often defied. They didn't ask us how we were doing, how our schoolwork was going, whether we had friends, or what we liked to do when not at school or the restaurant. It was work, work, work, with no time for swimming or bicycle lessons or fancy store-bought toys.

Pop and Mom developed unique reputations. Some customers thought that Pop was as friendly as all get-out. To many white customers, he was a nice guy, approachable, smiling. Others, however, saw his quick temper. He could be gruff and unsmiling, exhibiting a stereotype of Hoisan men, spitting out words in a machine gun–like flurry of harsh, curt tones. My sisters remember apologizing for him. Pop also lost his temper with at least one of his daughters at the restaurant. A nonfamily waitress hired during the war years recalled hearing Pop shout at Lai Wah in the upstairs dining area and even heard slaps. Lai Wah acknowledged being yelled at but didn't remember him hitting her.

Mom had a much better reputation at the restaurant. When she dealt with customers, she broke out in a smile that her children rarely saw. She could be charming, even though her heavily accented English was limited. And she could be tough. Once, a customer refused to pay his bill and wanted to leave. She stood between him and the exit until he paid.

From 1943 to 1948, the restaurant was open every day. Then, Pop and Mom decided to close it on Wednesdays because business had fallen off. If an American holiday—New Year's Day, Fourth of July, Thanksgiving, Christmas—fell on a Wednesday, our family celebrated in, well, a Chinatown way, with raucous meals at home with Chinese and American foods. Pop cooked exquisitely wonderful Cantonese meals, something he never did at the restaurant. But if such holidays were on any other day of the week, we didn't celebrate them, per se, because we were working. On Thanksgiving or Christmas, the Great China had special meals such as all-out turkey offerings that we ate, too, hurriedly, without fanfare, in between waiting on customers who liked the fact that our restaurant was open.

Even on the vaunted Chinese New Year, the Great China opened unless it fell on a Wednesday. Forget about special family celebrations, such as birthdays or even weddings. If they didn't fall on a Wednesday, we would "celebrate" by working; maybe there would be a birthday cake in between serving customers. On the weddings or receptions of two of my sisters—Li Hong in June 1944 and Lai Wah in July 1950—most of us worked, while a few of us attended the special event. When daughter no. five Leslie got married in 1954, however, the Great China closed because her wedding was to the son of a Chinatown gambling boss and thus a huge social deal in our tightly contained community.

My sisters and I were major support players at the Great China. Well, I wasn't in the earliest, busiest years because I was a toddler. My "job" was to stay out of the way. I sat quietly on the restaurant's front step, with my parents and sisters checking on me periodically. Or I crawled atop the one-hundred-pound rice sacks just inside the swinging front doors. As I got older, I was effortlessly rotated into duty. One might think that I, as the only boy, would have been treated like a spoiled brat. Had I felt the urge to act like that, I would have been ignored or dismissed. Like my sisters, I was obedient to a fault. And at that age, I certainly didn't feel especially privileged.

I'd go with Pop when he shopped for produce a few blocks from Chinatown. My first real task before I turned ten years old was washing and drying water glasses. Much as my older sisters did, I took on unglamorous but necessary chores, such as filling sugar jars, salt-and-pepper shakers, and napkin holders. I learned to work the clanky cash register and how to distinguish among different coins and paper currency.

Ultimately, I became a waiter when I was maybe ten years old. By then, the early 1950s, the rush of customers had plummeted considerably. That was fine by me. I never was a happy-go-lucky, smiling, cheerful kid. I could be grumpy or curt as a waiter. I wore a white waiter's jacket with two hand pockets and a left breast pocket, where I kept a ballpoint pen to write down customers' orders on a small writing pad that I kept in the left waist pocket. By the end of my shifts, the whiteness of my jacket was no longer pristine. Inevitably, it displayed ketchup or gravy stains and other smudges, and pen streaks on the breast pocket.

Author as a waiter taking a meal break in the 1950s with restaurant co-workers, pastry chef Chel Goong (*left*) and dishwasher Lo Wong Bock. (Author's Collection)

A sometimes-snarky tendency almost got me into trouble with some Chinatown guys who hung out for coffee and pie. I was a bit younger than those guys, some of them members of a lion-dance troupe that I, too, belonged to briefly. Every so often, I got mouthy, spouting off some smart-ass comment or sarcasm. One or more of the fellows scolded me for having a smart mouth and even threatened me. I meekly distanced myself from the machismo of my Chinatown brothers, preferring to live inside my head.

During slow weekend mid-afternoons, I read and drew. I was in my preteen to teen years. I'd read a paperback book or the *Oakland Tribune*. Scottish author A. J. Cronin somehow caught my attention. I don't know why, but I loved reading his *The Keys of the Kingdom*. I forget its story, but in reviewing it briefly after all these years, I was reminded that its main character, a Scottish Catholic priest, spent time in China. Maybe that's why I read it; it certainly wasn't for its religious theme. I also loved the *Tribune* sports pages for their war and military metaphors: Such-and-such team bombed such-and-such team; such-and-such team annihilated such-and-such team.

Author (*third from the left*) with two Oakland Chinatown buddies at an Oakland Oaks baseball game in the late 1940s, escorted by his sister Lai Wah (*to his left*). (Author's Collection)

Another medium, radio, was my inspiration for reading the *Tribune* sports pages. Before I had a lot of work responsibilities at our restaurant, I lazed around at our new house outside Chinatown and listened to radio shows, such as *The Lone Ranger* and *The Shadow*. Those shows sparked my imagination. Hollywood Westerns on the radio sucked me in, to the point where I begged my parents to buy me toy guns and bows and arrows, which I used on rare play dates with friends. I also loved listening to University of California football games. The late 1940s were the good old days of Cal football. Coached by Lynn "Pappy" Waldorf, Cal won thirty-three consecutive games from 1947 to 1950, starring such players as Bob Celeri, Jackie Jensen, and Johnny Olszewski.

My interest in sports spread to baseball and basketball. In the late 1940s, my sister Lai Wah took me and other Chinatown guys to cheer on Oakland's minor-league baseball team, the Oaks, in a cozy field in Emeryville, the tiny city northwest of Oakland. Those were fun times in the sun for us generally closed-in Chinatown kids, replete with hot dogs and soft drinks. The one downer was the Oaks' grouchy-faced manager, Casey Stengel, who marched past me and other kids seeking his autograph. He never acknowledged us except for a grunt. Stengel went on to manage the mighty New York Yankees.

Before Oakland got a Major League team—in 1968, when the Kansas City Athletics transferred to my hometown—I had only the Oaks to root for (and the San Francisco Seals to root against!). My favorite Major League player was Henry "Hank" Aaron, a southern Black outfielder who was a future star in the mid-1950s, with the Milwaukee, and, later, Atlanta Braves. It was in the *Tribune*'s sports section that I practiced long-division math by religiously following Aaron's daily exploits. I scoured the teeny box scores—how many hits he got, how many home runs, how many teammates he batted in—to calculate his batting average, practicing simple long-division math. When I wasn't obsessing over Aaron's statistics, I'd sit at the restaurant's counter, reading books and pencil-sketching Western forts, horses, cavalry soldiers, human hands and faces, and football helmets with faces of players.

Before my time as a waiter, my sisters worked as waitresses. Pretty and with different degrees of outgoing personalities, they were more popular than I was with our largely male customers, for obvious reasons. Over time, my sisters developed favorite customers, who rewarded them handsomely with tips that I never saw. Li Keng assiduously stashed away tip money during the busiest years. What helped was Pop asking her to serve a gambling tycoon, who left 50¢ tips, a whopping amount when a nickel or a dime was the norm. Smart and determined, Li Keng tossed her tips into an empty water glass she kept hidden. The next morning, she would take the coins to a nearby bank. By the time she was ready to go to college, she had accumulated an astounding $1,600. She didn't tell Pop and Mom about this money until she needed to. That was when Mom vehemently objected to her college plans because she believed that the restaurant needed Li Keng's services, and, besides, from her perspective, girls were to be married off, not go on to college and a career outside the home.

Besides, Mom was notoriously stingy. She didn't want to pay the fees Cal was charging then, a mere $27.50 a semester. It wasn't really the money. It was more a matter of her worrying that the Great China wouldn't have enough help during the super-busy war years. Defiantly, Li Keng said that she'd pay for her own college education. Neither was completely victorious. It took Li Keng six years to finish Cal, not the normal four, because she juggled school and work. This situation stressed her out to the degree of her getting psoriasis, which plagued her until her death at age ninety-two in 2018.

Pop drafted our first brother-in-law, Henry Lew, to help at the restaurant too. Newly married to my oldest sister Li Hong in 1944, Henry had a late afternoon job at the Mare Island Naval Shipyard in Vallejo as an electrician (and, later, at Hunters Point Naval Shipyard in San Francisco), so he waited tables at lunchtime. He also worked partial weekend days. As a reward, Henry ate lunch and took food to go for his dinners at his real job.

As captive restaurant workers who also felt the need to be social beings, Flo and I had occasional conflicts in our work schedules. In the mid-1950s, both of us were teenagers and, each in our own ways, feeling frisky. Flo had a boyfriend, Ed, while I had no female social attachments but had a few buddies. Sometimes, tension developed between us when each of us wanted to go out with friends instead of working. Somehow, we managed to work it out without hating one another.

The Great China's customers were a lively mix of the mostly white shipyard and military-base workers and Chinatown folks (mostly men, some families). Some of the men were avid gamblers who'd come to eat, often spouting off after a loss. At times, gambling bosses brought in female companions—white sex workers. On the other end of the respectability spectrum was Henry J. Kaiser, Oakland's industrial king of the mid-twentieth century and the major domo of the Richmond shipyards where Pop and Li Hong had worked. He loved eating at the Great China. Less famous but more important to our restaurant was Mr. Carlson, whose company, Carlson Confectionary, supplied the restaurant's sugar and flour. He and his family enjoyed eating at the Great China too.

Then there were some quirky characters. A family of Roma ordered the same thing: bowls of steaming white rice covered with brown gravy. One customer loved to pour ketchup on a piece of bread; Pop got upset at Nellie when she gave this customer a full bottle of ketchup rather than one with only a little. Florence recalled a well-dressed Black man who asked to "rent" a spoon only. Never one to turn down a sale, Pop said yes. Later, Florence noticed a newspaper photo of a Black man arrested on drug charges, the same guy who had rented the spoon for 50¢.

13

MOVING UP

Pop saved so much money from the Great China's early years that he was able to buy his first house with $16,000 in cash. This purchase was a big step up for our family, representing the beginnings of middle-class status and acceleration of integration. After fifteen years of living in rental properties, we burst through Chinatown's invisible walls in 1948 into a previously all-white neighborhood near Lake Merritt, Oakland's star attraction, only two miles away. It was a liberation made possible by the Chinese exclusion law's repeal and the profound effects of the end of World War II, including the erosion of discriminatory housing barriers.

An ever-alert Lai Wah, seventeen years old at the time, spotted a newspaper ad for a house near Lake Merritt. A newly licensed driver, she drove by it for a quick look. Impressed, she told Pop, who went with her to check it out. He instantly liked it and decided to buy it, almost on the spot, without first talking with Mom, who was upset about not being consulted in advance, but eventually approved. The house was spacious enough to accommodate our large family. Pop put Li Keng in charge of furnishing it. She went to Breuner's, a big furniture emporium in uptown Oakland, and chose couches, chairs, carpets, curtains, tables, and beds, worth thousands of dollars, which Pop paid for in cash.

I was too young to care, but my sisters were giddy about the move. We were on the cutting edge of some Chinatown families' expanding horizons. Our move generated interest (and envy) from Chinatown families, who thronged to our new house to see what going upscale looked like. Our new neighborhood eventually became known as "China Hill" for the growing Chinese presence.

We didn't abandon Chinatown completely, however, as the Great China was still our base. We slept at our new house but still spent most of our time in Chinatown. We were a family beginning to straddle an inside-outside Chinatown world. For the younger children especially, it was the start of joining a different, less self-consciously insular place.

The house's plain rectangular front deceptively hid the fact that its street level had seven rooms (living, dining, kitchen, breakfast, three bedrooms) plus a bathroom, and a middle staircase leading down to an unfinished basement beneath the living room. Two finished bedrooms and a bathroom were in the back on this lower level. A small backyard had a grassy lawn, next to a detached single-car garage that sloped down from street level. Our family needed all this space. When we moved, only Li Hong had married and was no longer living with the rest of us.

Even though this structure wasn't new—it was twenty-five years old when we moved in—it sure felt new, and expansive, to us. We were so used to the cramped Victorians in Chinatown built at the turn of the century. This new house was relatively modern, without the mustiness of the old rentals. This feeling of modernity lifted our spirits too. Having lawns in front and back gave it the feel of a suburban home, even though the green patches were relatively small and the houses next door on either side were close. Pop told us that we'd be living next to *lo fahn* (non-Chinese "foreigners"). As it turned out, the white neighbors on either side welcomed us. The only neighbor who didn't lived across the street. The older woman there yelled at her grandchildren to stop playing outside. "We don't want you to play with people like that," she said, referring to us.

Once Pop and Mom decided to close the Great China on Wednesdays, that day became family day, like manna from heaven. They took full advantage. First, they'd clean the house, and then they'd dress up nicely and head for lunch at a well-appointed uptown, white-run restaurant, which had white tablecloths, sparkly silverware, and cloth napkins. Sometimes, they went to the Washington Market near Chinatown for scrumptious bacon, lettuce, and tomato sandwiches, something they

Author's mother and father relaxing on one of their days off in the 1950s. (Author's Collection)

didn't serve at the Great China. Often, Gee Yuey Yung, the head chef, joined them. Sometimes, they'd go to a movie.

Gee Yuey Yung occupied a curious place in our family. He was a loyal employee, a compatriot of Pop's and a work partner of Mom's. One morning at the restaurant, Li Keng found Mom crying in the back booth. Mom said, "Your *Baba* thinks I am having an affair with How Chuey Goong [head chef]. I am not! How Chuey Goong and I work in the kitchen, and we get along well."[1] Pop indeed was jealous of Mom's relationship with Goong. She and Goong never argued the way she and

Pop did. As far as we children knew, no scandalous relationship developed between Mom and Goong. Despite their deep differences, she and Pop stayed together until his death.

Pop and Mom brought some of us children with them to the fancy American lunches, or we'd go with them to San Francisco Chinatown for *cha ngow* (Cantonese for "tea food," known today as *dim sum*). About the only decent dim sum place in San Francisco in the 1940s and 1950s was Hang Ah, in an alleyway near some tennis courts. We'd also go to San Francisco to visit Mom's brother-in-law, Jin Ting, whose laundry was near Chinatown. A stoic, taciturn man who wore a nice three-piece suit on our visits, he treated us to beef prime rib and gave us money in red envelopes. When he came to Oakland, he always brought goodies. We took family outings to Lake Merritt, too, an easy walk from Chinatown. When I was a toddler, according to family legend, I wandered off by myself, panicking my family since I was the precious only son. They scurried about looking for me and found me near another family.

Wednesday dinners were special, with Pop doing most of the cooking, complex Chinese dishes that couldn't be found in any Oakland Chinatown restaurant. Three generations of our family happily gathered for these feasts. Flo well remembered Pop's cooking. One favorite was *choon goon*, eggrolls. Others were a deep-fried red snapper stuffed with diced vegetables and yummy spices, turtle soup, eel with rice noodles, and pickled pigs' feet.

Lai Wah enjoyed family Wednesdays in the 1950s when she was married with one daughter, living a few blocks from our restaurant and caring for her mother-in-law, who was living with a disability. When she could, ever the dutiful daughter, she continued to help at the restaurant. Occasionally, Pop gave her money to take Mom shopping, to a movie, or to lunch while he prepared dinner. Despite the mental and possibly physical abuse she endured before she was married, Lai Wah didn't hold grudges against Mom and eagerly awaited her outings with her. "I remember those were the good days," Lai reminisced. "We really had a good time. I used to look forward to Wednesday. That was my escape from my mother-in-law."[2]

Pop loved his grandchildren—he had nine when he died—and gave them treats all the time. For Lai Wah's oldest daughter, Allison, he frequently fixed *gai lon* (Chinese broccoli) with *lop cheng* (Chinese sausages),

Author with his sisters, (*left to right*) Leslie, Li Keng, Lai Wah, Nellie, Li Hong, and Florence, in the late 1970s or early 1980s. (Author's Collection)

or, from the restaurant kitchen, he fed her beef prime rib, mashed potatoes, gravy, a milkshake, and pie a la mode. That explains Allison's pudginess as a child. He gave his oldest grandchild, Vickie, hugs when she visited the Great China in the late 1940s. Vickie lived in San Francisco with her mother, Li Hong, and her father, Henry. Pop sometimes shared his late-night at-home dinners with her. "He was showing that he really appreciated me being the first grandchild," Vickie recalled with fondness.[3]

In my early years, I felt the snuggly warmth, safety, and security of these family-day cocoons. I wasn't yet ready to connect more deeply, however, with my six older sisters. That came much later and unevenly because of our different personalities and life experiences. I was too much into my own life to care about my sisters, one way or the other. Besides, for the oldest ones, we simply were too far apart in age. And our gender difference was a natural cultural chasm, given their China roots and my Oakland ones over a period of gradual integration for all of us, with relatively quicker Americanization for me than for them.

I was alternately cordial and positive and distant and disinterested in dealing with my sisters. At times, I was surly, grouchy, and temperamental; at others, I was friendly, more involved, and engaged. Nothing that unusual, considering that most of us have been in each other's lives for eight to nine decades, living within an hour of one another, except for the years I was far, far away. In our unique universe as Pop and Mom's children, we've been friends, allies, and sometimes competitors linked in a China/Chinatown/assimilated American cultural sense.

I never got close to Li Hong, the oldest who was nineteen years my senior and who passed away when she was ninety-three in 2015. She married when I was only three years old and left Oakland for San Francisco. I hardly knew her other than to see her on family days. I'm more connected to her children, Vickie, Melvin, and Julie, who are closer to my age. She was a devoted stay-at-home mom who liked to eat, cook, and clean house. As noted earlier, she had learning disabilities, but that didn't stop her from occasionally breaking into a Chinese opera tune or a delightful chuckle.

Li Keng and I became close only when we were both much older, after our respective retirements. When young, I barely knew her, too (she was fifteen years older), except for family parties with her husband, Roger, and two children, Kirby and Karen. For more than three decades, she was a primary-school teacher, the first of Chinese descent in southern Alameda County. In learning more about her early working years, I admired her spunk and adaptability. Although disappointed she wasn't their first son, Pop and Mom loaded her with responsibilities as though she were a boy once she landed in Oakland.

Li Keng was obedient in her new foreign environment. She showed her smarts while working in Pop's lottery shop. She also worked hard as household help for a white family, and later in the family restaurant. At home, she was disciplined and determined, not carefree and fun-loving in the ways of her younger sisters. Beginning at the restaurant, when she was in her mid-teens, Li Keng developed different facets of her personality. To white strangers and colleagues, she was especially solicitous, even fawning, with a smile. To her own people outside family, she was friendly but less gushy. At Cal, she hung around other Chinese students. Her socializing with Chinese people continued into adulthood, even when she became a teacher in a mostly white community. She displayed her determination in her new work life, excelling as a primary-school teacher.

She didn't date much. Through mutual friends, she met Roger Wong, her future husband, who, like her, was a Hoisan immigrant. They went on group socials, where she and Roger grew closer. They married in 1954; she was twenty-eight, he a year older. They loved to play mah-jong with other Chinese immigrant couples. One such gathering became the Joy Luck Club, made famous by Oakland-born author Amy Tan, whose parents were founding members along with Li Keng, Roger, and a few other couples.

In somewhat of an upside-down occurrence, Li Keng found inspiration from "my baby brother Bill" (me). She boasted to friends that I had become a high-profile newspaper writer and commentator. Long harboring a desire to tell her own story, but too busy as a teacher and parent, she waited until retirement to take a writing class, where she polished her skills, encouraged by her teacher and fellow students. Her memoir, *Good Fortune: My Journey to Gold Mountain*, aimed at middle-school students, was published in 2006, when she was eighty years old. Some middle schools teach her book, and students at Peralta School in Oakland created an opera based on her story. She died in 2018, when she was ninety-two.

Lai Wah and I were ten years apart and have always gotten along well, even though our life journeys have been so different. She had an easygoing, accommodating personality and showed a flair for fun and for painting when young. Unlike Li Keng, Lai Wah attracted many guys and loved going out, a situation that frequently distressed Mom, who worried that Lai (and all the daughters) might get pregnant out of wedlock.

Also reflecting the socially conservative Chinatown culture, Lai, as extroverted as she was, was obedient too. With Li Hong and Li Keng taking on serious work responsibilities outside Chinatown during troubled times for Pop and Mom in the late 1930s and early 1940s, Lai Wah was assigned household chores, backing Mom up, and served as the designated caregiver for three younger sisters and me.

At nineteen, after high school but no college, she married Allen Chop from another Chinatown family. Traditional Chinese daughter-in-law duties made impossible any pursuit of an artistic life. She had to care for her ailing mother-in-law in Chinatown before she and Allen, an engineer, moved in the early 1960s to Sunnyvale in what today is Silicon Valley. She was a stay-at-home mom caring for daughters Allison and Alexandra. Her husband Allen died early on her, twenty-three years into their union. A few years later, she married a workmate, Daniel Webster, who had two daughters from a previous marriage.

With three grandchildren of her own, Lai worked in administration for a Silicon Valley company and was active in a senior center. Like Li Keng, she loved playing and teaching mah-jong. Her married social life included a mix of Chinese and white contemporaries, with travel, cocktails, and family parties. Our extended family loved picking cherries from Lai and Allen's Sunnyvale Eichler house. Lai died in 2021, at the age of ninety.

Nellie, the first Oakland-born child, was also a hard worker. The tallest of the sisters, at five feet four inches, she has a steady, friendly personality. Nellie was the first of our sibling line to go to Oakland High School.[4] A good student and well organized, she got a secretarial job at Oakland High while still a student. This job led to other administrative positions into adulthood, so she put off a college education. Off work, she loved movies and show business, but only as a consumer, although at home she'd break out in song every so often. She has a creative imagination.

She couldn't find a marriage partner until she was in her thirties, which is when she began to blossom as a poet and political activist, a committed socialist. She was the last child to leave home, as she cared for Mom after Pop died and I left home. Her marriage to James Balch lasted a decade, but her writing and activism carried on. She published four volumes of poetry, and many activists of all backgrounds greatly admire her writing and politics. Even into her late eighties, she attends progressive protest rallies and remains active with the Freedom Socialist Party.

Leslie, born less than two years after Nellie, was arguably everyone's favorite sister. Pretty and petite, with a nice smile and a magnetic personality, she was very popular among male customers at our restaurant. She attracted Donald Yee, who was from a well-off family and whose father was a Chinatown honcho. Mom especially was dazzled by Leslie and Donald's marriage, which was a huge Chinatown affair. Leslie was only nineteen. Privately, she had doubts but felt pressured by Chinatown culture and our parents to take the plunge.

Leslie and Donald had three children, Noel, Erin, and Dana, but their marriage fell apart after about ten years. Struggling with caring for the three children, Leslie worked waitressing jobs before becoming a middle-school secretary. Nellie and I, both without opposite-sex companions, went over to commiserate with Leslie at her mother-in-law's house or, later, her own place after her divorce. She had an innate capacity to listen to our woes with sympathy and empathy without whining about her own unhappy home life, dominated by a demanding mother-in-law and a troubled marriage.

She tried to hide her emotional wounds, but we siblings knew that her domestic situation was painful. In a way, she compensated by welcoming us into her home and listening to us rather than sharing her inner turmoil. Another compensatory move was playing tennis and bowling, two activities she loved and did well, despite her slightness. After her divorce, gaining primary custody of their three kids, she remarried, this time to Dennis Jow, a low-key Chinatown friend. A longtime smoker, Leslie contracted lung cancer, killing her at only forty-nine in 1985, a deeply felt loss for her siblings and children.

Florence followed Leslie, disappointing Pop and Mom yet again, and they let her know their unhappiness because she wasn't what they had wanted, a son. Maybe she sensed their unhappiness, as Flo, as we called her, exhibited a feistiness early on. She acquired the Cantonese nickname *Gai Na Oy*, loosely translated as "cackling chicken." She wasn't one to be stoic and silent when Pop or Mom barked at her. Like Li Keng, Flo was tough, determined, and very smart. She, too, worked hard at the restaurant and used her charm to get tips from male customers. She learned from her older sisters how to appreciate fine fashions obtainable at Oakland's array of middle- and highbrow clothiers, especially Joseph Magnin and I. Magnin. Flo especially loved Lanz dresses, a favorite item of many teenage girls of her day. She did well in school, including Cal, only the second child in the family to go to college to that point. (Nellie went to college in her thirties.)

Flo entered a serious boyfriend relationship earlier than her older sisters did. When she was twelve, she met Edward K. Wong at a roller-skating party of young people who went to the Chinese Independent Baptist Church in Chinatown. Ed, a handsome six-footer, was seventeen years old, a relative newcomer to Oakland. Ed's family had moved from Augusta, Georgia, of all places, in 1949, two years before he met Flo. Ed's mother, uncle, and older brother (his father had passed away) opened a grocery store, their business in Georgia, in Oakland, far from Chinatown. Ed, who had gone to a Baptist church in Augusta, liked to visit Chinatown to meet new people and get a social life, and the Chinese Baptist church was one place to do so.

Flo and Ed quickly became an item; they married ten years later in Oakland. Not long after, they moved to Sunnyvale, where they were practically neighbors of Lai Wah and Allen. That's where Ed, who earned a Ph.D. at Stanford, had gotten an electrical engineering job. Flo taught elementary school for five years before having Felicia and Bradley. Being a stay-at-home mom wasn't enough for her. As someone who studied English literature at Cal and who loved the arts, a creative storm was brewing inside her. At forty, she began drawing and painting, which has led her to a dedicated pathway in art and, later, poetry. She helped organize Asian American women artists and has had her work exhibited widely, and she had a book of poetry published when she turned eighty. A year or two later, she and Nellie joined Genny Lim, a well-regarded Chinese American poet, to form the Last Hoisan Poets, performing their work in a mix of their native dialect and English around the Bay Area.

Those of us siblings who are still alive, now in our eighties, get together frequently, except during the coronavirus pandemic. Even for those who've died, in our unique universe as Pop and Mom's children, we've been friends, allies, and sometimes competitors linked in a China/Chinatown/American cultural sense. Rarely, if ever, have we confronted one another in spite, anger, or jealousy. Rather, if one or more of us have a negative opinion of another of us, we may certainly feel it inside or might even hint our opinion, but face to face, we maintain a cordiality that won't upset the moment. I recall having only one direct, angry argument with one of my sisters within earshot of another. This disagreement was in the 1970s, and the reason is lost in time. That we've maintained friendly contact with each other is because of Pop's guidance and our time and place.

We're the children of rural Chinese immigrant parents who came to America under a legal cloud and whose characters were formed by a tiny Chinese village and a segregated urban American village under poor and working-class conditions. The cultural blanket that covered us was crafted more by Pop's belief in Confucian precepts of respecting elders and honoring family than the Western concept of individual rights and freedom. We children learned to adapt to American ways to varying degrees, while feeling the unarticulated psychological effects of exclusion and white supremacy. Subtle and nuanced cultural differences accounted for gradations of closeness or distance between and among my sisters and me. The four Oakland-born siblings have had a more shared American cultural experience wrapped in a layer of Chinatown than did our older China-born sisters.

Always, however, I was the boy, the only boy. In relative terms, Pop and Mom favored me, but I still had to do my turn at the restaurant—no favoritism there. I was destined for college, however, whereas my sisters had to fight to go, went later in life, or didn't go at all. At some family socials, I've felt somewhat disengaged. It's odd for me to note this feeling since family is a big deal to me. Was it the gender split that's baked into our sibling dynamics, with me being the only male in gatherings that were dominated by female (and womanly) chatter? Or was it—is it—because I happen to be someone who's somewhat shy and introverted, who doesn't crave social gatherings—family or no family—and doesn't mind solitude at home?

In our later years, I found myself excluded from sisters-only gatherings. Minus the late Leslie, the other sisters, at the instigation of Li Keng, celebrated each other's birthdays over nice lunches in Bay Area restaurants. Li Keng wanted the occasions to be sisters only. I knew nothing about them, but when I found out, I felt hurt even though, as I just indicated, I'm not a particularly social being. I insisted on being included, and I finally was. Those birthday lunches have ceased, as some of my sisters have died, the COVID-19 pandemic hit, and the rest of us have minimized our social activities because of age.

As for brothers-in-law, I've been closest to Flo's husband, Ed, seven years my senior. While our work lives were divergent—he was a brilliant electrical engineer, I a journalist—we shared a love of sports, politics, and grilling ribs. When both of us were younger, Ed and I bantered loudly at family gatherings over politics, he leaning conservative, me more liberal, and sports, he favoring the San Francisco 49ers, me the Oakland Raiders. That was our idea of macho fun, Chinatown-style. Both of us enjoyed our exchanges. Our tone, while noisy, was light and good-hearted, not angry or vehement. Neither of us took each other all that seriously. Ed's politics gradually moved left of center, and he became a Raiders fan too.

Our political jousts were a model of sorts for at least one sister, Nellie. For about four decades, Nellie's life was pretty circumscribed by Chinatown, general patriarchal traditions, work, and the old-fashioned wife trope. However, her white husband, James Balch, encouraged her to write and to attend San Francisco State at a time when feminism was blossoming. By her late thirties and into her forties, Nellie had found her voice in a most poetic—and political—way. Ed and I sort of helped her enhance her voice. After one of our raucous political debates at the family dinner table, Nellie, usually quiet, piped up, asserting herself on a related political subject, not the usual family trivia that dominated the chatter from many of the women. Her suddenly speaking out surprised us, but that told me that she was ready to come out of her traditionalist shell to become an outspoken radical socialist feminist.

Other than Ed, my other brothers-in-law, considerably older than me, intimidated me, not from a talking standpoint—I easily held my own there—but from the conventional stereotype of what a man is. Each was skilled in do-it-yourself home crafts. Each had the latest manly equipment, such as standup saws and other power tools, in their garages. Each was able to repair things that broke down in their nice houses, dress up their gardens, and be all-around handymen and home caretakers. Each had an engineering mind-set that eluded me. I much preferred what one (white) friend said that he favored when it came to home repairs: H-I-R-E; in other words, call someone to come fix it.

14

ASSIMILATION

Long before any meaningful adult interactions with my sisters and their husbands, I, of course, went through my own development process, starting with school. Lincoln School, where Pop went thirty-four years earlier, was my first "American" school, from kindergarten to eighth grade. I must have had separation anxiety when I started kindergarten in the late summer of 1946, as Pop had to carry me the few blocks to school, with me kicking, screaming, and crying all the way.

So began my Americanization. This process slowly but surely stretched me out of the Chinatown bubble into a much wider, whiter, and more colorful, complicated world chock-full of mysteries, contradictions, dilemmas, wonders, and possibilities. Not that Chinatown itself didn't have its own intrigues, but the outside world that Lincoln began to show me was a much larger canvas on which I could paint my future.

The first languages I heard as an infant were *Hoisan-wa* (spoken by Pop and Mom), English (spoken by my sisters), and blended Chinglish. Lincoln was where I first learned English formally. It was, after all, the only language of instruction used by white, mostly women teachers. We ethnic Chinese students spoke *Hoisan-wa* and Cantonese among ourselves, as well as English, but the Lincoln experience grew my English skills exponentially and shrank my Chinese language skills. I found that I really liked to speak, read, and eventually write in English. I did well enough academically that I, along with a handful of others, was promoted to the next grade level ahead of schedule.

Learning English quickly and easily had an unintended consequence for my generation of Chinatown kids: It subtly separated us from those who didn't pick it up as efficaciously or who may have been new immigrants themselves. So emerged the "FOBs" ("fresh off the boat") versus the "ABCs" ("American-born Chinese"), an intra-Chinatown rivalry that perhaps foretold different identity journeys into adulthood, the so-called FOBs holding on more dearly to a China-Chinatown sensibility compared with us ABCs, who more readily assimilated into the white-dominated American mainstream.

I don't recall any specific academic class, but I do remember enjoying recess, playing kickball and four square, and later the classic American sports of football, baseball, softball, and basketball at Lincoln Square on the adjacent block. Although the square had no grass or dirt field, concrete only, those games were addictive. I loved that time with my Chinatown buddies, something our immigrant fathers didn't experience in their farm-village youths. None had a clue about playing these American sports, so how could they be our role models?

Instead, we Chinatown kids looked to professional athletes whom we read about or, if we were lucky, saw in person, as I did at Oakland Oaks' games. I especially loved playing basketball, even though I never attended a professional basketball game. Two guys I played with a lot were Calvin Lum, who later became a physician, and Frank Chin, who developed into a towering and controversial figure in the Asian American literary world. Both were six feet tall, or close to it, to my squat five feet four inches. Our height differences didn't matter. I simply loved chucking up jump shots, even though I couldn't jump very high.

Lincoln Square and Lincoln School were two specific places where we young school-age children had oodles of fun. We played and passed time on other Chinatown streets and blocks too. One activity we kids engaged in perfectly blended our ethnic identity with an American tradition: going door-to-door, singing Christmas carols. That activity was something I did with some of my sisters and friends every December in the late 1940s and into the 1950s. Even though some of us went to one of the Protestant churches in Chinatown, those who didn't thought of Christmas time as a generic American holiday without it being a distinctive religious celebration. We just liked going around singing carols in front of Chinese-occupied Victorians and slurping down wonton soup or chow mein afterward.

Another activity that we Lincoln boys pursued during non-school time was adrenaline-pumping and profitable. During the two weeks of Chinese New Year celebrations, we'd toss lit firecracker packages or cherry bombs at each other across Webster Street when cars weren't whizzing by. No one got hurt, as far as I can remember. Chinatown was literally popping, and we guys loved it, especially selling our explosive goods to mostly white folks streaming into Chinatown during the New Year period. They also came in just before the Fourth of July. When we saw a police car or a beat cop, we'd hide our explosives-filled paper bags inside tire wells of parked cars.

My Lincoln years began my gradual cultural separation from Pop, thanks largely to my quickly developing English-language skills. Pop did his best to keep me grounded in *Hoisan-wa* and Cantonese and Chinese philosophy, as expressed by Confucian teachings. He sent my sisters and me to Chinese school, complementing some of my "American" school years. After a Lincoln school day, I grabbed a quick snack at the restaurant, then dashed off to Chinese school at four o'clock every weekday for two more hours at *Wah Kue Hawk How*,[1] two blocks from our home and restaurant. Older students were in one classroom, younger in the other, separated by a collapsible wall.

This school was less fun than Lincoln. The two teachers—a middle-aged man and an older woman—were very strict, using a ruler or bamboo switch to whack our butts or the backs of our legs at the slightest provocation. We learned by rote and repetition—no free expression or intellectual exchanges. During breaks, some of us goofed off by speaking English and tossed balled-up paper and small objects (erasers and so forth) at one another. A few of us munched French fries or chewed gum and candy. Our weekday instruction was in Cantonese; on Saturday mornings, it was in Mandarin, almost a foreign language in Cantonese-dominated Chinatown.

Having skipped a grade at Lincoln, I graduated from eighth grade in 1954, just before my thirteenth birthday. My next American school was Oakland High, a short walk from the house we moved to outside Chinatown. Going to Oakland High was a huge cultural leap away from

Pop and Chinatown culture. Although I was now in truly alien territory, I got along well, at least superficially, with school- and classmates who weren't ethnic Chinese. Drawing students from the city's wealthiest neighborhoods, Oakland High was the whitest of the city's five public high schools, whereas Oakland Technical High, in a less wealthy part of the city, had more Chinese American and Asian American students. The mid-1950s were when Oaklanders of Asian descent didn't even compose 2 percent of the city's 384,000 residents, 85 percent of whom were white and 12 percent African American.

Those numbers meant nothing to me. I just knew that high school was the first time I had been around a lot of bigger and taller white kids. Initially, I felt intimidated and didn't really want to attract attention, so I kept my head down and stayed quiet. Gradually, I came out of my shell, using my verbal skills to become reasonably sociable. I knew that I had to adapt to survive, my natural introversion be damned.

Sports helped me socially, sort of. All those hours of playing at Lincoln Square got me thinking that I had some basketball skills. Was it an inflated ego, or was I delusional to try out for the freshman basketball team? My relative shortness was all right for Lincoln Square, but not high school. Unsurprisingly, I didn't make the first cut. When it came to the opposite sex, well, I didn't do much better. At Lincoln, I was one of the smart guys, not one of the swaggering handsome dudes who caught the eyes of the cute girls. Indeed, I was awkward, if not pathetic, too insecure to pursue girls. Every so often, I nervously phoned a girl I liked, hoping to get a date, but I never got one.

My strong academic performance was what really helped me stand out in high school, except for my mediocre grades in certain science courses (chemistry, physics), shattering the stereotype that Chinese and Asian students are science whizzes. So did my writing sports for the school newspaper, my fallback position from not making the basketball team. My grades ranked fairly high in my class, mostly As and some Bs, for a 3.75 grade point average over four years.

Two teachers stood out for me. One was George Stokes, who taught history in the upper grades. Bespectacled with a crew cut and an arm disability, he had a big personality and spoke assertively. He challenged us to think critically and independently and to read widely. That was the most important lesson I learned from him. He opened my mind to different ideas and unleashed analytical skills beyond rote memorization. He suggested that we read skeptically and to not take everything at face value. His comments on my papers were pointed, provocative, and encouraging.

The other influential teacher was Blanche Hurd. A tall, slender, middle-aged woman, she had the misfortune of succeeding James Black, a very popular journalism and English instructor. Turns out she was perfect for me. She saw something in me that I didn't see in myself. For my senior year, all I wanted to do was to write about sports for the school newspaper. That wasn't what Ms. Hurd saw for me. She appointed me editor-in-chief of the yearbook, the *Oaken Bucket*, a position I hadn't thought about or coveted.

Early on, I was disastrous in that role. I didn't know what it meant or how to be a "leader." In dealing with my staff (i.e., classmates), I used the *I* word too frequently, implying that I was the only important person. Ms. Hurd took me aside and gently advised me to use *we*. The lesson was well learned, for the rest of my editorship and for life in general. In the end, my team and I produced a book that we could be proud of. It was superior to earlier versions, confirmed by positive comments from many students. Among our innovations were more candid photos, better internal organization, captions on group photos, and dazzling artwork by my old Lincoln schoolmate, the gifted Frank Chin, whose multiple talents shined brightly in high school.

Ms. Hurd also gave an early warning signal for my future. One day, in a quiet moment, she asked what career I envisioned. By now smitten with this writing and editing thing, I told her that I was interested in becoming a journalist. She listened attentively and then said, "You will have to be twice as good to succeed." *Twice as good.* Since that moment, when I was all of sixteen years old, I've heard that sentiment expressed over many years for (1) women, (2) African Americans, and (3) many other racial and ethnic "minorities," including Chinese Americans like me. That is, the world as we knew it in the 1950s—and still pretty much well into the twenty-first century—is a world where white men dominate and are still the driving force, still the standard by which all else is judged, despite movements aplenty since the 1960s to increase opportunities for non-white men and all women to gain representation, leadership, and power in all aspects of modern civilization.

My high school years grew and stiffened my cultural distance from Pop. More than ever, I was in my own little universe, even though I still lived at home with him and Mom and worked at the restaurant on weekends. We may have been physically close to one another, but my head and heart were somewhere else. I never discussed with my parents my academics or extracurricular activities, nor did they ask. I wasn't defiant or rebellious. It was more a matter of communication difficulties since, by now, my English was superior to either my native *Hoisan-wa* or Cantonese, the direct inverse of their language capabilities.

Part of my continuing integration and assimilation involved joining one of the school's fraternity-like organizations. I felt the need to be one of the guys. Oakland High in the 1950s had these all-male groups called "Hi-Ys." There was an unspoken hierarchy among these groups—one for jocks and tougher guys, another for studious dudes, and a third for a lesser mixture, a kind of unconscious caste system.

My group was Rambler Hi-Y, a collection of nerdy fellows, along with those active in student government and sports (swim team, in particular) and a few rebellious goof-offs. We wore cool jackets of lime green cotton with cream leather sleeves. Ramblers were one of two highly regarded clubs, although other Hi-Ys would vehemently disagree. The other was Trojan Hi-Y, whose members liked to think of themselves as macho jocks and studs, but the club had brainy and mischievous types too. Trojans wore shiny deep all-blue jackets, and it seemed as though top Trojans attracted the most conventionally pretty young women.

My best friend was a fellow Rambler, Stephen Johnson, an amiable fellow and a good student. I hung out with him more than I did almost anyone else, except perhaps for Frank Chin. Stephen and I enjoyed studying together at each other's homes and talking about serious stuff, like history and politics.

Another Rambler invited both of us to dinner at his parents' house (packaged fried fish sticks). This other fellow played a role in the only overt racial incident of any consequence while I was in high school. A tall, slender extrovert, he and I planned a double date to a school social, but he told me that a parent—probably his girlfriend's—didn't approve. I wondered why. Nothing explicit was said about my race and that of my Chinese American date, but the more I thought about it, the more wounded my feelings became. It was much later that I labeled this incident as "soft" racism. As hurt as I might have felt, I never expressed my feelings to this fellow or to Stephen.

Another time, Stephen and I went to the house of this other Rambler's girlfriend for a social gathering in her basement. Shortly after we got there, Stephen recalled, the girlfriend went upstairs to see her mother, the woman who had most likely objected to that ill-fated proposed double date. Minutes later, the girlfriend and her Rambler boyfriend told me that I'd have to leave. "That incident has been emblazoned in my brain ever since," Stephen told me more than a half century later. "It was the first time I had witnessed or been part of discrimination and I became aware" of such negativity.

My social skills with girls didn't noticeably improve throughout my high school years. I never had a girlfriend, per se. I thought that I was a "normal" teenage boy in that I liked girls and had private opinions about their looks and personalities. I became close to two young women classmates, both white and attractive. One served as a hall monitor with me, and I enjoyed having witty conversations with her. The other was on the newspaper staff with me. I felt at ease with both. We got along fabulously. But I didn't have the gumption to go beyond our mutually cheerful and comforting social chatter. Besides, dating them was a cultural taboo, in my estimation. I wasn't brave like my buddy Frank Chin, whose outsized personality and creative gifts made him a Big Man on Campus and a "babe magnet" for some white female schoolmates, despite his somewhat-gangly physical presence and an unconventional, long, thin face that wouldn't be described as classically handsome. He had what I longed for—charisma, that hard-to-define personal magnetism.

No one in my family ever told me that I couldn't be extra-friendly with young women who weren't ethnic Chinese. Nothing needed to be said. I simply understood that that restriction was the "norm" for short Chinatown guys like me. In fact, I never talked with family members about any of this socializing or dating stuff. I did have a few dates for events like school proms, to which I asked schoolmates who were Chinese American young women with whom I had friendly relations, but no strong connection the way I did with the two young white women.

Race issues overall weren't at the center of my little universe or that of other teenagers. If anything, we may have internalized the idea that we shouldn't get too serious about someone of another race. Like adolescents elsewhere, our concerns were looks and personalities and whether we fit in. More generally, the 1950s were relatively quiet on the political and social fronts, but things were brewing.

I didn't make a big deal of my Chinatown Chinese American identity, with which I felt comfortable sometimes and uncomfortable at others. I didn't want to bring too much attention to the fact that my parents were immigrants who didn't speak the perfect King's English, who weren't steeped in white American culture, who worked in lowly jobs, and who didn't have any social status to speak of. Yes, at times I was ashamed of who my parents were, what they did, where they came from, and how poorly they spoke English.

If anything, when I was in a largely white universe like Oakland High, these feelings of inferiority rested deep inside me without fully surfacing. Somehow, I managed to thrive in this foreign territory, as I got through high school with decent grades and the prestige of being yearbook editor. Without a lot of strategic planning on my part, I somehow rose to a leadership role, despite not having a Chinatown role model or mentor.

Graduation was a proud moment for Pop, Mom, and me, but that night, when we seniors celebrated, I came upon a profound realization that I hadn't really "belonged" socially with my white classmates. I went to a graduation party at somebody's home and immediately felt out of place. Many classmates were drinking heavily and dancing wildly. I didn't drink booze then and wasn't a wild dancer. Feeling very awkward and way out of place, a Chinatown guy in an all-white world, I left quickly. It was so weird: During school hours, I had no problem easily mingling with white classmates after the initial awkwardness of my freshman year. The graduation party scene, however, shook me emotionally.

There was only one college choice for me: Cal, five miles up the road in Berkeley, where Li Keng and Flo went. Cal was almost like Chinatown's neighborhood college. It had a reputation, in fact, of being a high-status place for the Chinatowns and Chinese American communities of northern California. Such was the social and cultural naïveté of Bay Area Chinatowns that Cal was the pinnacle of an American higher education. This comment is not to disrespect Cal in the least, for it was—and still is—a much sought-after destination for people of all backgrounds seeking a first-rate college education. It is widely considered one of the best, if not the best, public universities in America, and some argue that it is among the very best American universities, period.

Chinatown kids of my era simply weren't imbued (yet) with the intense desire for social climbing so prevalent these days among some young people and their ambitious parents, the goal of crashing through the all-but-impenetrable ivy-covered walls of certain East Coast universities. Psychological effects of the Chinese exclusion phenomenon blinded us to the remote possibility of becoming a part of America's elite. Many of us and our parents didn't even know that the Ivy League institutions existed. We knew of Stanford, the upscale private university in Palo Alto, thirty-three miles south of San Francisco and Oakland, but it was thought to be too expensive—and too white—for working-class Chinese American families.

So, it was Cal for me. My academic start was a trace embarrassing. Freshmen had to take an entrance English exam, which I didn't pass, so I had to take what was called "Bonehead English" to meet Cal's standards. You'd think that I would've passed that entrance exam, given my growing affinity for writing in English, but guess again.

Before enrolling in any class, I strolled into the basement of Eshleman Hall near the famous Campanile bell tower to sign up for the *Daily Californian* sports staff. There, I met Ron Bergman, a funny guy with an older sensibility and a lively, quirky intelligence. Already a Navy veteran, he was in his early twenties, old to me, as I had just turned seventeen. The first time I saw him, he was hunched over a manual, hunt-and-peck, clackety typewriter, writing something like, "There's this guy Bill Wong looking over my shoulder. . . ." That was iconoclastic Ron, the *Daily Cal*'s sports editor who went on to an acclaimed sportswriting career at local newspapers. He wrote hilarious and poignant columns and covered the famous Oakland A's of the 1970s and 1980s when they won a bunch of World Series. His book *Mustache Gang* was the definitive account of those A's teams owned by the eccentric Charles O. Finley.

Ron and I became good friends, despite our decidedly different cultural backgrounds. He was a blunt, straight-talking, secular Jewish American with a sarcastic sense of humor whose political and cultural ideas seemed grounded in the 1950s. I was a mild-mannered, somewhat introverted, somewhat cerebral Chinatown Chinese American without a whit of religious affiliation. Both of us loved sports, sarcastic humor, and good

Chinese food. I became his Chinese restaurant consultant. In the 1970s, we had fiery meals at Soon Lee, across the street from the old San Francisco Seals ballpark. Soon Lee served spicy cuisine from either Sichuan or Hunan, not my much blander, but still delicious, Chinatown Cantonese. I learned to love, even crave, this spicier, tastier cuisine.

Along with Ron, Mike Berger was a *Daily Cal* sports editor who also became a good friend. Mike had a quick wit and dry sense of humor. I loved talking politics with him. Both of us read political magazines, such as the *Reporter*, the *Nation*, and the *New Republic*, and we'd exchange views on various articles. Mike went on to a successful career as the *San Francisco Chronicle*'s sports editor and later lived in Tokyo with his Japanese wife.

I became sports editor at the end of my sophomore year, an amazing ascension that I had never envisioned. I was pleased as punch, however, to become sports editor with so little actual experience. Outgoing sports editor Ron introduced me in his last column: "He likes to call himself Bill Wong, although we all know his real name is Mao Tse-Tung. The kid is only 18 years old. Which proves that you don't have to be an old man to edit a page of sport. He's going to prove that you don't have to be good either." By the way, he insulted everyone in this farewell piece.

The highlight for me of being sports editor was going to Los Angeles to cover the Cal football game against the University of Southern California (USC), the pricey private institution known for its winning football teams. For a naïve teen like me, going to Los Angeles was heavenly. The press box at the Los Angeles Coliseum was way up there. A greenhorn like me was blown away by the professional atmosphere of the press box and the privilege of getting statistical sheets as the game proceeded, and free snacks and soft drinks. I loved going into the locker rooms of both teams right after the game to snatch quick interviews with important players. It didn't matter that the players towered over me. I reveled in being among these sweaty, smelly behemoths, especially the massive USC Trojans' star linemen, Mike and Marlin McKeever, to catch a pithy quote or two to include in my game account.

As sports editor, I wrote a column, "The Chinese Bandit." That name may sound like an awful, even racist, label, but remember, this was 1960, before a full-blown civil rights movement and before I had gained a mature consciousness of my own racial and ethnic identity. Why "Chinese

Bandit"? In 1958, Paul Dietzel, coach of the Louisiana State University football team, famously called his defensive team "Chinese Bandits," after characters in the *Terry and the Pirates* comic strip. He did so reportedly because he wanted to instill pride in these unsung players.[2] I didn't take the term as a racial slur. Rather, I took a fancy to that culturally dissonant nickname.

Alas, my rarefied status as sports editor abruptly ended after only a few months. Campus politics that I had nothing to do with nor had much interest in torpedoed my precious standing in my young college journalism career. That greatly annoyed the selfish me, engrossed in the sports world, not the political one. I wasn't yet politically attuned, yet as sports editor, I was a de facto member of the paper's editorial board, which consisted of the top news-side editors, who were more passionate and knowledgeable about politics than I was.

The late 1950s and early 1960s were heady political times at Cal, on the cutting edge of the budding student power movement. A sharp example of that for me was the surprising visit to the *Daily Cal* office one summer day of Tom Hayden. A few colleagues and I happened to be hanging out there. In he strolled, a tall, handsome man about our age from the University of Michigan. A leader on his campus, Hayden told us that he was on a scouting trip to check out Cal's student activism, which was well known in college circles across the country. He later became famous as, among other things, an antiwar activist, California legislator, and husband of Jane Fonda, the even more famous actress and antiwar activist.

In the 1950s, American politics were rife with deep divisions related to the so-called Cold War between the democratic United States and the Communist Soviet Union, which had been an ally during World War II. The ripple effects of the Cold War landed at Cal, where the dominant political issue on campus in the late 1950s was whether faculty members would pledge loyalty to the United States to show conservative doubters that Cal's professors were indeed pro-American and anti-Communist.

This overarching contretemps spilled over in indirect ways to the *Daily Cal*. Our liberal-leaning editorial board chose to endorse Michael Tigar[3] of the leftist SLATE student political group for a top student government role. Cal's cautious and, in a few cases, more conservative administrators—the grown-ups—didn't at all like whom we smart-ass student

Front page of the *Daily Californian*, announcing the staff's resignation after the Cal administration suspended the staff in late October 1960. (Author's Collection)

editors had backed. Our editorial board took a big risk because Cal's administrators had leverage over our partially student-funded newspaper. (We student journalists controlled only advertising revenue, which wasn't enough to cover full operations.)

To punish us for this stance, the administration suspended the *Daily Cal*'s editorial board, including me, in late October 1960. In effect, we were fired, a move we didn't acknowledge. Instead, we resigned in noisy protest, igniting a huge brouhaha that got lots of local news coverage. Even though my own involvement was peripheral, I was loyal to my colleagues and the *Daily Cal*. We didn't go quietly.

Off campus, I helped produce an alternative newspaper, the *Independent Californian*, supported by a local independent journalist, Orr Kelly, and distributed them around the campus. Our actions got more local news coverage, and for a while, we felt empowered. After several weeks, though, we burned out. Meanwhile, the Cal administration recruited inexperienced and more politically conservative students from fraternities and sororities to run the *Daily Cal*. We former staffers were left out in the cold.

This episode changed my college journalism plans for good. After a spell of uneasiness, the Cal administration decided to try to make peace, sort of, with those of us "fired." Its solution was Solomonic. It retained some of the new staff and brought back some of the old. I was one of the few survivors of the old editing corps, and, as such, I was named managing editor, the second top news post. I can't say that I was the ideal choice since my only experience to that point had been on the sports side, not on the more serious—and, arguably, more important—news side. But the powers that be must have trusted me to join the new interlopers to keep the *Daily Cal* alive. I moved out of my comfort zone, sports journalism, into a potentially more stressful and scarier arena, campus political news.

As for academics, I was in the College of Letters and Science, a grab bag of liberal arts and social science classes. Cal was famous for its huge lecture-hall classes in such subjects as economics and political science. I took those lower-division (freshmen/sophomore) courses, lost somewhere with hundreds of others in the back of Dwinelle and Wheeler Halls. I majored in journalism, taking as many undergraduate journalism courses as possible. Cal didn't offer a bachelor's degree in journalism, however, so I got your garden-variety Bachelor of Arts degree. The journalism classes weren't affiliated with the *Daily Cal*, which was like an extracurricular activity.[4] Maybe I spent a bit too much time at the *Daily Cal* or I was distracted by still working at the Great China, but my overall grade point average was something like 2.75, somewhere between Bs and Cs, nothing to brag about, and not a rating that would get me into a prestigious graduate school, which, by the way, wasn't something I gave any thought to.

Had my parents and I talked about my growing interest in newspaper journalism—which we didn't—they would've said something like, "That's not something that pays well" or "That's not something that will bring honor to the family." They made not-so-subtle entreaties to me that I should become a medical doctor, a stereotypical calling for Chinese Americans/Asian Americans that was, in their perceptions, prestigious and high-paying, a status symbol they could boast about in Chinatown. If not a doctor, then maybe I could be an architect. I didn't feel those vibes, whereas I felt good about newspaper writing.

My involvement in the *Daily Cal*, especially after the loyalty-oath kerfuffle, contributed in major ways to my burgeoning political education. The politics that jolted the *Daily Cal* staff in 1960 certainly provided a lesson in the Cold War era. Before our firing, in May 1960, the infamous House Un-American Activities Committee (HUAC) held controversial hearings at San Francisco's city hall. Hundreds, if not thousands, of college students, some from Cal, protested vehemently. I was still very much a political novice, so I wasn't among the protesters, but nonetheless, I was aghast at police spraying firehoses at the protestors as they ascended the elaborate marble staircase of city hall. As it was, other *Daily Cal* editors and I were paranoid over rumors that HUAC had our names on a purported Communist sympathizers list because we had supported a leftist student politician.

While the *Daily Cal* dominated my Cal years, I almost took a politically safer path in the leadership of Cal's only Chinese American fraternity, Pi Alpha Phi. I joined in my sophomore year out of a desire to bond with other Chinese American guys. Out-of-town members lived at the frat house near campus. Since I lived at home in Oakland, I hung out at the frat house on Friday and Saturday nights, a big social time for me.

Not many frat brothers had grown up in Chinatowns. Many were more well-to-do Chinese Americans, even some from outside California. It was a good experience for me to get to know guys with whom I shared an ethnicity, but whose socioeconomic standing was higher than mine. Some were socially "faster" than I was too. We bonded over booze and other manly activities that would have shocked our families. I was popular enough to be considered for the presidency heading into my junior year, posing a dilemma since I had a *Daily Cal* leadership role.

Should I be a newspaper editor or a fraternity leader? Should I choose to hang with my own ethnic brothers, or should I continue to learn more about campus politics with more young white men and women (and a few Asian Americans) in pursuit of what I was beginning to love as a possible career? I was genuinely torn. I chose the *Daily Cal*, a decision I've never regretted.

15

CHINESE LESSONS

As passive and uninvolved as he was throughout my "American" school years, Pop was quite the opposite when it came to my Chinese education. In addition to putting me through Chinese school, he spent time drilling me, and me only, with Confucian lessons. This focus was his way of demonstrating his Chinese identity, wanting me to learn Chinese thoughts, ideas, and philosophy, even while we were living in Oakland, a thoroughly American city that happened to include our tiny Chinatown bubble. I can't recall Pop ever explaining why he wanted me to study Chinese stuff. I sensed, however, that his mind-set was to inculcate in me a Chinese identity to perhaps counteract what he saw as my growing American identity. To him, and perhaps to his Chinatown contemporaries, maintaining a Chinese identity was more important than adapting to an American one since America wasn't all that hospitable in his many years here.

The problem for me was I liked my American schools, but I half-resented and half-hated my Chinese schools and the special lessons Pop gave me. I didn't have the nerve to tell him that, as I was a good Chinese son who obeyed his parents, especially the father (a very Confucian thing). I may have been mouthy with my sisters, friends, Chinatown guys, and schoolmates, but not with Pop, who directed me to listen to him, Mom, and other elders and not to disrespect them, which I didn't, at least not directly. I embodied the filial piety thing. I had two faces, one I showed my parents, and one I showed everyone else.

Pop eagerly supplemented my formal Chinese-language schooling with one-on-one sessions in his restaurant office during down times. He'd recite Confucian precepts (rules, commands, orders) that were rhyming phrases in Cantonese and ask me to repeat them. This learning was strictly rote, with no discussion of what these phrases meant. Chinese school and his personal teaching weren't enough for him. When I was about ten, Pop sent me to a tutor in Chinatown for private Confucian lessons. I went to where this man lived, where, at a counter-desk, he did what Pop did: Recite in Cantonese and listen to me recite back. Again, no discussion or explanation took place, just rote memorization. What a wasted effort on Pop's part, I'm sorry to say so many years later. I can't recite anything I presumably "learned" from Pop or the tutor, nor can I remember any of those phrases.

While not a highly educated man, Pop had an affinity for Confucian teachings. He started learning the iconic Chinese philosopher's classic writings—or, more precisely, interpretations of Confucian teachings by his many disciples—while at his village school in China. The teachings of Confucius, who lived about 2,500 years ago, and those of his most dedicated followers were thoroughly ingrained in Chinese education, society, and culture for more than two millennia, until the twentieth century.

Not a religion per se, Confucianism is like a moral code of living harmoniously and humanely and was a major way China got and maintained social stability. The most virtuous Confucian values were respect for elders, faithfulness to friends, loyalty to the emperor, honesty, and sympathy for the poor. Lying, cheating, and treachery were among the least virtuous values.[1] For many centuries of imperial rule in China, those chosen for government work had to pass examinations based on the Confucian classics. This system was, in effect, a meritocracy (*but for men only*). Aspiring government workers had to show their worthiness based on talent and skills, not on family connections or wealth. Outsiders greatly admired these examinations as exemplifying Chinese civilization.[2]

At some point in his Oakland life, Pop acquired six scrolls of Confucian-related teachings. The author of those scrolls was Zhu Xi,[3] a Gee clan member since *Zhu* is the Mandarin transliteration of the *Hoisanwa Gee*. One sister remembered Pop boasting about Zhu Xi because of his historically famous standing in China's philosophical and intellectual firmament. According to the *Stanford Encyclopedia of Philosophy*, Zhu Xi "is generally ranked as second only to Confucius . . . in influence . . . in philosophic acumen in the Chinese philosophical tradition."[4]

Pop was especially proud because Zhu Xi was in his clan line. Confirmation of this latter fact is found in Pop's genealogy book that I inherited and had translated.[5] This book has two major sections. In the first portion, listing an older Gee clan line, Zhu Xi appears in the twelfth generation. In the second portion, listing Pop's Gee clan line, starting with the settlement of one branch moving to Hoisan, Pop is the twenty-third generation, and I am the twenty-fourth.

My ignorance of Zhu Xi epitomizes a profound identity gulf between Pop and me. This gulf is the essence of our unique relationship in which, at one level, we are joined by blood and some culture (Chinatown), one generation to the next, and at another, we were kept totally apart from one another by time, place, and culture (American) too. To know-nothing me, after learning of his exalted status in Chinese history, the fact that Zhu Xi's name was in Pop's genealogy book was a jaw-droppingly big deal.

In plain English, this famous Chinese philosopher and interpreter of Confucius preceded Pop and me in our clan line, albeit by about nine hundred years. Am I delusional to think that a writing gene in our DNA links us, however tenuously, to the great Zhu Xi? Li Keng, Nellie, Florence, and I have been or are writers of nonfiction and poetry. By no means are we writer siblings anywhere close to Zhu Xi's league as far as philosophical and cultural influence. Yet more than once, my sisters and I have asked one another how each of us came upon a need to tell stories in the written form. Maybe I am delusional.

During the twenty years I shared with Pop, I was oblivious to his getting the Zhu Xi scrolls and hanging them in our dining room. To me, they were simply part of the house's furnishings, nothing remarkable, and Pop's thing, not mine. They meant nothing to me. Did he ever tell me about them, or read them to me, or explain their meaning? Maybe, and if he did, what he said is long forgotten. And I never asked what they were, what they said, and what they meant.

After both parents died, I inherited the house and eventually sold it, taking possession of some of its furnishings and wall hangings, including those scrolls. Still incurious about what they were, I put them away in

The last panel of a Gee clan historic figure's code of moral family living. His signature, Zhu Xi (Mandarin transliteration), is in the lower left corner. (Author's Collection)

the garage-basement of my own house. Out of a vague duty to a long-deceased Pop, I kept them, but I didn't hang them prominently inside our house as he had done. Then, one day during my more focused search for Pop's past, now more curious than ever about what I didn't know about him and finally realizing how important these scrolls were to him and wondering why that was, I looked for them, photographed them, and had them translated.

The scrolls are framed in bamboo. Four panels display five columns of twenty-six Chinese words each. In all, these four have forty-six precepts or maxims—general rules intended to regulate family behavior or thought—derived from Confucian works. The other two show four larger words each. The first title panel says, in essence, "Go through life with poems and classics." The sixth panel means, "Pass down loyalty and filial piety to the family."[6] This panel also has Zhu Xi's red-stamped signature.

What was it about Zhu Xi's commentaries that attracted Pop? I don't have the luxury of hindsight. Had I absorbed Pop's and the tutor's lessons when I was young, I might have deeper insights into Pop's mind. In reviewing the translation of the forty-six maxims, however, I can feel Pop's presence and spirit. Even more astonishing, I see myself reflected in some of Zhu Xi's writings. I'm not saying that these maxims fit Pop or me to a T, for they—like rules, commands, orders, or lessons of many religions and belief systems—are ideals to strive toward, and we mere mortals often fall far short of reaching them. In addition, some, if taken literally, are woefully outdated, especially those that support a strictly patriarchal system, unsurprising in that they were written so long ago.

But for some of what Zhu Xi gleaned from Confucius as virtuous conduct and behavior, Pop embraced the essence and tried his best to pass it along to me, with some success, I believe, even though, as I said earlier, I didn't think that I had absorbed any of the Confucian lessons he and the tutor tried to teach me some seventy years earlier. It must have been osmosis, or something similar, an undetectable, unconscious, irrational mind-meld, with no discernible effort on my part.

What were some of Zhu Xi's most noteworthy lessons for living a good life? Exhibit orderliness, mindfulness, modesty, humility, altruism, reverence of ancestors, simplicity, thriftiness, honesty, ethical behavior, sympathy, and harmoniousness; be spirited and active; avoid profligacy; think of others, not yourself; and be virtuous.

Here are a few examples, in translation, of his maxims that exemplify some of those lessons:

- Be thrifty in satisfying your own needs, but generous in hosting a reception.
- Strive to lead a simple and thrifty life; through such example, your children will learn the principles of living.
- Show sympathy and solicitude to your relatives or neighbors who are in adverse circumstances.
- Fortune amassed by unjust means cannot be enjoyed for long; violating moral principles will bring about destruction.
- In a family, parents and children, husband and wife, the older and younger should each do their duty. They should all abide strictly by the rules of behavior and use appropriate language.
- A man who values money more than his parents is a bad son.
- One who is spiritless and lazy can achieve nothing.
- Do not keep in mind a favor you have bestowed on someone else, but do not forget to repay a favor you have received.
- Do not be envious of other people's happiness. Do not take pleasure in other people's misfortune.
- When a family lives together in harmony and peace, even if they are poor and can hardly make ends meet, they will enjoy plenty of happiness.

Pop's reverence for Zhu Xi's code for family harmony represented his moral compass for life, despite his own seriously amoral or even immoral real-life China and Chinatown experiences. Likely inspired by Confucius and Zhu Xi, Pop had his own homegrown philosophy. Whether these sayings were truly original with him or merely sensible guides common to his class of Chinese isn't something I have explored. Nonetheless, he had a handful of pithy, metaphorical sayings that have stuck with my sisters and me. I call them Pop's aphorisms.

A family favorite is *You how, mo me*[7]—literally, "Have head, no tail." My loose interpretation: "You start something, but you don't finish it." The message: Be responsible and finish what you start.

Another was *Cheh aye (dai) pow*—literally, "Dragging a big cannon." Someone who "drags a big cannon" exaggerates, gilds the lily, tells the big lie, bullshits. The message: Don't drag a big cannon.

Flo remembered more, including *Imm hoong siu*—literally, "no empty hand." When visiting neighbors or friends, bring a treat or a gift as a matter of courtesy.

A fourth was *A uh gaw maw aye uh*—literally, "give someone a tall hat to wear," meaning to praise someone freely, even effusively. Be nice and be positive.

A fifth was *You loy, you wonk*—literally "have come, have go," or give and take, life is a two-way street, full of compromises. Don't expect to have your way all the time.

Recall what I said earlier about not remembering any repetitive recitations, in Cantonese, of Confucian (or Zhu Xi) precepts from Pop or the Chinatown tutor. Guess what? I think that I got what they were saying, after all. Through my life experience with him, watching him, listening to him, seeing how he carried on his life, I learned from Pop to live modestly, not excessively; honor, don't embarrass family; respect others, especially elders; work hard; be responsible; and follow up on what you say you're going to do (at least I try most of the time!). He taught us good values. I got his basic message. I believe in loving and honoring family, treating others with respect, and not behaving boorishly. These values are hard to explain, but I know them when I feel them.

16

FAMILY TENSIONS

Pop adhered to the essence of some of Zhu Xi's maxims, especially those that addressed the importance of family honor and harmony, even though he and Mom were a badly matched pair, at least by Western standards. Li Keng said that the two were "like oil and water." The two stuck out their thirty-seven-year marriage despite constantly being at each other's throats, screaming and shouting at one another. We children could clearly see and feel the internal discord. We wondered why they stayed married. Our perspectives were undoubtedly swayed by our straddling of varying degrees of the broader American/Western cultural norms that stressed individual rights, not family or group solidarity.

Between Pop and Mom, each of us kids had our favorite, and it was overwhelmingly Pop. I liked him better than I did Mom. Almost all my sisters felt the same. Despite his hot temper, he was really a softie at heart, gentle, compassionate, sensitive, with even feminist tendencies. He quickly got over whatever set him off, and he didn't hold grudges. More than once, I'd see him break into a winning smile after bellowing loudly. Even though he didn't like not having a son until I came along seventeen years (and more girls!) into his marriage, he didn't resent having daughters.

He was attentive to their needs. He bought them a standing professional-style hair dryer, the kind women's hair salons had, so that they could dry their hair more thoroughly. He bought care necessities in bulk,

Kotex for the girls, Kleenex and toilet paper for the family. Some of the girls liked Campbell's noodle soup, so he bought cases of it, customizing it by adding rice noodles.

Pop demonstrated his positive fathering concerns in so many other ways. Whenever one of us got sick, he used his herbalist training to prescribe herbal cures. When Li Keng graduated from Cal, he bought a new Chrysler sedan for her to drive to her new teaching job south of Oakland. On weekends, he used it for business and family purposes. Pop was empathetic to Lai Wah on their drives home from the Great China. He reassured her he didn't have to worry about her future because of her upbeat and accommodating spirit, in contrast to the fiery independence and occasional defiance of Li Keng and Florence. That made her feel good.

He made sure that we had some of the latest technology. In 1952, he bought our first television set, influenced by a Chinatown bigwig who was the first in his social circle to do so. One sister recalled going over to this man's house to watch TV and finding it exciting. Her enthusiasm undoubtedly sparked Pop to get this new, increasingly popular entertainment gadget. Our first TV set was more a sleek piece of furniture, a blond-wood cabinet with a small-screen black-and-white TV, record player, and radio.

Pop liked to encourage his daughters to explore popular American culture, such as going to the movies. He'd give Li Keng money to take Lai Wah or Nellie to one of Oakland's many movie houses. He also gave Li Keng money to buy comic books at the open-air stand down the street from our restaurant.

Mom, too, had a temper, but unlike Pop's, her ill feelings didn't evaporate quickly. I couldn't help noticing this gap in temperament—his quick recovery, her lingering grudges. She had her happy and quiet times, but I saw her miserable and unhappy a lot, too, and she often took it out on her daughters, and even on me. She had a long memory of offenses, hurts, and ill feelings. After arguments, Mom often stopped talking to her feistiest daughters, Li Keng and Flo, for days, even a week.

The recurrent issue for Mom was money. With her daughters, the issue was more a personal manifestation of Chinese patriarchy. That she had given birth to five girls before a boy undergirded her feelings for a long time, and she didn't like having to care for Pop's first daughter, Li Hong, by his first wife either. My sisters suffered from Mom's predicament, to varying degrees. If she had had a son early, she wouldn't have had as many children, easing the financial burden and the enormous caregiving responsibilities foisted on her.

Mom was especially hard on Li Keng, her first born, and on Florence, her fifth. Mom and Li Keng constantly argued, most likely rooted in the fact that Li Keng wasn't a boy. Mom never praised Li Keng for her dedication and hard work—until, ironically, she graduated from Cal. Mom told four male diners, "This is my daughter Li Keng. She just graduated from UC [University of California] and is the first child to do so." The men smiled. The irony wasn't lost on Li Keng: "I guess she was complimenting me."

As tough as Mom was on Flo—again, rooted in Flo not being a boy—Flo benefited from Li Keng being the first to suffer Mom's wrath about going to college. The fiercely independent-minded and determined Flo, inspired by Li Keng's defiant model, wanted to go to Cal too. Unlike in Li Keng's case, however, Mom didn't actively block Flo. Maybe by then, Mom was worn down.

By the mid-1950s, our family's finances were in much better shape than they were when Li Keng sought a higher education, and Mom's insecurity over money had waned. Flo used her talent for persuasion to soften Pop and Mom to her desire to go to Cal. She told many customers, within earshot of Pop and Mom, that she loved children and wanted to go to college to become a teacher.

Pop was more supportive of Flo in many matters. In her middle-school years, Flo and two classmates wanted to take summer swimming lessons at Oakland High, but she didn't have a bathing suit. She asked Pop for money to buy one, and he gave her $15 in plain sight of Mom, who bolted out from the kitchen and snatched the money from Flo's hand. Mom said, "You can't go swimming. I am taking the money back." Flo recalled, "Mom told me I would drown. 'Who do you think you are, Esther Williams?'" She pronounced the name of the famous actress-swimmer with a *Hoisan-wa* intonation, *Esta Weeyim*. All ended well for Flo, as Pop secretly gave her money again for the bathing suit. "Don't tell Mom," he warned her.[1]

Lai Wah had a similar incident with Mom and money. When Lai was graduating from high school, she wanted to buy a fashionable, maroon-colored suit for $30, which she didn't have. She asked Pop for the money, which he gave her from his office cubbyhole. Not one to miss a thing, Mom saw the transaction, rushed out from the kitchen, and yanked the money from Lai Wah's hands. That caused a scene and embarrassed Lai to tears. Later, Pop slipped her the money again with a familiar caveat, in *Hoisan-wa*: *Mo gong nay gah mah heng* ("Don't tell your mother"). She got her suit.[2] When Mom found out, she had no recourse other than to grumble.

Even after our family fortunes improved, Mom still guilt-tripped her children over her sacrifices and hard work. On her honeymoon in Canada in the summer of 1961, Flo insisted on buying Mom a cashmere sweater to assuage her ongoing lingering guilt. When she and Lai Wah moved to Sunnyvale with their husbands, they bought Mom rosebushes for our Oakland house, partially out of guilt. They wanted to soothe Mom's unhappiness about their moving away from Oakland.

Sometimes their guilt-ridden gestures worked, and sometimes they didn't. Mom expressed her displeasure at a gift by saying that Pop, who had died, wouldn't have liked it. That projection technique of communicating, by the way, was a favorite of Mom's and exemplified how some Chinatown folks let you know how they felt. *So-and-so* wouldn't like that, or *so-and-so* didn't like what you just did, never *I* don't like that, or *I* didn't want you to do that.

Mom was difficult to please, and she let us know it. When Lai Wah got her driver's license, she drove Pop and Mom home from the Great China, Mom first, Pop later. Once, Lai had a date for a dance in San Francisco, and she told Mom that she couldn't drive her home. Mom had to take a taxicab. That was unfortunate because, en route, the taxi driver stopped abruptly, tossing Mom in the back seat and bruising her. (No seat belts then.) As Lai was getting dressed for her date, Mom burst into the house and screamed at her, calling her a "terrible person" because she had almost gotten her killed. Shaken up, Lai left for her date, but her evening was ruined. "Of course, [the incident] devastated me," Lai remembered. "I went to the dance, and I was so miserable that I left the dance within an hour. I asked the guy to take me home."

That was one incident of mental abuse, but there were times of physical abuse. "Mom broke a lot of coat hangers on me, the wooden ones. Every time I looked at her sideways or looked at her wrong—*pow!* She didn't stop," Lai remembered years after Mom had died.[3]

One way Pop coped with Mom's anger at him was hitting the bottle, especially after work, when he cooked himself dinner at home. He'd fry up a pork chop or two and steam some white rice. He'd sit on a stepstool chair with a low back, rather awkwardly, his knees crammed into a white metal cabinet next to the stove. The aromatic smells of the frying pork chops wafted from the kitchen into nearby rooms. Always, he accompanied his meal with a shot or two of whisky.

That was his chill time, away from Mom, who was already in bed. By then, only Nellie, Flo, and I were living at home with him and Mom. Each of us would saunter into the kitchen, drawn by the delectable smells of Pop's cooking. Nellie ironed the family's clothes. Flo's job was to clean up Pop's kitchen mess, a greasy fry pan, grease spatters everywhere, a pot crusted with the remains of cooked rice. At times, Flo didn't act immediately. Seeing the piled-high sink and soiled stovetop, Pop yelled at Flo, who yelled back that she'd get to it soon.

Pop did enjoy drinking booze, at home and at tong gatherings. He'd down shots of whisky or Haig & Haig scotch, and sometimes *Ng Gah Pay*,[4] a potent, nasty-tasting Chinese liquor. He got drunk, but he didn't turn mean or abusive. On special holidays, such as Chinese New Year, he went alone to the tong gathering. Once, we at home got a phone call from him. He was quite drunk and said that he didn't remember where he had parked the car. One or more of my sisters went to help him find his missing car and drive him home.

It was during those late-night dinners that Pop obliquely expressed to Nellie how he felt about marriage. Nellie was feeling sorry for herself. Here she was at home while her sisters were out having fun or were married with children. Nellie was single, living at home in her mid-twenties, practically an "old maid" without marriage prospects, according to the dominant and sexist conventional wisdom of the time. Pop was his forlorn self, weary from all the hard work, beaten down by constant harping from Mom. He was happy in his late-night space, but melancholic as well. Somehow, the topic of marriage emerged. Pop harrumphed, "Ah, marriage!" in a manner that Nellie interpreted as something negative, or "Don't think that your problems are solved by being married," or "Marriage is a lot harder than you think."[5]

The relationship between our parents was imbalanced, with Mom the aggressor, the verbal abuser, and Pop the sometimes-passive victim.

At times he screamed back, but he also tried to please her by buying her clothes and jewelry. Often, that wasn't enough, yielding the unsatisfactory outcome some of the daughters felt when they tried to appease Mom with a guilt gift. Yet they stayed married, out of deep cultural beliefs based on Confucian precepts that one did not divorce, no matter what, that husbands had the upper hand. Chinese women of their time absorbed the cultural belief that virtuous women married only once.

Of course, they wouldn't be the first married couple in human history to stay together without visible signs of love and affection. The institution of marriage is strong, if painful, in many cultural settings. For Pop and Mom, and other Chinatown couples of their era, staying together as a family was more important than being "happy" in the relationship. The moral codes of Confucius and Zhu Xi were inexorably influential on the ideal of family harmony, even if little was harmonious in the marriage.

Notwithstanding their ill feelings toward one another, they proved to be good partners. Unlike other Chinatown men, Pop chose to bring his wife to America and did all he could to provide for her and all their children. For her part, Mom worked extremely hard throughout the marriage, caring for us and the household, with the Great China years demonstrating the height of her work loyalty.

17

BITTERSWEET SUMMER

The summer of 1961 was, well, bittersweet for our family. In the spring, Pop became quite ill, losing weight, and was largely bedridden, either at home or in a hospital. The illness, related to a failing liver, perhaps from the effects of too many shots of whisky over too many years, exacerbated perhaps by long-term consequences of his shooting wounds and lost kidney from twenty-one years earlier, sapped his strength to the point he could no longer work, imploding our family's universe for the past eighteen years, the Great China restaurant, in the middle of April 1961. Pop was in his mid-sixties, and this time was only the second when he couldn't work since he had been an immigrant teenager. We knew that the end was near.

But our clan also had reason to feel joy that fateful summer. Florence, Pop's sixth and youngest daughter, was about to be married. She and her fiancé, Edward, were most torn by the polarizing emotions. They certainly wanted Pop to be around for their early July wedding. His deteriorating condition was such, however, that Mom arranged for a Gee relative, a man we called Lin Goo, who lived in Las Vegas, to walk Flo down the aisle.

A physically weak but spiritually determined Pop assured Flo that he'd be around when the wedding day came. The reassurance made the betrothed couple feel better, but who could really say what Pop's condition would be on the big day? Flo and Ed decided to go ahead with their plans. Pop couldn't attend the Christian wedding ceremony at a fancy Oakland church outside Chinatown in the mid-afternoon or the sumptuous banquet at a San Francisco Chinatown restaurant. Six weeks later, Pop died. Cause of death: cirrhosis of the liver. He was either sixty-five or sixty-six years old, depending on which of three birth dates was true. He was buried facing west, toward his beloved China, in a beautiful Oakland mountainside cemetery.

Pallbearers at Pop's funeral were members of his tong. That happenstance puzzled the thoroughly Americanized me because one would think that Pop's relationship with his tong would have been permanently severed after his near-fatal shooting by a tong hitman two decades earlier. My confusion was further accentuated when I saw a photo taken about six years after the shooting of Pop standing among many tong brothers on Chinatown's main drag during a national gathering of his tong. His continuing links to the tong that had apparently ordered his attempted murder—and that, conversely, supported several of his business ventures—say something significant about rural Cantonese Chinatown culture totally untethered from the surrounding white America that American-born descendants like me find difficult to fathom.

A month after Pop died, I began my senior year at Cal. I was emotionally torn—happy for Flo and Ed, very sad about Pop's passing—but I was also excitedly anticipating the coming school year. I was managing editor of the *Daily Californian*, at least for the fall semester, extending that role I had had in my junior year after a colleague lower in the hierarchy manipulated his way above me to become editor-in-chief for the fall semester. I finally became editor-in-chief in the spring semester of 1962. As such, I had a nice corner office and felt good about being one of the big men on campus. Did I become arrogant and obnoxious? I might have seemed so to some folks, but I never believed that my status really went to my head.

The editorials I wrote were well within mainstream liberalism, even if I couldn't articulately define the term. At times, I was even naïvely idealistic. For example, I wrote an editorial extolling President John F. Kennedy coming to Cal and giving a speech in the football stadium. It's a big deal anytime an American president visits a college campus, especially one who was very popular among my college generation. My edi-

Bill Wong
Editor

Author at his desk when he was editor-in-chief of the *Daily Cal* in 1962. (Author's Collection)

torial thanked him for coming to Cal and was almost hagiographic. Activist students further to my left, however, criticized that editorial. They wanted me to join them in denouncing Kennedy's actions at the Bay of Pigs, the failed invasion of Cuba to try to overthrow Fidel Castro, the Communist revolutionary who had taken over the island nation in 1959.

My Cal years deepened my interest in newspaper journalism and educated me well in basic American and international politics. Those topics mattered more than the liberal arts classes I took, some from star professors whom we lowly students never actually met. Upon graduation, one of my journalism teachers helped me get a summer reporting job at the *San Francisco Chronicle*, which hired several fresh college graduates as temporary substitutes for its reporters, who staggered their vacations throughout the summer and autumn. A Stanford guy and I were the chosen ones that summer. I may have thought myself to be hot stuff, but I really knew very little about the complex world around me. I had exited my Chinatown bubble only a few years earlier, and other than a few brief vacation trips and a high-school journalism convention in New York City, I had seen almost nothing outside Oakland, San Francisco, and Berkeley.

The *Chronicle* was one of two major morning newspapers in San Francisco, so getting a job there, even a short-term one, was a major achievement in my still-young life. Yet I felt unsure about being a rookie reporter with the biggest metropolitan newspaper in the area, a big leap from the *Daily Cal*. I was the only Chinese American on the news staff in a city that has had a significant ethnic Chinese population for more than a century, the place of America's first Chinatown. The paper had one African American reporter that summer as well. Otherwise, its staff was mostly white men, the demographic profile of establishment American print journalism of that period.

My desk was in a back row of the so-called city desk section, which handled "hard" or "breaking" local news—crimes, fires, government meetings, and events unrelated to sports, the arts, and culture. Abe Mellinkoff was the city editor. A well-groomed, natty dresser with wavy salt-and-pepper hair, he favored suspenders, immaculately ironed shirts, and colorful ties. His visage was serious, and he groused a lot. His newsroom rival was Bill German, another gruff guy less sartorially splendid or charismatic. He was the news editor, in charge of the copy desk, wire-service news, and the design and organization of the main news sections.

Star reporters, all graceful, colorful writers, sat in the front row, facing Mellinkoff and his assistants. Most were middle-aged men. One, Carolyn Anspacher, was a woman perhaps in her fifties or sixties who wrote beautifully. Some of the star men reporters smoked up a storm, and maybe a few had bottles of booze in their desk drawers. These stars took notes from reporters in the field to craft colorful, easy-to-read stories, the *Chronicle*'s hallmark. There were even rumors a few of these stars wrote stories from a nearby bar. In the middle were budding luminaries, including Ron Fimrite, a gifted writer who later became a star at *Sports Illustrated*, and Warren Hinckle, who went on to a maverick career as a compelling raconteur, stylist, and provocateur.

My story assignments were the simple, one-note variety—government meetings, crimes and fires, the foundational content of local newspapers. One story assignment I can't forget was the Miss Chinatown contest, held annually in San Francisco's Chinatown. One might assume that since I was a Chinatown native, I'd have an affinity for a Miss Chinatown pageant. That would be a mistaken assumption. Oakland's Chinatown, while vibrant on its own, was distinctly minor league to San Francisco's, and my Chinatown didn't have such a glittery event.

At age twenty-one, I hadn't yet developed fully formed racial-ethnic, cultural, social, and political identities. In fact, I gave virtually no thought to these deep matters. Of course, I knew that I was of Chinese descent, but since I had been encased in a Chinatown bubble when the dominant white culture looked down at us yellow folk, I wasn't yet wholly proud of who I was from a racial-ethnic perspective.

A Miss Chinatown beauty pageant was something I hadn't given much thought to, yet I felt vaguely embarrassed by its existence. For one thing, it seemed a silly copycat to the white Miss America–type pageants where young women of a certain appearance (thin, curvy, unblemished, good-looking, preferably blonde) paraded around in bathing suits and ball gowns that would shock (or excite) Chinatown elders. I also wasn't "woke" in a gender sense, but I sensed the inherent sexism in such pageants. In short, I wasn't yet in a professional or enlightened personal position to even think about saying "no" when an assistant city editor told me to cover the Miss Chinatown contest. My feelings were decidedly mixed and confused. Did I get this story because I was Chinese American or because I was a rookie?

I asked several contestants, "What are your measurements?" In hindsight, that was a stupid, sexist question, but one I had observed being asked by veteran print reporters at beauty pageants like Miss America. In those prefeminist days, reporters expected beauty contestants to provide their bust, waist, and hip sizes for inclusion in pageant stories. Alas, I got a well-deserved denunciation for asking contestants such a personal question, one that in a Chinese cultural context was taboo. I asked it because I thought that my editor would ask me why I didn't include such information in the story. Ultimately, my story didn't include such information, and my editor never asked me for it. Nonetheless, I still felt ashamed.

My *Chronicle* stint ended in November 1962, as scheduled. Neither the Stanford guy nor I was offered a permanent reporter job, as sometimes happened. I wasn't devastated; I simply hunted for another newspaper reporting gig. I found one at the *San Leandro Morning News*, a step down from the *Chronicle*. San Leandro is a small city just south of Oakland. The paper had a tiny staff, and the position I was hired for was an odd combination of general-news reporter and weekend sports editor. I covered many government and school-board meetings in San Leandro and adjacent small towns Castro Valley and San Lorenzo. On weekends, I edited the sports pages, with no writing.

One of the other reporters was Curtis Castain, a tall, affable, athletic African American man about my age. By appearance and racial-ethnic and cultural backgrounds, we couldn't have been more different, yet we became fast friends, hanging out together and grabbing breakfast after our shifts ended at midnight. Unlike me, he had construction skills and, being the nice guy that he was, helped fix the garage door at my family's China Hill house. My mother, not used to Black people other than as occasional restaurant customers, couldn't have been happier.

Curtis and I loved sports, especially track and field. His love was more authentic, as he was a track and field athlete, a hurdler. One spring, we drove down together—about a four-hour trip one way—to the Fresno Relays, at the time one of the big track-and-field events in California. Curtis happened to have relatives in Fresno, with whom we stayed that weekend and ate delicious fried chicken. Eventually, as our careers veered in different directions, we grew apart, one of my life's regrets.

A genial, middle-aged fellow named Paul Spindler was our editor. He didn't grouse the way Mellinkoff and German did at the *Chronicle*. Curtis and I liked him, and he liked us. The *Morning News* newsroom was a much more congenial work setting, a comforting environment to a still inexperienced reporter.

Six months later, I caught wind of a reporting job at the *San Francisco News Call Bulletin*, which had once been three separate newspapers—the *News*, the *Call*, and the *Bulletin*. While I liked the San Leandro gig, I was eager to get back to the big city. I got the job. At first, I worked an early morning to mid-afternoon shift, covering, yes, routine local stories (crime, fires, meetings). Since this newspaper was an afternoon edition, our deadlines were early afternoon, with a final deadline of mid-afternoon so the paper could feature a front-page, red-boxed stock-market closing price and the latest breaking news for late afternoon street sales.

The most exciting late-breaking story I worked on was an early afternoon earthquake, close to our deadline. I happened to be on rewrite duty, meaning that I and a few other reporters were tasked with handling fast-breaking stories covered by reporters in the field. When the quake shook, the city editor, Harry Press (yes, that was his name) barked at me to start writing. I reached for a half-sheet carbonized paper packet and put on a headphone to get facts from our police reporter. I typed furiously, using a different packet of paper for each sentence, calling out "boy" (for "copy boy") for a young assistant to take the sheet to an assistant city editor to start editing and moving the story to the copy desk. This work was high-stress for the minutes it took for me to rap out a "just the facts" story, but it was an exhilarating adrenaline rush.

After a few months of an early morning shift, I was moved to the night shift, reporting to work when all the other reporters were going home. I became the only reporter on duty, quite an awesome responsibility for someone with only a year's experience. Now I had the entire city to cover at night, when anything could happen. I wasn't quite alone. A photographer also worked the night shift. Sometimes, he'd have his own assignments, and sometimes the two of us would do a story together. The night photographer I remember best was a white guy in his fifties with a weathered face. His tousled hair was streaked with gray, and he dressed sloppily. He was somewhat surly, but he loved to talk about the paper, staff, and city, and, as different as we were, I kind of liked his company.

When we went on the same assignment, he drove a beaten-down company car since he knew San Francisco streets, hills and all, a lot better than I did. His driving concerned me since I could smell booze on him. Some assignments required only a reporter, so I drove alone, getting to know the city better than ever.

As at the *Chronicle*, I was the only Chinese American reporter. A veteran *News Call Bulletin* reporter (yes, a white guy with a vaguely European accent) told me that I was breaking a yellow color line at San Francisco newspapers, a fact that had never crossed my mind until he mentioned it. At the time, 1962–1963, I hadn't grasped the concepts of equal opportunity or racial equity and justice. I just wanted a newspaper job.

I learned a lot from veteran (white male) reporters. Accompanying one to a homicide scene, I observed one quizzing police detectives on minute details of the dead body and the crime scene, details like dress, posture, how many gunshots, where, or what type of deadly force. Ghoulish, maybe, but essential for good crime-scene reporting. I also noticed how casual, sarcastic, and snarky some of these older reporters were, a sure sign of a culture of cynicism that infected newspaper newsrooms.

The reporter who told me that I was a yellow pioneer helped Mom unravel her dicey immigration history. This reporter was working on a story about the Chinese "confession" program, which encouraged Chinese who had immigrated illegally during the exclusion era to "confess" their status, clearing the way to legal status and possible U.S. citizenship. I told him about Mom's status, and he recommended that she participate in the program, which had the unannounced—and controversial—intent of finding Communist sympathizers in the Chinese American community. He even brokered a meeting with the senior federal immigration official in San Francisco, cutting through the dreaded "red tape." I accompanied Mom to the immigration office, which was intimidating to a mother and son mostly closeted in a Chinatown and rarely, if ever, interacting with The (White) Man.

As nervous as each of us was, we got through the process without incident. I was her "witness," testifying that she was indeed my mother and helping her understand the process, using Chinglish as best I could to soothe whatever nerves she had. The process cleared a path to her becoming a legal permanent resident, which could, if she wanted, lead to official citizenship. She died before achieving that higher legal status.

One of the big San Francisco stories in the early 1960s was civil rights protests advocating for equal-opportunity hiring. Having gotten my early political education at Cal and being enamored by what I understood to be the civil rights movement as it related to African Americans, I decided to attend such a demonstration on my day off, a Friday, either in 1963 or 1964. That casual decision got me into trouble with my union. The protest site was the elegant Sheraton Palace Hotel, in the heart of the city's commercial strip along Market Street. As hundreds of protestors rhythmically shouted slogans in front of the hotel, I took notes. After the protest, I went to the *News Call Bulletin* office. Hardly anyone was around as I typed up my notes and left them at the city desk in case editors wanted a record of what I had seen.

The following Monday, the paper's union chief, a grizzled veteran with whom I had had almost no interaction previously, pulled me aside. Without collegial small talk, in an even tone without histrionics, he told me that I shouldn't have been "working" on that story because it was my day off. I had broken a union-management rule, he said. Don't do that again. I apologized and pledged fealty to the rules. I was certainly chastised, but it made me wonder about the efficacy of work rules versus a good breaking story one saw in the moment, even if one were officially off duty. By no means was I anti-union—quite the contrary. I liked being a member of a journalists' union. In this case, I wasn't thinking about union rules. As an eager, wide-eyed young reporter, I was simply thinking about a good story breaking in front of me, regardless of whether I was officially on duty or specifically assigned to it.

By the spring of 1964, I had grown weary of the stories I was covering. Maybe I wasn't as jazzed about being a newspaper reporter, after all. I was tired of schlepping out to the next fire and seeing the same deputy chief overseeing his troops trying to douse yet another set of raging flames. I felt the slow, steady creep of cynicism seep into my young journalistic soul and wondered, "Is this all there is to being a newspaper reporter?" The cumulative numbness began to course through my veins.

At the same time, I had grown restless at home. It was just Mom, Nellie, and me living in that big house. Pop was gone, and so was the newly married Flo. While I appreciated the meals Mom cooked and the shelter—I had moved into one of the downstairs bedrooms far from hers—I had little to say to her, or she to me. I got along with Nellie, but being seven years apart, our interests were different (me, sports, news; her, movies, TV). Until then, in my early twenties, I hadn't had much of a feeling of wanderlust, to get out there to see the world. Now an itch to go somewhere else, to experience life more broadly, to be somewhere less familiar started forming oh so steadily. Getting a draft notice in the wake of an acceleration of America's involvement in a war in Vietnam (where was that?) certainly made me scratch that itch more intensely.

18

WANDERLUST

The Peace Corps

In the late morning of November 22, 1963, the wall phone outside my basement bedroom rang, waking me up. I had worked until midnight and was still asleep when the call came. The caller was Patricia Mar, a friend who was one of the few Chinese American reporters on the *Daily Cal* when I was there and was now a reporter at the *San Francisco Examiner*. Every so often, we hung around together with other former *Daily Cal* pals, and it was at one of those sessions that I had complained about being bored with the stories I had been covering and that there hadn't been any exciting news recently, locally or nationally.

"Hi, Bill, I've got some exciting news for you," she intoned, in the deadpan way I had heard many times before. "President Kennedy's been shot."

"What?" I exclaimed, still not fully awake and not sure of what I had just heard. "What are you saying?"

"Kennedy's been shot," she repeated. She had few other details, including whether he was going to be all right or was dead.

Stunned and shocked, I hung up, not knowing what to think or do. Not only was the news that Pat had conveyed "exciting"; it was enormously devastating for a nation—and much of the world—that had never imagined such a tragic whopper of a news story. Kennedy's assassination shook me up in ways I hadn't experienced before. I liked the fact that he had been elected, a young (only in his early forties) and seemingly forward-looking political figure, a sharp, progressive step from the dour, dull Eisenhower years. Like many other Americans, especially younger ones, I was starstruck with the perceptions about Kennedy and his family's "Camelot" fantasy. Recall that romanticized editorial I had written a year earlier at the *Daily Cal* and how warm I had felt when Kennedy had blessed us with his presence on the Cal campus.

Kennedy's inauguration speech ("Ask not what your country can do for you, ask what you can do for your country") pierced the conscience of young Americans like me more than anything any other politician had said in our lifetimes. His apparent idealism and creation of the Peace Corps spoke to me and others my age in an inspirational way that few public figures had ever done in our still developing lives. (Many decades later, I no longer hold Kennedy in such high esteem.)

At about the same time, I had gotten a piece of mail that I had dreaded—a notice from my local draft board to possibly serve in the military. In my dreamy naïveté, I wasn't fully tuned into the realpolitik of the Kennedy administration's ratcheting up military involvement, begun under President Dwight D. Eisenhower, in a war allegedly to "fight Communism" in Vietnam.

Together, the Kennedy assassination and the draft notice set my active mind spinning with thoughts that mashed together my unrest with being a newspaper reporter and still living at home with Mom. And I felt this vague stirring within me, a nascent wanderlust, a desire to get far away so that I might discover more of me than I knew from my rather cosseted life thus far.

As instructed by the draft notice, I went for a medical examination. Doctors found a little something that I had not heard of before or had felt was a problem: a pilonidal cyst on my tailbone. That somewhat-bad news turned out to be good news for me. Instead of being classified "1A" for the draft, meaning that I could be called up for military service at any time, I was nudged to a less urgent "1Y," which didn't exempt me, per se, but reduced the chances I'd be called to service quickly.

So, where did all my active brain cells take me? Ah, the Peace Corps, Kennedy's marvelous project that gave idealistic Americans a golden opportunity to do something good for people and countries less fortunate than ours. On that elevated philosophic ground, I applied to join the Peace Corps, almost on a whim.

My reasoning wasn't wholly noble. I've never seen myself as a clever, scheming career thinker, someone who's coolly strategic in master-planning my life. Rather, at that point, I responded to whatever opportunities presented themselves, such as the *San Francisco Chronicle* summer job. This time, though, I had a plan, vague as it was, to do something Big with my life.

Moving forward assertively in the Peace Corps application process was also a way to scratch a persistent itch I had developed about searching for my Chinese roots. I was hoping, through the Peace Corps, to get closer to where Pop came from. Still in its infancy, the Peace Corps didn't have a presence in China, which only a dozen or so years earlier had ended a bloody civil war the Communist Party had won. The United States was still in a Cold War with the Communist Soviet Union, so the thought of the young, liberal, democracy-loving American president's well-regarded public-service project going to a new Communist country was unfathomable. China wasn't ready to get any help from a country at the polar opposite of the political and economic spectrums.[1]

Well, if not China, then where would my Peace Corps dream take me? I asked to be assigned somewhere close to China. The Peace Corps said, "How about the Philippines?" I knew little about the Philippines. Some Filipinos lived and worked near us in Chinatown, but I had never had much curiosity about them or where they or their forbears came from. The only thing Mom said, when she learned of my assignment, was, in *Hoisan-wa*, "Be careful. They steal gold out of your ears." Her comment struck me as odd . . . and racist. Besides, I didn't wear gold in my ears. Mom didn't like that her only son, now twenty-three years old, was soon going to be leaving her and going to a place far, far away and, in her mind, dangerous. She couldn't stop me, though, and I was ready to defy her if she tried.

When the Peace Corps accepted my application and told me that I was going to the Philippines, I didn't have a clue what was ahead, and I still didn't know what I was looking for and why. The cynicism that had germinated in my early newspaper reporting days hadn't yet fully enveloped me, or at least not the naïve altruistic part of me who wanted to serve my country peacefully. My ongoing curiosity and inexplicable idealism blanketed any self-doubts and insecurities that sometimes swelled up.

The biggest adventure of my life began at Northern Illinois University in DeKalb, west of Chicago, the training site for my designated Peace Corps group. I had very little experience traveling far and flying on airplanes. With no guidance from family members, I relied on official Peace Corps documents suggesting things like what kinds of clothes to pack or not pack. After landing at O'Hare Airport, I found my way to a bus that would drive us aspiring Peace Corps Volunteers (our official title, or PCVs) to DeKalb. As we awkwardly gathered near the bus, me wearing a tan raincoat in the humid heat of the Midwest, I noticed that I was a distinct racial minority, along with an Asian American woman and an African American man.

On the bus, I happened to sit next to a young white woman with a pretty smile, Letitia (Lettie) Morse, from Stroudsburg, Pennsylvania. She looked at me and wondered whether I might be a Filipino on the Peace Corps training staff. I told her, no, I was Chinese American from Oakland hoping to join the Peace Corps. Was this a prima facie case of we Asians all look alike? I wasn't offended by Lettie's apparent ignorance, for she was nice, friendly, and free of malice. We chatted on and became friends in training and have stayed in touch for more than a half century. Lettie later told me that she knew very few Asians in her part of Pennsylvania, the Pocono Mountains. In one of life's many ironies, she ended up marrying a Filipino, a prominent politician, Jesse Lladoc, in Ormoc City, where she was assigned, on Leyte island in the Visayas region, about halfway between Manila and Mindanao.

Our Illinois contingent was seventy-four in number, almost two-thirds women, the overwhelming majority white, and most of us in our early- to mid-twenties. We came from twenty-eight states, with California and Ohio having the most, nine each. We were the "A" portion of Group XIII (the Peace Corps loves Roman numerals), headed for the middle and south of the Philippines, while the "B" part with similar numbers was simultaneously training in Hilo, Hawaii—lucky them! "B" was going to the northern regions that included the capital city, Manila. Our entire Group XIII numbered about 150 at the beginning of training.

The two months of training in Illinois were intense: sixty hours a week for eight weeks. About 40 percent of that was devoted to learning Cebuano, the predominant dialect of the areas our cohort was going to.[2] The impression I came away with in the language training was that once we reached our assignments, we'd need whatever dialect we were learning to better communicate with the people there. That was a safe and sane assumption because a PCV's tour of duty was roughly two years, plenty of time to immerse oneself in the culture. The ability to speak a little of their language would show the Americans' respect and willingness to be part of their culture.

This immersion mind-set was hardly mainstream American cultural thinking, in part because the arrogance of us "exceptional" Americans usually meant that we didn't have to speak any language other than English. Whatever the philosophical underpinnings of the theory behind Kennedy's creation of the Peace Corps were, we PCVs had a sharply contrasting mission from that of other young Americans—a larger portion of whom were non-white—drafted to fight a war against Vietnamese and other Southeast Asians.

Besides 210 hours of language training, the other training time was split among history, political, and cultural studies; the educational system of the Philippines and teaching methodologies; health matters, physical education, and recreation; and the Peace Corps itself. As we were learning about the history and culture of the Philippines, I felt a special connection because the Chinatown culture I had come from had broadly similar values. Both put a premium on family and group relationships, not individual rights, as in the white mainstream Judeo-Christian Western/American culture.

We also learned our mission. Our group was to teach English, math, and science and tutor teachers of those disciplines. Teaching English and teaching teachers of English how to better teach English were entirely new enterprises for me and most others assigned this task. This Peace Corps education mission was also American arrogance writ large. To think that inexperienced young adults, many fresh out of college, could impart substantive knowledge to teachers in other lands who might be twice our age or older, with a great deal of teaching experience, was ludicrous on its face. At the time, none of us as far as I know ever questioned our educational mission. Most of us tried hard, I believe, to do our new jobs in places and conditions that were strange, uncomfortable, and intimidating.

We also got a dose of international intrigue. From our narrow, provincial perspective, we trainees saw ourselves as do-gooders, using whatever skills we learned and our American personas that had been imbued with individual rights and freedom. From a wider political perspective, however, some politicians, analysts, and commentators looked at the Peace Corps skeptically, certainly as a "soft weapon" in the ongoing Cold War between the democratic West, led by America, and the Communist East, led by the Soviet Union and China.

Through that lens, we PCVs could be viewed as instruments of U.S. foreign policy to gain whatever advantage we could over Communist nations. In other words, doubters could see the Peace Corps more conspiratorially. Sure, young Americans went into the jungles and villages of so-called Third-World countries to uplift the natives and maybe spread democracy and freedom. But were we undercover spies working for the CIA (Central Intelligence Agency)? In one session, we trainees were alerted to the possibility that host-country people might look on us as spies, not as idealistic do-gooders. That idea took some of us aback, as it was designed to. It essentially told us to be alert when we got to our assignments, even those in tiny rural villages. We shouldn't be surprised if someone suspected us of being spies for some grand nefarious purpose having nothing to do with teaching English or helping a village find better drinking water. But the spy talk in training was just that—talk.

In our two months of Illinois training, each of us was being evaluated as to whether we'd be good candidates to send overseas. A few chose to leave the program on their own. A small number were "deselected." Most in my "A" portion made it to the next level, Hawaii, to join our "B" colleagues, a welcome change from the bland, boring surroundings of central Illinois, whose main feature during the late summer and early autumn was seemingly endless fields of tall corn stalks, a beautiful but unexciting vista.

Hawaii had become a state only five years earlier, but it already had a reputation for being paradise. I had only a vague impression of the islands way down somewhere in the vast Pacific Ocean—yes, it was paradise, but with a lot of Asian and Native peoples, making it a unique American state. Our six-week stay there, however, was no vacation. We merely touched down and quickly passed through touristy Honolulu on the island of Oahu, on our way to our destination, Waipio Valley, on the northern part of the big island of Hawaii. While our Illinois experience was largely classroom learning, our time in Waipio Valley was designed to expose us to a living experience close to what we might have in the Philippines, a tropical village setting. The sharp contrast to pallid Illinois was most welcome. Now, we'd be doing stuff outdoors, not being confined to a drab classroom.

One major lesson, or test, was spending a night alone in a small hut on stilts somewhere deep in a forested area, surrounded by nothing but nature. Not all of us were so tested. Awaiting the word as to who would be given this challenging lesson, I was highly anxious. A sudden jolt of fright surged through me when I learned I'd be one of the lucky, or unlucky, ones. Why me? Was my capacity to survive in question? Was I on the edge of "deselection"? Was this night out alone the ultimate test for me making it or getting sent home? I was too anxiety-ridden to ask, nor was I ever told why I was one of the chosen ones. Being a good trouper, I mentally prepared for this new adventure.

Until then, my whole life of some twenty-three years had been spent in a city, a built environment of concrete, steel, glass, motor vehicles, lots of people, and relatively little natural greenery, flowing rivers and streams, and wide-open spaces where, at night, one could marvel at the jillions of blinking lights in the blackest of black skies. Sure, I'd been on a brief camping trip with a brother-in-law, but I was hardly relaxed or comfortable in the great outdoors.

When my turn came for a night out in the jungle, I was given a sleeping bag; camping gear, including a little cooktop, a few pots and pans, and utensils; and some food (raw pork pieces, uncooked rice). A staff member pointed the way and gave me general instructions. Loaded down, with the rolled-up sleeping bag hanging over one shoulder, the other things stuffed into a backpack, I headed by foot in the direction I was told to go. That was almost my undoing. Trudging off, my head filled with a fear of the unknown and a quest to calm my jittery nerves, I came upon a stream. Oh, no. Even though the water flowed gently, I froze. For me, it seemed like a torrent.

Frighteningly, I conjured up the first time I had tried swimming lessons at the Oakland High School pool—I wasn't yet a student there but merely starting a multi-week course as a preteen. It wasn't a cheerful memory. As I was standing poolside with other kids about my age, someone knocked me into the shallow end of the pool before I felt ready. This sudden plunge scared me to no end. I stiffened as I hopped up and down, swallowing some water. I frantically waved my arms, as the other kids, oblivious to my situation, happily splashed away without any cares in the world. I had to immediately climb out, unsure of what to do next. I eventually slipped back in, but that little accident instilled in me a fear of water ever since, to the degree that I've never learned how to swim.

I knew that I had no other choice, so I waded in carefully, not knowing how deep the water ran. My gear felt heavier. My breathing got faster and more pronounced. I began to panic. My grip on some of my gear loosened, resulting in a portion touching the stream. That panicked me even more. I somehow managed to reach the other shoreline without completely losing my overactive mind and my gear that suddenly seemed unmanageable. The stream was quite shallow, after all, but how was I to know? Now damp from my knees down and still unnerved, I trekked on, breathing heavily. Eventually, I found the hut.

I felt some relief, as I had completed the first part of this test, although not without feeling a bit terrorized. I climbed into the hut, unpacked my stuff, and set up the cooking gear to prepare dinner. I don't know how I did it because at that point, I hadn't cooked much of anything. The pork and rice, usually one of my favorites, was barely edible, but at that point, I didn't care. With nothing else to do, I climbed into the sleeping bag and tried to fall asleep as easily and quickly as I could. No surprise, that wasn't the most restful night in my life. After tossing and turning, I awoke to the light peeking through a window. I felt even more relief—I had survived the second portion of the test. I packed up quickly and headed back to the training camp, with less concern and a lighter gait. The stream didn't present the same unknown challenge, and I found my way back.

A slight cockiness swelled up in me—"I did it! I did it!"—as I approached my destination. A few of my training mates saw me coming. They smiled and waved, and I was so happy to see them, as they greeted me warmly with applause and cheers. I was pleased with myself for having done something difficult that I had never done before.

Another training exercise was to corral a pig (yes, a real oink-oink pig) and, uh—how do I say this without offending animal-rights activists?—kill it with a knife. This exercise called for a few of us to act as a team. Two or more of us had to grab and hold a squealing, squirmy pig, while one of us was told to stick a knife into its neck and twist it, thus incapacitating the animal. Exactly why I volunteered to do the dirty deed, I can't say even after all these years. Until then, I had been neutral about animals in general, and home pets in particular. Our Chinatown household never had animal pets. I was familiar, however, with the killing of live chickens and ducks for food at a store across the street from our restaurant. I had no feelings one way or the other. Such a happenstance was just something that happened in Chinatown. But I had never killed an animal myself.

Without much thought, as my mates held on tightly to the pig in question, I stuck the knife into its throat and twisted it. Each of us looked at one another as the animal went limp after a few herky-jerky moves. Its blood spilled on the ground. My mates laid it down; none of us said a word. We backed off, letting others handle the next step, which was to prepare it for roasting for our next meal. I walked away shaken, even as some of my colleagues congratulated me for my "bravery."

Those of us who survived training headed off for the real place, the Republic of the Philippines, arriving in early November 1964. The Philippines is a nation of more than seven thousand islands in the South China Sea. It was once a U.S. colony, after several hundred years of Spanish occupation. It's been fully independent since 1946. Its history adds up to identity confusion. Largely a Malay people, Filipinos have been whipsawed by Spanish Catholicism; American democracy and Hollywoodization; an erratic independence marked by wealthy oligarchical families controlling political and economic power, sometimes through blatantly corrupt means; and rampant poverty. Its population was approximately 30 million when I was there. Now, it is about 110 million, amazing growth in almost sixty years. Its economic performance since independence hasn't matched that of other East and Southeast Asian nations, such as China, Japan, South Korea, and Singapore. The Filipino diaspora is everywhere, ranging from doctors, nurses, and other medical and white-collar professionals, to nannies and service workers.

My assignment was at Iligan City High School as an English teacher. Iligan City is on the northern coastline of Mindanao, the big island in the south. Its residents were primarily Catholics. Much of Mindanao was where many of the Philippines' Muslim (known locally as "Moro") faithful lived. Indeed, the informal Moro capital was Marawi City, just up the interior mountains from seaside Iligan City. We were made aware of serious tensions between Catholics and Moros, but in my time in Iligan, I never saw those tensions break out into violence. We read about such violence erupting, however, in other Mindanao cities and communities, such as Cagayan de Oro, Davao, and the Sulu Archipelago south of Zamboanga in the southwest.

I had no preconceived notion about what my housing arrangements would be like. They turned out to be quite nice, a far cry from the imagined hut-on-stilts like I suffered through during my Hawaii training. I lived in a nice corner two-story house of an attorney named Voltaire, whose father was a judge elsewhere in the Philippines. Up a few steps, the house had a stylish wood-lined office on one side of the first floor and decent living and dining rooms on the other, with several bedrooms upstairs.

Voltaire was a lively, wiry fellow about my height, but decidedly skinnier than I, who, while not portly, had more flab. Wearing his black hair in a slick, well-parted wave, he was charming with a quick smile and wit. Often, around the house, he'd go shirtless, while wearing dark trousers. That inspired me to do the same, although I felt self-conscious because of my modest flab. Voltaire was extroverted, chatty, and friendly. His English was so good that I saw no need to use whatever Cebuano I had managed to learn. Indeed, it would have been insulting if I had tried to converse with him in my baby Cebuano. I didn't see him do a lot of lawyering. He was an assistant to the Iligan City mayor, but I never learned what that title meant. All I knew was that he was connected and was around the house a lot and not all that often at the mayor's office.

I was the second PCV he hosted. The first was John Holmstrom, a tall, strapping fellow from Washington State. John was a Stanford graduate, so he and I had a natural "rivalry," Stanford versus Cal, which can be a Big Deal to fervent alums of both universities, which are about forty miles apart. As two American foreigners living together in a sociable Filipino attorney's nice house, we didn't engage in any serious trashing of one another's alma maters. We got along just fine, sharing the strangeness of our individual and joint situations. John's assignment was also at Iligan City High, teaching math. John had a dry sense of humor and easy manner. I was fortunate to live with two guys who were easy to get along with. My Chinese ethnicity made no difference to either of them, and I didn't make a big deal of it either.

Voltaire always had buddies hanging around the house. The most ubiquitous was Eufracio, or Fraz, taller than Voltaire, slender like him, and very handsome, with a warm smile. A teenage houseboy cooked and cleaned the house. Upon my arrival, Voltaire and Fraz took me to a Chinese restaurant! Maybe my Chinese face meant something to them, after all. They ordered their favorites. The sweet and sour meatballs were pretty good, if somewhat tiny. The other dishes were familiar but not as voluminous or tasty as those served in San Francisco's or Oakland's Chinatown.

Quite surprising to me, we next went to a hotel nightclub, where a pretty, heavily made-up young woman wearing a tight gown belted out familiar American pop tunes, backed by a small band. This night was the first time I had seen Filipino singers and musicians, who performed well. I was entertained, helped along by a few ice-cold homegrown San Miguel beers. I later learned that Filipino pop bands and singers played all over Southeast Asia, showing a talent for pop music modeled after American entertainers.

Because Fraz and a few other guys hung around often, our house often resembled a frat pad. We drank lots of San Miguels, shot the bull, roasted one another gently and humorously, played cards, and listened to Voltaire play his violin beautifully, European classics mostly.

Oh, I worked, too, teaching English at the high school and advising English teachers. This job was sometimes nerve-wracking, awkward, and uncomfortable, but also energizing and exciting. Since I had never been a teacher of anything, I had to find the way on my own, using the training I got in Illinois and Hawaii, but what I learned there wasn't sufficient to make me feel fully confident as a teacher. Yet there I was, teaching eager, bright-eyed Filipino teenagers English, their second (or third) language. My guess is that the students I had, mostly younger teens, were from poorer families since Iligan City itself, although the site of a new steel mill, was like most of the Philippines, working and lower class, unlike the handful of wealthy suburbs of Manila. My students knew some English since it was one of the languages of instruction in Philippine schools. They preferred to speak their native Cebuano dialect when not being forced to use English in the classroom.

Author teaching at Iligan City High School, the Philippines, in 1965.
(Author's Collection)

Well-intentioned interlopers like PCVs from wealthy societies trying to do good in poorer societies must weigh the pros and cons of a familiar dilemma: Should we try to change or embrace indigenous values? In some of my American schools' experience, teachers, especially in high school, encouraged me to think for myself and to express myself. That instruction was a big change from my Chinatown homelife, where I wasn't urged to speak out at all.

At Iligan City High School, I wanted my students to express themselves freely. Like my own Chinatown upbringing, Iligan City High School students weren't culturally grounded to question authority and offer their opinions. In response to mildly provocative questions from me, they rarely, if ever, did so. Sometimes, an adjacent student side-whispered to the student I had addressed, possibly offering an answer to help his or her mate. That interaction, subtle but noticeable, showed an aspect of Filipino culture that resembled what I had experienced in my Chinatown—people don't want to be shamed or embarrassed—that is, in the colloquialism of Asian enclaves of America, "lose face." Without openly shaming students and as gently as I could, I tried my best to discourage those assisting gestures because I wanted to encourage original and unique thoughts and ideas. I'm pretty sure I didn't change much cognitive behavior in my time teaching high-school English.

While I quit journalism to join the Peace Corps, I incorporated something from my former professional life in my new teaching life. I asked my students to create a "newspaper"—that is, to write brief stories that I typed out at home and somehow crudely "printed" up as a single-sheet "newspaper." This assignment, of course, offered a way for them to practice writing English.

Trying to help veteran English teachers of Filipino descent be better teachers was a greater hurdle for me. The teachers I worked with were much too polite to critique what I tried to do to help them. We had cordial relationships overall, but in reflecting on that experience, I can't help but think that my efforts were pretty much a joke, if not an outright insult to teachers much older and experienced than I was.

At first, my Chinese face puzzled my students and fellow teachers. Voltaire and Fraz, however, never seemed to question my American-ness, at least not overtly in my presence. Others in Iligan City weren't sure of who I really was. I didn't "look American," an image stereotyped as being white, preferably blond, an image thrust upon many Filipinos through colonization and Hollywood films. To many Filipinos, I was *Inchick*, meaning "Chinese" in their dialect, because of my physical appearance. Once I spoke, though, I really mystified them: How could this Chinese guy speak such fluent "American" English?

In an American context, my Chinese ethnicity was a distinguishing feature in a society that was overwhelmingly white, but increasingly non-white. Since I had spent the first twenty years of my life mostly inside a Chinatown bubble, I generally felt comfortable with my ethnic identity. It was later that I began to wonder just who I was. My Philippines experience accelerated that questioning process.

Before I got to the Philippines, I didn't know the racial-ethnic dynamics there. It wasn't until I was there, living among Filipinos in Mindanao and later in Manila, that I gained deeper insights into the status of ethnic Chinese in a country that was predominantly ethnic Malay with doses of Spanish, Chinese, and other white European. It became quite clear to me that ethnic Chinese in the Philippines weren't well regarded. The main reason: Chinese, a minority tracing their ancestral roots primarily to Fujian Province, dominated local economies.

At a visceral level, I got quizzical looks and a few squeals of surprise. However, I never felt the ignominy of being targeted for racial abuse other than the *Inchick* label, which wasn't threatening or hostile. Overall, the Filipinos I interacted with—some who likely had Chinese ancestry but never revealed that fact to me—were warm, gracious, and friendly. Others were diffident and standoffish, but that's no different than my experience in other places I've lived, including Oakland and other parts of America. Such is life.

Filipinos have a well-deserved reputation of being hospitable, especially outside metropolitan Manila. Given our American-ness and the general admiration for things American, we PCVs were always invited to *meriendas*, ritualistic midday social gatherings where generous amounts of food, sweets, and nonalcoholic drinks were served. There was often a quid pro quo for their hospitality: We were asked to sing! Singing in public has never been my thing since I can't carry a tune, but I belted out some pop hits nonetheless to avoid losing face and causing my hosts to lose theirs.

One of the craziest, maybe riskiest, adventures I had with my housemates in Iligan City was to hunt for wild boar in a jungle area and, if we got lucky, catch it and prepare its meat. I was more passive than aggressive, in sharp contrast to my Hawaii training incident of knifing a pig. Eventually someone caught a boar, and others stripped it down to extract some meat that was pickled in some acidic liquid. My Filipino mates dared me to eat the raw pickled meat, which I did, overcoming fears that doing so could sicken me. I didn't get sick, thank goodness. This example showed me, an urbanized American, willing to be "part of the culture" into which I had been thrust. Presumably, had I not indulged in the raw wild boar meat, I might have insulted my hosts or been labeled a scaredy-cat.

During weekdays, we Americans worked, but what about a social life? Most of us were unattached and still at a stage of life where we were seeking closer-than-just-friends relationships. Other than the guys night out, quaffing San Miguels, I had no close relationship with any eligible Filipinas. Most of the teachers at Iligan City High were women, some single and pretty, who certainly caught my eye. I knew, however, that trying to pursue anything more than a professional friendship would be a big taboo, and I simply didn't have the kind of bold rebellious nature to break sensitive social conventions.

In Manila, things were different. The bustling, chaotic capital was teeming with fun legal and illegal activities as well as standard urban pastimes, such as hanging out at cafés, restaurants, and bars. It also hosted the U.S. embassy, with its cafeteria that served such American staples as hamburgers, French fries, and milkshakes. Some of us Peace Corps folks might have had a dim view of the embassy—the fanciful CIA connection?—but we enjoyed the privilege of the cafeteria. One could always tell who the PCVs were—grubbier, more casually attired, perhaps even in need of better grooming. We didn't care. We just wanted a good old burger, fries, and a shake.

As for socializing, some Manila-based PCVs and those from nearby communities would go on "group dates," quite innocent, really. We'd head out to an American-like diner in the city's tourist district, or a Chinese place nearby, or some bar that featured singing from staff and customers. I had a lot of fun sitting at a bar with several PCV guys, fast-talking sports, politics, and culture trivia. One-on-one dating was much more difficult, at least outside Manila. It happened for a small number of PCVs, as some Filipino men, even married ones, found young American women to be quite comely for a possible relationship or even marriage. We American men found a higher barrier in trying to develop a serious relationship with Filipinas, who were more restricted by prevailing Catholic norms. Love relationships occurred between and among us Americans. There were even some American-Filipino love relationships, but those were rarer.

Robust public disclosures of gay and lesbian relationships hadn't yet broken out in the mid-1960s, whether in America or in the Philippines. That subject wasn't prominent in my universe, but I saw something in Iligan that, on the surface, made me wonder about the possible extent of gay relationships. That "something" was Filipino men holding hands with one another while walking in public. That sight initially shocked me privately, but I learned that this behavior wasn't necessarily a sign of homosexuality. When Fraz once reached for my hand as we strolled down a street in Iligan, I was self-conscious about responding, but gradually I got used to it, and it didn't happen all the time. I saw Fraz and

Voltaire hold hands and didn't think that they were gay. They weren't. They liked women, a lot.

Every so often, our staff leaders convened meetings in Manila or at a beautiful retreat center in Zamboanga at the southwestern tip of Mindanao, to which some of us grunt PCVs were invited. I wasn't privy to how the selection process worked, but I was invited to a few, for which I was quite thankful. They were like a mini-vacation that combined group therapy, where we could unload our feelings, both good and bad, and social activities, where we could eat, drink, dance, gossip, and have fun, like tossing a football.

Depending on individual dispositions and circumstances, our assignments could be stressful. I was fortunate in that I had John as a housemate and a congenial host in Voltaire. Other PCVs weren't as lucky in that they didn't have another PCV close by or they lived in a household that felt more culturally claustrophobic. In general, we're talking here of contrasting cultural experiences, with Americans used to the freedoms of movement, speech, and conduct; looser family ties and commitments; and the independence of thought and action. We Americans can be direct, blunt, judgmental, and seemingly insensitive, expressing ourselves without hesitation or any consideration for someone else's feelings.

That isn't how Filipinos interact with each other, and certainly not with Americans. Because America was once a colonizer, Filipinos could appear subservient to PCVs. An important Filipino cultural characteristic was *pakikisama*, or getting along with one another through smooth interpersonal relationships. Their relationships with one another were more nuanced, indirect, and roundabout, less in your face.

To get through as smoothly and graciously as possible during our two years of service, the burden was on us Americans to listen, learn, and adapt to our immediate physical, social, and cultural surroundings. After all, we were in their 'hood, not our own. This adjustment wasn't always easy or seamless. A handful of PCVs during my time chose to depart early or were sent home involuntarily. Some of us, on the other hand, chose to extend our initial two-year commitment.

I saw Filipino politics up close and personal since Voltaire worked for the Iligan City mayor. Filipino-style politics was akin to a Wild West version of American democracy. Institutionally, the Philippines' national political structure was a carbon copy of the American system—executive, judicial, and legislative. In the time I was there, it was a burgeoning democracy, volatile, wild, and chaotic. Filipinos took their politics seriously, to the point that many local politicians employed their own well-armed militias.

The scariest moments for John and me were the day or two we were effectively held hostage, along with Voltaire and the houseboy. Word on the street was that anyone associated with the mayor was in danger. Since John and I lived with mayoral assistant Voltaire, that meant us. John and I were told to not leave the house. We didn't. We hung around, nonchalant yet concerned. I didn't know what to think, all the while feeling a weird combination of excitement and fear. Occasionally, we peeked out the windows to see what was happening on the streets. Since Voltaire's house was on a corner, we had a good view of intersecting pathways. We saw nothing extraordinary, certainly no gunmen skulking about. Ultimately, nothing happened, and we were again free to leave the house.

In 1965, Filipinos elected a president who later became internationally infamous, Ferdinand Marcos. At the time of his election, he was quite popular and didn't let on that he had a dictatorship in mind. That came later, in September 1972, after I had departed. Marcos's glamorous, charismatic wife, Imelda, she of the many shoes, was his co-conspirator. Both were members of oligarchical elite families who dominated Filipino politics.

In June 1967, the Marcoses invited Manila-area PCVs to Malacañang Palace, the presidential estate. Many of us were excited to attend since this was a rare opportunity to stargaze. It was a sumptuous affair, with lots of good food and drink. The reception was scheduled for the mid-afternoon, but President Marcos showed up almost two hours late, and Imelda made an appearance shortly thereafter. We hardly cared about their tardiness. We merely ate and drank to our hearts' delight. When they arrived, many of us circled them. They were, after all, the Philippines' biggest celebrities. After blessedly brief formal remarks, they graciously posed for countless photos.

After he declared martial law, Marcos and his people played hardball against one of his chief rivals, Senator Benigno "Ninoy" Aquino Jr., a member of another oligarchical family. After being exiled, Aquino returned to the Philippines, only to be assassinated at Manila International Airport in 1983. Exactly who ordered the sensational political murder is still a matter of dispute, but the Marcoses were strongly suspected of being involved.

Long before Aquino made his own international headlines, a few Peace Corps friends and I met him in a chance encounter on a farm in Tarlac province, Luzon island, of which he was governor. It was the most casual of meetups, as we were tourists that day. He was standing by himself, without a militia or aides. He was handsome, down to earth, and curious about us. We felt his charisma, a man destined for higher office.

This example was one of many of PCVs meeting Filipino politicians. Our access to them couldn't have been simpler. I won't go so far as to declare that we young Americans were, well, celebrities in our own right, but I go back to my personal observation that Americans in general were admired by many ordinary Filipinos. Even local politicians and officials saw us as status symbols. For many Filipinos, associating with Americans was a social plus.

Not all Filipinos had unadulterated admiration for Americans. The mid-1960s were a politically perilous time in Southeast Asia. We young American do-gooders may have seemed far away from our agemates fighting a war to the west of us in Vietnam, yet some of us saw the war's deleterious effects. America used the Philippines as a military base of operations for the Vietnam War, in Subic Bay for the U.S. Navy and Clark Air Base for the U.S. Air Force. Accompanying those American military facilities were "rest and recreation" towns that featured bars, strip joints, and houses of prostitution. That image of Americans—soldiers, sailors, and airmen relaxing in sometimes drunken stupor in those towns next to military bases—couldn't have been in sharper contrast to that of PCVs in villages, towns, and cities.

Some Filipino activists didn't at all like their country being used as American military support. We saw how they felt. One evening, a group of us "good" PCVs were wandering along Manila's expansive Rojas Boulevard near the imposing U.S. embassy compound. The chants of protestors in front of the embassy caught our attention. As we got closer to the scene, a youthful crowd shouted anti-American slogans and waved anti-American banners. Some of them saw us and started toward us. For a moment, a few of us tensed up. We felt threatened. That reaction quickly eased when several of the young men looked at us, grinned, and said, "But not you!"

My duty in Iligan City ended in the early summer of 1966. At about the time I was ending my teaching assignment, the Manila-based PCV editor of *Ang Boluntaryo* ("The Volunteer" in Tagalog), or *Ang B*, as everyone called it, was ending his service. Since I'd written for *Ang B* and was even a faraway co-editor for one issue, here was a chance to stay on and do something for which I had real experience, and to avoid as best I could the draft back home. I asked for the editorship and got it. That meant moving to Manila and working out of the Peace Corps headquarters. As cushy a gig as the editing job sounds, I took it seriously since it got me back into something I knew best—print journalism.

It might seem extravagant for a Peace Corps program to have a publication of its own. Since the program had more than seven hundred volunteers at one time in the mid-1960s, having a publication that could communicate news and stories of common interests wasn't thought to be extravagant at all. I didn't care why the publication existed—I just cared about writing for it, which is what I did from my Iligan City post. I even submitted an article by one of my students, who was fifteen years old. She wrote about visiting relatives in a poor village. These relatives, she wrote, treated her and her city family well, whereas when the villagers went to the city, she and her family didn't reciprocate in a similar fashion, a cultural insight best told by an "insider," not an outsider like me.

The Peace Corps headquarters was a dignified two-story house in a nice neighborhood of Manila, near the tourist zone. Inside were the offices of the director, deputy director, other senior staff members, and their assistants. Behind the main building was a low-slung office building where lower-level staff members had their offices. That included the editor of *Ang B*, me. Our backlot crew of twenty-somethings got along well, gossiping and carrying on casually out of sight of the older big bosses.

I felt rusty, having been away from newspaper writing for about two years. I enjoyed reading newspapers in the Philippines whenever I could and noticed similarities of some of them to American tabloids in tone, headlines, articles, and commentaries, while one or two aspired to the gravitas of the *New York Times* and the *Washington Post*. When I was in Iligan City, a little general store (*sari-sari* in the native argot) was located a few blocks from Voltaire's house. I'd go there weekly to buy TIME and *Newsweek* magazines, the overseas editions printed on flimsy, almost-tissue paper (to be lighter to cut down on transportation costs). I gobbled up the contents of both.

I admired the way the two magazines covered the news in longer, deeply reported and colorfully written articles, accompanied by beautiful photos and inviting graphics. Each had to find ways to cover the major news of any given week that retained some immediacy but also gave readers greater perspective and even historical context that daily newspapers didn't. Call me derivative, but I wanted to fashion *Ang B* into an amateurish imitation of TIME and *Newsweek*. Before my editorship, *Ang B* was mostly a gray, dull-looking, sixteen-page sheet with no photos, a few line drawings—not at all inviting to read.

The few stories I wrote from Iligan City were a departure from the usual fare of essays and opinion pieces from PCVs, some griping about popular insider topics, such as lack of communications with staff leaders or questions about our mission. I chose to write human-interest features about such topics as the Iligan City High marching band or the junior-senior prom, the big social event of the school year.

Among the changes I instituted in the nine issues I oversaw were increasing the number of pages to a range of twenty-four to thirty-two, including photos, and loosening up the design, with lengthier headlines as a graphic device and more "white space" to ease a reader's eye. These were stylistic changes, less important than articles' content. More and deeper stories covered staff changes, new and departing PCV groups, and other inside developments of the Peace Corps/Philippines program. I'm proudest of the increased number of stories that featured the work of PCVs in the field—those working with Filipinos living with disabilities, with ethnic minority tribes, helping increase rice production and rebuild a city after a typhoon. There were so few Black PCVs that a white female colleague and I interviewed the five serving at that time about their experiences. On a lighter note, I included brief items intended to get a chuckle, such as the following: "A sign above the second-floor comfort room door in a downtown Manila theater: TOILET PAPER AVAILABLE AT THE TICKET COUNTER. *Excuse me, gotta run. . . .*"

After a year, I relinquished the editorship to two sharp, newer PCVs, Larry Katzenbach, a nephew of Nicholas deBelleville Katzenbach, the attorney general in the Lyndon Johnson administration, and David Briscoe, who had been with the Associated Press in Utah.

19

LIFE PARTNER

My moving to Manila in the summer of 1966 had a lasting consequence for me than extending my service and further distancing myself from the dreaded draft: I met my future life partner there, although I didn't know it at the time. I was fresh on the scene at Peace Corps headquarters, and we Manila-based Peace Corps Volunteers (PCVs) heard that four PCV secretaries would be arriving imminently. Among the male PCVs, that was exciting news. Many of us guys were, shall we say, desperate for convivial female companionship, so news that four new female PCVs were headed our way gave us hope that we might have a chance of catching someone's eye.

On the day of their arrival, several of us taxied out to Manila International Airport to see firsthand who they were. We had seen their photos and were impressed. One of the four was Joyce Ann Mende, of Springfield, New Jersey. Her photo showed a pretty face with a faint smile and her brunette hair styled short with blonde streaks. The three other women looked sharp too. Joyce was designated to be the secretary to the deputy director, whose office was on the second floor of the main headquarters building. The other three had provincial assignments.

The airport greeting itself was perfunctory. A few senior staff members and we PCV hangers-on greatly outnumbered the four. Some staff officials gave brief welcoming remarks, as the young women, looking weary and distracted, fidgeted, probably muttering to themselves, "Where are we? What is this? When can I get some rest?"

I didn't make special eye contact with any of them, including the beautiful Joyce. I was just happy to see new blood, especially of the female variety. It was a few days later that, in my *Ang B* editor capacity, I asked Joyce, who was twenty-one years old, for an interview for an article about her as a new PCV secretary.

"What did you do in America?"

"I was a belly dancer," she asserted, with that faint smile.

I laughed out loud.

That coy response told me a lot about her personality and sense of humor. (She hadn't been a belly dancer.)

As Joyce got accustomed to her new job and surroundings, she showed her sociability, positive attitude, can-do spirit, and especially her quick New Jersey–bred wit. During breaks, she'd wander back to where I worked, and we'd have some laughs, gossiping up a storm. As pretty, pleasant, and outgoing as she was, I felt nothing special stirring in me toward her. In fact, in her early months, she gave me the distinct impression she was interested in a couple of other PCV men taller and handsomer than I.

I learned that her father was a small businessman, a florist, and her mother a homemaker, and that she was the oldest of four (two sisters, one brother). I could tell that she was smart, but she said that she hadn't gone to college. Instead, she had studied at Katharine Gibbs, the exclusive secretarial school (white gloves, hats), worked a year or two in New York City, and traveled to Europe with two friends. Then, the Peace Corps beckoned her after she had tasted overseas travel.

Quickly, she became one of the Manila-area PCVs who enjoyed hanging out together, during occasional U.S. embassy lunches or after work, hitting American-style cafés, Filipino dive bars, and restaurants. One favorite was a Chinese restaurant called Kowloon whose Cantonese food was pretty good, despite heavy doses of MSG. I was the only one in our group who was of Chinese descent, and, given my Chinatown experience, I sometimes offered to lead the ordering or give ideas, playing the role of a cultural informant, kind of a show-off.

Being a cultural informant is a familiar undertaking of some nonwhite people in the company of white people in "ethnic" situations, such as eating out at purportedly non-American establishments. Some of us non-whites scorn this role because of its white-supremacist or imperialistic implications. I have vacillated in my own views of this role, from being a supplicant to subconsciously resisting (at least in my mind) while stoically complying.

More than once, I tried to persuade the other PCVs to eat "family style" (i.e., sharing multiple dishes), the way I was accustomed to in Chinatown. That happened on occasion. On others, depending on who was in our group, one or two preferred to order one dish for him- or herself, leaving it up to the rest of us to either do family-style or individual-style. I never made a major ethnic case out of this so as not to introduce a potential point of cultural tension in an otherwise convivial gathering.

Bar-hopping nights were loads of fun too. One favorite spot was a tiny corner bar called Taboy's, named after the middle-aged proprietor who loved to belt out popular American tunes, louder as the evening wore on and he consumed more alcohol. He was especially fond of "Bye, Bye, Blackbird." Sometimes, we sang along in our own semi-drunken stupor. We were a loud, happy lot.

One night, maybe a year into her tour of duty, Joyce and I happened to be sitting next to one another at Taboy's. This arrangement wasn't by my design; it just happened. Each of us chugged San Miguels, sang along with Taboy, and were having a grand old time. Next thing I knew, in the bar's darkness, Joyce leaned over and planted a firm but soft lip-to-lip kiss! Oh, my! I knew that we got along fabulously—just friends, you understand—but had no idea she had special feelings for me. She said that she kept looking at my (to her) "luscious lips" and wanted to know "how they would feel."

That definitively changed our relationship. We became a pair, although we didn't openly advertise it. I liked her a lot, her warm personality, wit, bright outlook, and positive energy. I loved the feeling of having a close female companion. At the same time, I felt unmoored in that I had never imagined having a serious relationship with anyone. I had no one special at home and didn't know what I'd be doing once my service ended. Rather than group dates, Joyce and I started going out as a couple only. One of our favorite spots was a low-rise penthouse bar on scenic Rojas Boulevard overlooking Manila Bay, quite a romantic spot, where we slowly sipped Tanqueray gins with a lemon twist. The sunsets were gorgeous, and we were both goo-goo-eyed.

I was taken aback emotionally in the most pleasant sense by Joyce's forwardness. Before Joyce, I had only had two serious "girl friends," one white, the other Chinese American. Mom, of course, wanted me to marry a Chinese woman. It raised her expectations when I dated one just before I left for the Peace Corps. My seriously dating—and possibly marrying—a white woman was an unspoken taboo subject with Mom and, by extension, me.

Joyce coming on to me didn't make a lot of sense, however, in part because of our obvious differences—or maybe that's why it made all the sense in the world. The most obvious difference was our race-ethnicity. She's "white," French-German (Alsatian) on her father's side and Slovak on her mother's. She didn't make a big deal of her white ethnic roots the way I do of my Chinese heritage. She was simply an "American," one from a "mixed marriage"—Catholic mother, Protestant father. That was another difference between us. In California, a "mixed" marriage was interracial. In New Jersey, it was interreligious. Another obvious, although thoroughly superficial, difference was the fact she was at least four inches taller than me.

Other less obvious differences were our origin stories, I from Oakland's Chinatown, she from a New Jersey suburb. The only Chinese people she had seen were waiters at a Chinese restaurant in her overwhelmingly white hometown. She went to Mass on Sundays with her mother and siblings. I wasn't part of any organized religion.

Getting serious with Joyce altered my termination plan. I decided to extend my service to leave when Joyce's term ended. We decided to travel for a few months with another PCV, Patricia Fewer, of San Francisco, who was also part of Joyce's group ending her term.

20

BACK TO CHAOS

Joyce, Patty, and I departed Manila with sadness and anticipation in early March 1968. A travel agent mapped out a journey that spanned about four months, with stops in Hong Kong, Thailand, India, Nepal, Israel, and Greece on the first leg and London and parts of continental Europe on the next. In London, we picked up a car I had asked my sister Nellie to help me buy.

Ah, the car, a green two-seat Triumph 250 sportscar, for the three of us! What was I thinking? The car had a back bench seat that accommodated one of us crunched in sideways. It also had a classic stick shift. Since Joyce didn't know how to drive a stick shift, Patty and I alternated as drivers. The three of us rotated sitting sideways on the back bench seat. What an adventure!

We drove around London and the British countryside and ferried over to France—the start of our continental leg that included Belgium, Spain, Italy, Switzerland, Germany, Denmark, and the Netherlands—before heading back to London to drop off the car for shipment to Oakland. Our final leg was Ireland—first to Dublin, then to County Cork to kiss the Blarney Stone (Patty and I did, but not Joyce), and last to County Kerry to visit Patty's relatives. In early July, we flew to New York City, ending up in Springfield, New Jersey, where Joyce's family lived.

This trip was one of a lifetime. We did it on a very slim budget, staying mostly in youth hostels. I had less than $600 for the four months, after paying for all the plane fares. It may seem mindboggling now, but in 1968, one could do that with a shoestring budget and a copy of *Frommer's Europe on 5 Dollars a Day*.

We had to have been an odd sight: a short Chinese guy with two taller, attractive white women, schlepping around Asia and Europe as a threesome. Yet there were no disapproving or unfriendly incidents, except for some with Parisian vendors and low-grade hoteliers, who were just plain nasty, out of disdain for non-French-speaking American tourists.

Along with timeless tourist attractions—the Taj Mahal, the Himalayas, Jerusalem, the Parthenon, Trevi Fountain, the Uffizi Gallery, Buckingham Palace, and so forth—our trip coincided with epic news from America that cast a somber shadow on what otherwise was a joyous trip. While in Israel, we heard that President Lyndon Johnson, hailed for his leadership on landmark civil rights legislation but denounced for escalating the Vietnam War, announced that he wasn't going to run for reelection. We were shaken to the core when we learned that Martin Luther King Jr. and Senator Robert F. Kennedy had been assassinated, while we were in Greece and Germany, respectively.

As much fun as we were having and as far away as we were from these monumental political events, we couldn't avoid asking one another, "What were we coming home to?" The social, political, and cultural earthquakes of 1968 were shaking up everything in America, our beloved country that we had served in the name of peace. We weren't prepared to acknowledge the delusion of the politics that we had essentially been shielded from while ensconced in the isolated safety of the Philippines. It was a weird duality for us, touched deeply by the mind-blowing events at home and dazzled by the sights that assaulted us daily in famous and historic places we had seen before only in photos, on TV, and in the movies.

Culture shock is a mild way of describing our state of mind as we settled into the basement of Joyce's family's home in the heat and humidity of an East Coast summer. Joyce's parents and siblings were welcoming, kind, and generous, but we must have seemed like spaced-out zombies to them. On one of our European stops, we met the then-boyfriend of one of Joyce's younger sisters, a U.S. embassy Marine guard. Each of us was dressed in casual attire. To this straight-arrow, buttoned-down Marine, we looked like hippies, a label he used to describe us to Joyce's sister.

Joyce's father, Herman, a tall, taciturn man, owned a small florist shop. He had a bipolar disorder that infused family dynamics. He was lively and talkative at times, quiet and sullen at others. He never treated me badly. In fact, I know that he loved our give-and-take political discussions, knowing that I was a liberal Democrat while he was a rock-solid Republican. On his death bed, Joyce told me that he asked, "Where's Bill Wong?" I was a day away and missed saying goodbye in person. Joyce's mother, Margaret, was a friendly and often cheerful homemaker who tended to Herman's many needs. She was always in the kitchen, cooking up a storm, or straightening up the split-level house, making sure that the pillows were plumped and the carpets were vacuumed. I enjoyed getting to know Joyce's siblings, Christine, Karl, and Karen, and looked forward to our times together.

Somewhat suspended in our own transitional space, we weren't all that cheerful with Joyce's family. Rather, the three of us huddled in the basement, watching TV for hours on end, a pastime we hadn't engaged in for years. One event we watched in horror was the Democratic National Convention in Chicago, at which the police beat up antiwar protestors. This violence reinforced our already fragile feelings about coming home. What was next for three idealists, fresh from an exhilarating overseas experience, who watched news so out of sync with our home country's celebrated values of freedom and justice for all?

Washington, D.C., was next. Joyce and Patty had made better plans than I for the first step back into normal American life: They had lined up jobs at the Peace Corps headquarters as desk officer assistants (i.e., secretaries) again. I found a job at the National Committee for Support of the Public Schools, writing and editing this nonprofit organization's monthly newsletter. I saw this job as a way of easing back into journalism, sort of. It just so happened this committee had indirect ties to journalism. Agnes Elizabeth Ernst Meyer, a journalist who had married financier Eugene Meyer, started the committee as a philanthropic gesture because she believed in the value of public education. The Meyers purchased the *Washington Post* in 1933, and their daughter, Katharine Graham, was its publisher during the famous Watergate scandal in the 1970s.

This backdrop gave me psychological comfort as I felt my way mincingly into the fringes of the stratified culture of our nation's capital. As a staff member of this nonprofit organization founded by a prominent Washington, D.C., doyenne, I took Joyce to a fancy reception in the Meyers' palatial home, where I felt, well, like a Chinatown working-class guy way out of his element but enthralled by the grandness of the place and the haughty, accomplished, and powerful people I was with for a few hours, sipping champagne and noshing on bite-sized appetizers.

Before we began working, I flew home to Oakland, while Joyce, having had enough of flying, followed by train to meet my family. She stayed in San Francisco with Patty. This trip home was my first since the one-month leave I had had a few years earlier. It was an emotional visit in that my family was meeting Joyce for the first time. I was anxiety-ridden yet excited, because I wasn't sure how both sides—Joyce and my family—would feel toward one another. I needn't have worried. She impressed my clan with her calm, friendly, sociable, and sincere manner. My sisters thought that she was beautiful.

The most awkward moments came when Joyce and Mom met, but neither let whatever feelings they might have had overwhelm their common cordiality. We also told my family of our forthcoming wedding plans—we had gotten engaged in Hong Kong, during the first leg of our trip home from the Philippines—which triggered conversations as to who might attend the big event in Joyce's hometown three thousand miles away. Both of us were relieved that the visit went about as well as could be expected.

We found apartments in Arlington, Virginia, across the Potomac River. Joyce and Patty rented one unit, and I another nearby. We were so chaste in those days. A good Catholic young woman like Joyce simply didn't live with a man before marriage. I wasn't of the same mind-set, but I didn't want to force Joyce into devaluing her moral beliefs for my sake. Even though Joyce and I were a couple, the three of us did a lot together. We shared meals (this period is when I started cooking), did our laundry, watched TV (Neil Armstrong's moon landing), gossiped about work, and went around D.C. like tourists.

Joyce and I set a late November date for our wedding at her old church, St. James Catholic. That location wasn't ideal for my California family—too far and too expensive for most of them. Only Mom and my sisters Lai Wah and Nellie could attend. Joyce's parents were generous in offering their modest home for my family. As it was, we planned a small wedding with fewer than fifty guests. Joyce decided to pare down the list of potential attendees from her side, because I only had Mom and two sisters. The wedding ceremony itself, on a Saturday, was casual, informal, and almost without pomp and circumstance.

Steve Lenton was my best man. He and I had known one another casually at Cal. He had shown his left-leaning political activism there at a time when Cal was bubbling with the beginnings of "student power." After graduation, he was a PCV in the Philippines before I joined, and then he became a highly esteemed regional director in the program. He was charismatic, and Joyce and I liked him immensely. Eileen Wagner, Joyce's high-school friend, was her maid of honor.

On the morning of the wedding, I was relaxed, so much so that I asked my about-to-be brother-in-law Karl to toss a football in front of the Mende house. Karl towered over me, being about six feet five inches tall, and he was a high school football player (lineman). The two of us trotted up and down the street, alternating passes and catches to our hearts' content.

I was happy that Mom had traveled across the country for the first time in her sixty-five years to see me get married, even though I suspected that she still hadn't fully accepted my choice of a bride. She'd never say anything directly to me, or maybe even to any of my sisters. Whatever she might have felt inside, she wanted to see her only son get married, even if it were to a woman not of her preference. As it was, good karma infused our ceremony in that, by sheer coincidence (or was it?), a Cantonese-speaking Catholic priest from Hong Kong, Father Mark Tsai, was a guest visitor at the church. The presiding (white) priest asked whether we'd want Father Tsai to co-officiate the proceedings. That would be delightful, we said. Mom would at least be able to understand what was being said during the ceremony.

As further evidence of how casual we were in planning the wedding, we hadn't thought about who would drive the newlyweds from the church to the reception at the Mende house, many blocks away. We never thought about renting a limo. Joyce suggested asking our good friend Patty Fewer to drive us in our scruffy red Volkswagen hatchback sedan. A photo of us smiling through the back window is a favorite. Joyce's mom prepared most of the reception food. The intimacy and warmth of the Mende home added a loving touch to our special day.

Author marries Joyce Ann Mende in 1968. (Author's Collection)

Since we had no immediate honeymoon plans and had to report to work on the following Monday, Joyce and I drove off toward Washington, D.C. Our post–wedding reception meal was at a Howard Johnson's along the way, perhaps in Delaware, where I had my first ever crab roll. Now, we could live together in my apartment, while Patty lived by herself in the apartment she had shared with Joyce.

21

CAREER RESTART

My work at Agnes Meyer's committee was transitional. It gave me valuable time to assess my next steps toward resuming my newspaper career. I was in my late twenties, with a thin work résumé. The conventional wisdom was that one starts a steady career climb in one's twenties, increasing one's salary and promotional prospects. By 1969, I should have accumulated seven years in the business world, with presumably a growing savings account. Not by great design, I defied convention.

My future wasn't with Meyer's well-intentioned nonprofit committee, or even with her wider empire that included the *Washington Post*. I lacked confidence in my journalism experience, nor did I think that the great *Post* would consider me a prospective reporter. I never applied for a job there. I didn't believe that the real world cared about or would give me career credit for my Peace Corps time.

Something continued to nag at me about my Chinese roots. I read about the East Asian journalism program at Columbia University in New York. It would be a good blend of my interests, I thought. I applied but was rejected. What about a plain old graduate journalism program? I applied at several universities, including Columbia, which had a sparkling reputation of training top-quality journalists sprinkled among elite news organizations, especially in the hallowed Boston–New York–Washington corridor. I was no longer blissfully ignorant of the power elite in

America, as I had been when I was a cloistered Chinatown teenager headed for college. I sensed that I needed to try to get in the door of ivy-inflected institutions on the other side of the American continent, far from my California comfort zone, to rise in newspaper journalism. Lo and behold, Columbia said yes. Joyce wasn't permanently affixed to her job and was eager to get back to her home area. The idea of living in New York City excited us.

We found a five-story walkup studio apartment in the Upper East Side of Manhattan, rent-controlled at $156 a month, a relative bargain. We didn't get a lot for our money—a tiny room with a corner kitchenette and a small bathroom. Fitting our Arlington apartment stuff into that studio apartment was almost an art form, which Joyce managed well. The challenge for me was how to get quiet time to study, while Joyce watched TV. We did it without strangling each other.

Our apartment location wasn't ideal for me to get to Columbia, which is on the Upper West Side of Manhattan. I had to catch a crosstown bus and then transfer to a subway going north to the campus. Meanwhile, Joyce found secretarial work at the Ford Foundation in midtown Manhattan. Her salary was our household's main income. Although my Columbia fees were in the low thousands, it was more money than we had saved up, so I got a part-time job at Columbia to supplement Joyce's income. My job title was "portal engineer," meaning that I had keys to open doors.

I was among the oldest of my class of about one hundred domestic students. There was a smaller contingent of international students. Most of my domestic classmates were fresh college graduates, in their early twenties; I was twenty-eight. That I was married and lived far from campus meant that I had little time and opportunity to get to know most of my classmates well, other than during class time. I got closest to Dick Barnes, a fellow Californian who was also married and living far from campus. Joyce and I socialized with him and his wife, Bonnie. He's one of the few classmates I've stayed in touch with.

Our first assignment was designed to test our mettle, to see how quick and intrepid each of us was in what, for most of us, was a new and very complicated place. Professors handed each student a slip of paper with a street address or significant place written on it. Our job was to find the place or address and return several hours later with a "story." My slip of paper said, "Hester Street," historically a center of Ashkenazi Jewish culture in lower Manhattan. I found the street on a map, checked out the proper subway line, and off I went. I strolled around several blocks; went into some businesses; talked with merchants, customers, and folks in the street; and came up with a "story" that "passed" this first of many tests.

The Columbia journalism school has a wonderful advantage over other J-schools. First and foremost, it's in Manhattan, the nation's center of finance, business, news media, and broad political and cultural trends. It had a stellar faculty, including Melvin Mencher, known for his reporting expertise, and Fred W. Friendly, the renowned TV news executive. Star journalists came regularly as guest lecturers.

Non–New Yorkers might feel anger, frustration, pity, anguish, envy, jealousy, admiration, love, or various combinations about New York City, especially Manhattan, for it is a unique American city, the nation's most populous and, arguably, its most colorful, busy, multilayered, multicultural, and narcissistic. You've heard the cliché: If you can make it in New York City, you can make it anywhere. "It" isn't well defined, but you get the point. For journalists in training, there is no better place to start.

For the most important assignment, the equivalent of a master's thesis, I chose to write something about Manhattan's Chinatown, a vibrant, thriving enclave echoing some of the same vibes as San Francisco's and Oakland's Chinatowns. This topic was organically in groove with my ongoing search for my own identity. With no preconceived notion of what the major themes of my project would be, I went to Manhattan's Chinatown many times, talked with many people, including those with official titles and many without, to learn about the issues, concerns, and problems they were confronting and trying to resolve. The time context was crucial for me to narrow down my topic. America was immersed in the political, social, and cultural quakes that were accelerated by mindboggling political assassinations, the Southeast Asia war, and the so-called countercultural revolution. These forces had compounding effects on America's biggest city, including its Chinatown.

There wasn't an "Asian America" before World War II. The Chinese Exclusion Act had effectively kept the Chinese American/Asian American populations small and irrelevant to the national political and cultural scenes. In the early 1940s, Pop and I were among about seventy-eight thousand ethnic Chinese living in the United States. Put another way, for every ten thousand Americans, six were of Chinese descent. Chinese Americans were the most numerous in the relatively tiny Asian American population. We and Japanese Americans, Filipino Americans, and Korean Americans—the three other major Asian groups—began to grow and integrate into American life after World War II. Inspired by the civil rights movement of the 1960s led by African Americans and some white Americans, other non-white communities found distinct identities to begin to free them from the political and cultural bondage of white supremacy.

An Asian American movement started in the San Francisco Bay Area in the mid- to late 1960s. While I missed that movement's birth, I saw it blossom in Manhattan's Chinatown, echoing what was happening in California, a sometimes strident and "un-Asian" cry for empowerment and a reclamation of rights, status, and dignity so long denied during the Chinese exclusion era that had also negatively affected other Asian Americans. Radicalized New York Chinese Americans had formed a group called *I Wor Kuen*, described in some quarters as Marxist-inspired, like far-left groups in white and Black America, such as the Black Panther Party. Their activism was one of the major themes of my master's paper about political awakening in New York's Chinatown. Overall, what I learned at Columbia was refreshing because it got me back into a journalist mind-set after being away for six years, and I learned a great deal about a big Chinatown on the other side of America.

It was impossible for university students to stay above the political fray. Outside political forces ended our school year prematurely. On May 4, 1970, several weeks before our last official day, Ohio National Guard troopers opened fire on unarmed protesting students at Kent State University. Four students died, and nine others were wounded. Some killed or wounded were bystanders. Kent State students, as elsewhere, were protesting the American bombings in Cambodia, part of the highly contentious Vietnam War. This sensational incident riled students across the country. At Columbia, I marched in protest along with my classmates, an unusual activity for those of us headed for a vocation that professes neutrality ("objectivity") in politics. Columbia was among many universities that closed early because of the political turmoil. That jeopardized us getting our master's degrees since technically we didn't finish the school year. Eventually, we got our degrees.

Before the shutdown, news media recruiters came to campus to interview many of us for possible jobs. Months earlier, during the winter break, we had gotten a preview of this recruiting ritual. Some of us had spent a week at a newspaper or magazine to see what life was like inside a big-time newsroom. This opportunity allowed eager prospects to impress newsroom bosses with our brains, ideas, questions, curiosity, and enthusiasm.

I spent my week at *Newsweek*. In 1970, *Newsweek* was one of the three major weekly news magazines, with TIME and *U.S. News & World Report* being the others. Each was influential in its own way, offering insightful summaries of the biggest stories and trends of the week. Recall that I had read the overseas editions of TIME and *Newsweek* regularly at my Peace Corps post in the Philippines five years earlier. Every morning for a workweek, I went to the Madison Avenue offices of *Newsweek*, where I observed reporters and top editors deciding which stories to feature in the upcoming edition. Over meals and drinks, we students asked a lot of questions and tried to show off our best sides. These visits were "soft" recruiting tactics, as editors could see firsthand which of us might be a possible hire. I heard that some *Newsweek* editors and reporters were "impressed" by me, but I never got a job offer.

During the on-campus recruiting effort in the spring, I met the *Wall Street Journal*'s recruiter, Michael Gartner, a senior editor, and made my pitch for him to hire me, including showing a few articles I had written in my two years as a San Francisco Bay Area reporter. Gartner, not too much older than me, was down to earth and easy to talk to. He had a straightforward, direct, yet friendly approach, unlike the stereotype I held of newspaper editors being a tad arrogant and dismissive. Something worked in my favor. The *Journal* hired me and said that I would be assigned to its Cleveland, Ohio, bureau.

Where, you say? Yes, Cleveland, as in "mistake by the lake," as it was derisively called in those days because of its economic and image problems. Joyce and I said to one another, "I'm a California guy, you're a New Jersey/New York gal. Where's Cleveland?"

This job offer was solid, so I said, "Why not? What the heck, let's do it."

22

JOURNALISM REDUX

From the buzz among my classmates, getting a job offer from the *Wall Street Journal*[1] was something to crow about since it was the only nationally distributed newspaper at that time and one that influenced national policy. I heard that three classmates also got *Journal* job offers. Until I got to Columbia, I hadn't read the *Journal*. I knew its sterling reputation as being a newspaper catering to, well, Wall Street, big-money corporate interests, something I paid little attention to. Business stuff I found, well, boring. Little did I know how myopic I was.

Joining the *Journal* was a journey into the unknown. The paper had a highly formatted, rigid front page of six columns, a gray, intimidating, uninviting presentation with only an occasional line drawing, never a photograph, illustrating stories. In its first and sixth columns[2] were news feature stories about economics and finance, certainly, but also politics and current events. A lighthearted, quirky story of little or no financial consequence was in a middle column.

In Cleveland, the *Journal* had a news, advertising, and printing-press complex near the city's business district. The news team consisted of a chief, four or five reporter-writers, and a small support staff. Other than me, the journalists were all white men, most in their thirties and forties. In racial-ethnic terms, I was likely a rarity among *Journal* reporters.

More broadly, if anything, I was one of only a small number of yellow journalists on leading American newspapers in the 1970s. Another was Frank Ching, who was with the *New York Times* in that decade. He switched to the *Wall Street Journal* and opened its Beijing bureau in 1979. *Ancestors*, Ching's important book that traces his clan[3] back nine hundred years, was published in 1988. William F. Woo, a Shanghai native, started in mainstream American newspapers five years before I did. He was a reporter for the *Kansas City Times* and went on to a distinguished thirty-four-year career at the *St. Louis Post-Dispatch*, where he became editor-in-chief; he later taught journalism at Stanford University.

A generation or decades before Ching, Woo, and me were Gobind Behari Lal (*San Francisco Examiner*, Hearst Newspapers) and Louise Leung Larson (*Chicago Daily Times*, *Los Angeles Times Sunday Magazine*) in the 1920s,[4] Bill Hosokawa, Kyung Won Lee, and perhaps a handful of others. Hosokawa, a Seattle-born Japanese American, worked at the *Des Moines Register* right after World War II. In 1946, he joined the *Denver Post*, where he was a columnist and a senior editor for thirty-eight years. Lee, a Korean native who had come to America when he was twenty-two, worked for local newspapers in Tennessee and West Virginia, starting in 1955. He is best known for his investigative work at the *Sacramento Union* in California, in particular a series stretching over five years that helped acquit Chol Soo Lee of murder charges in a San Francisco Chinatown gangland shooting.

After my initial nerves and a natural feeling of uncertainty when faced with an unfamiliar city and a new job at a newspaper whose stature was way above the papers I had worked for, I began to relax in the Cleveland bureau. Our leader was Everett Groseclose, a handsome Texan with a slight drawl and easy but serious demeanor. Two reporters, Jim Hyatt and Ralph Winter, were especially helpful, offering advice and support.

A *Journal* bureau reporter almost had to have a split personality. One side focused on meat-and-potatoes financial and economic stories, tied to specific industries, what some of us called DBI: dull but important. Stories emanating from this side filled the *Journal*'s inside pages. We had a rotation system: Weekly, one reporter was responsible for reporting and writing these "routine" news stories. The other side of the split personality concentrated on lengthier, more deeply reported Page One news features, which took on a wide array of topics, such as politics, social issues, and culture as well as economics and finance. The center column's more whimsical Page One feature was called an "A-hed," after the headline font type. These Page One news features were relatively luxurious assignments. We got weeks, even months, to complete them and often traveled to gather facts, background, and atmosphere to make these stories entertaining to read. This part of the job was more fun, exciting, expansive, enterprising, and, ultimately, rewarding.

Top editors in New York and the bureau chief wanted aggressive output on both fronts, but reporters knew that the Page One features gained one greater attention and possibly better bureau placement and more money. Our reputations rested more on how many Page One features we produced. Accounting for that production became a competitive game among reporters. The math was daunting. Five days a week (no weekend publication), there were three Page One slots and often a back-page feature slot (thought to be second tier, but still important). When I joined, the *Journal* had about 150 reporters worldwide, most in American bureaus, with the greatest number in New York. An outstanding annual performance was ten to fifteen Page One features. Several of my bureau mates were unabashedly ambitious, but not obnoxious, about producing these attention-getting features. I got the message, but, being a *Journal* rookie, I understandably never reached those heights.

One appealing aspect of the *Journal* was editors encouraging reporters to come up with their own Page One feature ideas, the more original the better. We also got such assignments from our bureau chief and from New York. Generating one's own features felt liberating—and scary—for a rookie like me. After my earliest features (all assigned by the bureau chief) got to New York, I got the shock of my young *Journal* life when I saw what editors there did. I barely recognized the rewritten first parts of those stories. The facts were there, but their packaging was quite different—livelier atmospherics, action verbs, adjectives galore. They were much more "readable," in other words. My colleagues could barely suppress their chuckles when they saw my initial reaction. "Don't sweat it," they said, "This has happened to all of us." This heavy editing at the start of a new reporter's output was the *Journal*'s way of inculcating its preferred style. The lesson: Learn how to write in the *Journal*'s Page One style, or else. The consensus was that a new reporter was given a year to adapt to the *Journal* style and culture.

That style was, in essence, this: Start with a memorable anecdote illustrating the core of the story. Punch it up. Find six or eight compelling examples to further illuminate your story's thesis, in graphic, colorful detail. Always include a "nut graf," a paragraph summarizing the theme. Always include some paragraphs questioning the theme, called the "however" or "on the other hand" portion. And always use pithy quotes that move the story along. These major feature stories demonstrated that the *Journal* wasn't a dull, boring financial rag, as was its reputation among those who didn't read it. In fact, the *Journal* won plaudits for its insightful civil rights stories in the 1960s and 1970s, a big departure from Wall Street interests and values.

It took me about a year to adapt to the *Journal*'s newsroom culture, to feel comfortable with how the bureau chief and New York editors handled major feature stories. I grew to appreciate the *Journal*'s high standards—multiple sources, with names and relevant titles, benchmarks I had not experienced in my early San Francisco newspaper days. In my two years in Cleveland, I wrote some interesting major features, including one explaining why a big-name downtown hotel had turned shabby, several about institutions of higher learning, another on more humane plant shutdowns, a profile of a small store owner, and, one dear to my heart, the struggles of the Cleveland Cavaliers professional basketball team.

In the time I was there, the *Journal* was internally disjointed. Although wrapped in one package of two sections, it was almost like two different newspapers. One part was its reporting staff, whose stories were fact-based without any noticeable ideology except for accuracy, depth of reporting, and colorful writing. The other part was its editorial-page staff, who expressed points of view, opinions, and commentaries that were rock-solid conservative politically and economically. Never the twain shall meet, although the general perception was that the *Journal* was a conservative establishment rag that answered only to America's moneyed interests.

On a personal level, I was gratified that my racial background wasn't an issue in a city and state that had a white-and-black profile and a negligible Asian presence. Not once did I believe that my white colleagues regarded me in racial terms or questioned my professionalism. Off work, when Joyce and I went around town, we got some stares, but nothing overtly racist or insulting.

The only time I felt racially uncomfortable at work was when bureau chief Groseclose and I were invited to play tennis with two local executives. I don't recall why we were invited to play, other than it being standard procedure for how business journalism was sometimes done. At one point, I must have told Groseclose that I played tennis. He did, too, so when the chance came to play these two executives, he asked me to join him. There I was, in my tennis whites, along with Groseclose on an exclusive clay court in a fancy Cleveland suburb, the kind of place I rarely saw. It was a sunny, not too humid day, and after we played (I forget the results), we relaxed with tall, cool drinks and idle chatter with no overt business quid pro quo.

Part of my discomfort had to do with how well or how badly I thought that I played. I never considered myself very good at tennis, and I didn't want to embarrass myself in front of my boss or these two executives. I guess I acquitted myself adequately. The other part of my discomfort had to do with feeling intimidated in a place of white upper-class privilege, a private tennis club with clay courts, not my usual venue of a public hard court. I simply wasn't accustomed to being around wealthy white people in their social hangouts.

In my second year in Cleveland, the spring of 1972, I got depressing news from Oakland: Mom wasn't doing well. She had cancer and didn't have long to live. I felt terrible about this news and knew that I had to do something, to go home to help my sisters care for Mom, so I asked for a transfer. Fortunately, the San Francisco bureau had two openings, and my Cleveland performance was good enough to warrant a move. With great relief and a feeling of job security, Joyce and I packed up and drove to Oakland in the summer of 1972.

23

HOME, AT LAST

It felt good to be home after being away for eight years. In that time, I had accomplished what I had set out to do: "Test" myself outside the security of the Chinatown bubble. I had seen some of the vast outside world and gone to places I hadn't even thought about or even known existed. I had met people from all over the country and in the Philippines that had I stayed home, I would never have met. I had met my future life partner, a huge milestone, and I had gotten to know myself better, advancing my quest to further reckon with my identities and my burning desire to continue doing so.

After all that, I felt the need to make up lost time with Mom, perhaps to assuage my guilt for having left her in the first place. Guilt was somewhere inside me, much like the guilt that my sisters felt about Mom. Apparently, she had that power over her children that went unarticulated in the years we spent with her in China and Oakland. I didn't allow any submerged guilty feelings to interrupt what I had chosen to do for those years away from home. Maybe I had rationalized that since my older sister Nellie was home with Mom, my going away to find myself was perfectly okay, if self-centered.

Into my early twenties, I didn't feel particularly close to Mom, even though I lived with her. Already, for a long time as I was growing up, she and I had grown increasingly distant in ways akin to my relationship with Pop. Now, it was time for me to resurface my strained relationship with her by exploring how I could help her deal with the cancer slowly eating away at her.

When we got back to Oakland, Mom was mobile, but it was obvious to us that she was deteriorating. In retirement, she had mellowed considerably. She learned English formally for the first time at classes offered by a Chinatown social-service agency, and she delighted in hand-writing letters in English to some of her children. We, too, were delighted to receive such carefully crafted letters.

One of the first things Joyce and I did was invite her to our apartment, close to the family house. Pleased to be invited, she brought along Goong, the former Great China head chef and her platonic companion after Pop died. My goal, beyond appearing to be a "good son" by cooking her a meal, was to renew and perhaps deepen my connection to Mom at a time of her personal crisis and to let her get to know Joyce better, and vice versa. As you might imagine, Joyce and Mom had a substantial distance to travel to become closer, language and cultural gaps being the most obvious. Both were willing to give it a try.

My cooking was still in its toddler stage. In its infancy, I had cooked a meal for Joyce's parents when they drove from New Jersey to visit us in Cleveland. I had tried out simple Chinese dishes, nothing too challenging. The only Chinese food Joyce's parents had eaten was at a place in their New Jersey hometown, far from any Chinatown. Among the dishes I had prepared was stir-fried *bok toy*, Chinese greens, a vegetable unfamiliar to Joyce's mom. After giving it a try, she averred, "Oh, that was different."

For our dinner for Mom and Goong, I prepared a classic, down-home *hom ngooey jing gee ngook beng*,[1] a steamed ground-pork patty topped with a chunk of salted fish. Pop and Mom cooked that for us all the time. When done right, it's scrumptious. The steaming process yielded a thin watery sauce infused with pork fat and the oils from the fragrant salted fish. I loved to scoop up pieces of pork and the gravy and spoon it atop steamed white rice in a bowl and, as rapidly as I could chew and swallow, shovel portions of this wet, meaty, fishy conglomeration into my eagerly awaiting mouth, almost breathlessly.

Neither Mom nor Goong replicated my speed-eating technique, in part because as grown-ups, they were more disciplined, but mostly because my version wasn't anywhere close to what they were used to. In a word, it was too dry. I had neglected to include ingredients that would have "softened" the meat. Mom and Goong were also much too polite to say anything negative about that dish, but I knew that I had missed the mark by a wide margin. Our invitation alone, however, greatly mitigated any disappointment they might have felt about the quality (or lack thereof) of my cooking.

As Mom grew more ill and was less able to get around, some of my sisters, Joyce, and I shared time caring for her at the Chinatown senior apartment she had moved to. That became an important bonding time for all of us. We'd rotate time slots to be with Mom for hours at a time, helping her cook and attend to any of her personal needs. I was gratified to have made the decision to return home from what had been a good job in Cleveland.

One day, I made a move that I had avoided for the longest time. Since Mom's time was short, I wanted to talk with her about some unresolved issues, foremost among them my decision to marry Joyce without informing her directly. I went to her apartment alone and sat next to her, lying in bed. I reached out and held her hand, something I rarely, if ever, did, at least as an adult. In a sometimes-tortured mix of Chinglish, we shared our feelings as best we could about my marriage to Joyce, a woman Mom certainly hadn't envisioned as the potential mother of her grandchildren.

Because of our respective language inadequacies, neither of us could precisely express our feelings. Even if we spoke the same language fluently, I'm not sure that we'd have been able to convey the depth and truthfulness of hard-to-express feelings on such a culturally and racially sensitive topic. In the end, we were able to declare a truce of sorts to our unspoken conflict and to reassure one another that we loved each other. The concept of "love" was differently defined in Mom's Chinese universe and my hybrid Chinatown-American universe. I was tense from the get-go and even felt choked up a few times, but as we talked, I began to relax and to feel a smoother flow of my *qi* ("chi").

Mom died in October 1973, more than a year after I had returned to Oakland. She was seventy years old. As inevitable as it was, Mom's passing was nonetheless painful for my sisters, me, and our families.

In my early months back, I had to overcome feeling like a stranger in the place where I had been born and spent the first twenty-three years of my life. Being in the Bay Area again was soothing and scary. I liked being around my family and having Joyce and my family get to know one another. It felt good to be familiar with the area, revisiting old haunts and introducing Joyce to places I had learned to love. The two of us eased into socializing with some of my sisters and their spouses, barhopping in San Francisco, and spending weekends in the Napa Valley wine country. Joyce and I also hosted dinner parties for family, friends, and colleagues.

One challenge for me was learning all the political, social, and cultural movements that had exploded in the Bay Area while I was gone. The Bay Area was one of the hottest anti–Vietnam War venues since there was a Selective Service office in downtown Oakland. In addition, Oakland was a center of African American discontent in the form of the Black Panther Party. Across the bay, San Francisco was ground zero of the "sex, drugs, and rock 'n' roll" countercultural revolution. And in Berkeley, the student power movement that had exploded through Cal's free speech movement just as I was flying off to Peace Corps training in the summer of 1964 was still very much alive.

Oakland's Chinatown itself looked different. In the early to mid-1960s, it was in a metaphorical coma after the World War II boom years. The war-related industries—shipyards, military bases—slowly began to close. Other heavy industries followed suit. Other parts of the U.S. economy started to crank up to accommodate the return of the men (and some women) who had been participants in the war. Before the war, areas to the east and south of Oakland, for instance, were largely farmland and fruit orchards. Those areas soon blossomed with tract housing for the white middle-class families who fled Oakland. New freeways facilitated this out-migration, as did the low cost of gasoline.

The cumulative effect of these inexorable forces had a crushing impact on my Chinatown. Its war-years liveliness faded as more families, mine included, sought housing outside the bubble. Many of my peers and those of my older sisters got jobs elsewhere too. Some family businesses, like the Great China, hung on, but we saw a marked decrease in patronage. When I returned, however, I noticed an uptick in Chinatown. One square block typified that change, the one bordered by 8th, Franklin, and 9th Streets and Broadway. For much of the mid-twentieth century, that block had low-rise, two- to three-story, architecturally bland buildings containing various apartments and retail businesses, including a huge warehouse store, Simon Hardware, which sold goods to Chinatown and non-Chinatown customers alike.

What I saw when I got back was a tall apartment building, maybe ten to twelve stories. On the 9th Street side were still unoccupied ground-level retail storefronts. The housing units weren't all inhabited yet, but from that point on, into the late 1970s, they began to fill up. The empty storefronts gradually perked up with Chinese and Asian supermarkets, jewelry stores, and other small businesses. This singular example of growth reflected general Chinese and Asian immigration patterns that greatly expanded the number of newcomers from Asia and elsewhere. Some of the new immigrants and refugees from Southeast Asia injected much-needed life as well in a rundown neighborhood east of Lake Merritt.

Working at the *Wall Street Journal*'s San Francisco bureau in the financial district gave me a chance to renew my acquaintance with that city's big Chinatown, only a short walk away. Weekly, I strolled up for lunch at my favorite hybrid cafés—Jackson's, Ping Yuen, and Woey Loy Goey. It was also about this time that I learned about *East/West Chinese American Journal*, a weekly newspaper published out of San Francisco's Chinatown. Its publisher-editor was Gordon Lew, a bilingual, biliterate Cantonese-language teacher, journalist, student of history, and businessman. In the mid-1960s, Lew, Kenneth Joe, and Ken Wong worked or wrote for three different San Francisco Chinese newspapers. Each was keenly aware of extraordinary times in China and America, whose relationship was beginning to percolate like a tea kettle after years of icy coolness. From 1966 to 1976, the Cultural Revolution shook up the Chinese educated class and disconnected a generation from mainstream society. In America, all sorts of political, social, and cultural disruptions were rocking our society.

The three men noticed that no local English-language American newspaper was addressing what was most important to them—the profound impact on Chinese America of these transnational developments. They filled that void by launching *East/West* as a platform in two languages to express Chinese American perspectives on what was happening in China and America.

During one of my lunch forays, I dropped by *East/West*'s offices, a narrow, dark space in an alleyway. The staff member I met was Richard Springer, a soft-spoken white guy with a quick laugh and easy smile. We became friends. He urged me to write for *East/West*, but I wasn't ready since I was new to the *Journal*'s San Francisco bureau and wanted to get acclimated there.

By now, there was no turning back in my accelerating quest to learn more about my racial identity and to try to reclaim whatever I could of Pop's speck of a place in the grand old American experiment. I started reading *East/West*, and I got to know Springer and Lew better, which led organically to my writing about Chinese America and Asian America for the *Wall Street Journal* (my day job) and for *East/West* on a freelance basis. In addition to Springer and Lew, I wanted to connect with Ken Wong. He had a back or spinal condition that distorted his stature. Wong appeared to be reserved, but he had a droll sense of humor, which showed in his English writing as a reporter and then a columnist for the mainstream white establishment *San Francisco Examiner*, breaking the yellow-glass ceiling.

Through this extracurricular activity, I began learning about San Francisco Chinese American politics, intracommunity disputes, personalities, and issues. One new organization that intrigued me was Chinese for Affirmative Action (CAA), which began in 1969, during a time of ferment and activism among Chinese American and Asian American intellectuals and activists. One of its founders was Ling-Chi Wang, a brainy, courageous immigrant scholar unafraid to speak out on issues he knew a lot about. Wang was a founder of the Asian American Studies Department at Cal in the late 1960s and taught its first course, later becoming its chair as well as director of the Ethnic Studies Department. He's that extraordinary blend of ideals, ideas, and action, which he's used to carry on a life of scholarship and political activism. He's made a career of almost unobtrusively confronting the powers of Chinatown, white San Francisco, and beyond.

After hearing more about CAA's founding and its work in Chinatown, I wrote a feature about the organization for the *Journal*. I believed that CAA deserved greater exposure, as America was undergoing seismic political, cultural, and social shifts, and what was happening in San Francisco's Chinatown was a microcosm of these changes. My CAA story in 1974 appeared as a front-section back-page news feature, almost as prestigious as a Page One feature. The fact it appeared at all in a newspaper of the *Journal*'s stature was notable, a rarity in that there had been almost no mainstream national print coverage of a burgeoning Chinese American/ Asian American movement.

The spark for CAA's founding was the Wang-led protests to include Chinese American and Asian American workers in the building of a new hotel in Chinatown. The project didn't have yellow workers, despite being in a city with many Chinese Americans and other Asian Americans. With persistence and passion, the organization sustained itself under the long-time stellar leadership of Wang and executive director Henry Der through initiatives and programs advocating for fairer representation of Chinese Americans and Asian Americans in private and public employment, fairer treatment of such employees, and more and better portrayals in the mainstream mass media.

24

ROOTS CONNECTION

I adjusted smoothly to my new *Wall Street Journal* environment. Herb Lawson led a staff of four or five white men reporters, all cordial, welcoming, and helpful. Lawson was a soft-spoken, easy-going, talented editor in his mid- to late thirties. The other reporters were in the same age range; I had just turned thirty-one.

The routine in San Francisco was like that in Cleveland. Each reporter had beats that produced some Page One features and a lot of inside stories. My beats included agriculture and paper products. Since California is a leading agricultural state, I wrote features related to farming. One of the scariest reporting assignments was about the intense battle in the mid-1970s between the United Farm Workers (UFW) and the Teamsters for control of farm laborers in California. I went to the Coachella Valley in southern California to report on this dispute.

I spent days observing picket lines and tense confrontations. This period was at the height of Cesar Chavez's UFW leadership and the union's famous strike of lettuce growers that led to a nationwide boycott. Liberal Catholic priests sided with the UFW. I asked to interview a tall, slender priest in his thirties. One morning, he and I met at a diner near the fields. For a few minutes, we were the only customers. Before our food came, a group of maybe six beefy men strolled in. They were Teamsters. After a minute or two of perusing menus and chitchatting, several noticed the priest, familiar to them as a protest leader. At first, good-natured bantering was aimed at the priest, whose back was to them and who paid them no heed. I had a clear view of them but said nothing about them to the priest. Our food arrived. The priest and I started eating. Suddenly, the Teamsters' chatter turned more menacing.

Within minutes, two of these big guys arose from their chairs and headed over to our table. One of them stood over the priest's left shoulder. Without saying a word, he swung his left arm in a sideways motion with great force, his fist in a tight ball, viciously swatting the priest squarely on his face. Thwack! The blow propelled the priest back in his chair but, surprisingly, didn't knock him over. His nose started bleeding profusely. He and I were stunned.

I tensed up and held my fork tightly, making sure that I kept my gaze straight ahead, not at the thugs. My heart started racing. I kept silent, staring at the priest. The other guy, not the swatter, addressed me sternly: "Keep eating." Having done their dirty deed, the two guys walked back to their table. A diner employee ran over with a towel for the bleeding priest. I remained frozen, unable to continue eating. Still sounding agitated, the Teamsters trundled out without eating. Police officers eventually showed up and talked to the diner staff, the priest, and me. Emergency medical personnel came to attend to the priest.

After I departed the diner, my reporter's mind cranked into gear, all while I was trying to lower my heightened blood pressure. After talking to my bureau chief in San Francisco, we decided not to file an immediate "news" story about the violent incident since the *Journal* didn't publish breaking local crime stories. Instead, I began my news feature, published later, about the UFW-Teamster dispute with the diner incident, which illustrated well the bitterness between the two unions.

That politically infused story was but one that I wrote while in the San Francisco bureau. For others, I traveled to Sacramento, the state capital, several times to write about economic and business issues between Governor Jerry Brown and the state legislature. Another big California issue I covered was Proposition 13, a voter initiative to drastically reduce property taxes. I wrote a profile of William B. Gould IV, the first African American on the Stanford Law School faculty and an early job-discrimination legal expert who later headed up the National Labor Relations

Board in the Bill Clinton administration. Hearkening back to my college sports writing days, I wrote major features on the Golden State Warriors winning a championship under Coach Al Attles, the Oakland Athletics baseball team hoping to continue its World Series championship streak, and the Oakland Raiders' success under coach John Madden. Most exhilarating was a reporting trip to Hawaii to write about Honolulu's controversial mayor, Frank Fasi, and the state's struggling sugar industry.

Nothing, however, beat my features on my yellow universe. Doing those fulfilled my inner obsession with finding my racial-ethnic identity as part of my national identity and gave a public view of many facets of an American subculture invisible to so many people. The story about CAA was but one such article. Another was prompted in the early Sunday morning hours of Labor Day weekend in 1977, when a horrific mass shooting at the Golden Dragon Restaurant in San Francisco's Chinatown got huge local coverage and some national exposure and generated deep concerns across the Bay Area. One Chinatown gang had sought revenge on another Chinatown gang. Five people were killed and eleven wounded, including tourists. No gang member was killed or hurt. It was San Francisco's worst mass killing, and it even evoked stereotypes of "tong wars" that occasionally had beset Chinatowns of yesteryear.

As a journalist, I wanted to dig deep into its essence. The story's aura gnawed at me. How could I write about it in a way that the *Journal* would publish? I proposed a Page One feature that put the massacre into historical and cultural contexts. My story wasn't about the crime itself or even gang rivalries; it was more about the social, political, and cultural isolations of Chinatowns and Chinese America rooted in historic systemic racism that bred such conditions as youth alienation and feelings of inferiority. My story ran on the *Journal*'s Page One about two months after the incident.

Upset with the racism aimed at Vietnamese refugees, I wrote an opinion piece in 1975 for the *Journal*'s editorial page—not my usual space—that reviewed America's history of systemic racism against people of Asian descent. This piece had to be one of the first, if not the earliest, condemnations in a major American newspaper of American anti-Chinese, anti-Asian racism, a "suddenly" hot topic during the coronavirus pandemic starting in 2020. A year after writing that opinion piece,

I wrote a Page One feature on how those refugees were faring, having fled their homelands after they had helped the ill-fated American misadventures in Southeast Asia.

The United States and China resumed formal diplomatic relations in the 1970s, a huge development that yielded many possible stories. I tackled several angles, including one about how Chinese Americans were helping American companies do business in China and another about how Chinese Americans felt after visiting their ancestral homeland.

Even before my yellow-inflected San Francisco and California stories, I wrote a review of a play for the *Journal*. Remember my Oakland schoolmate Frank Chin? In 1972, his groundbreaking play, *The Chickencoop Chinaman*, debuted at the American Place Theater in New York City, the first such stage production by a Chinese American/Asian American playwright. Joyce and I drove from Cleveland, where we were living at the time, to New York to attend its opening night. My review highlighted the play's unique cultural and historic contexts.

These Chinese American/Asian American–themed stories and commentaries were rare, if not pioneering, at the time they were published. In the 1970s, America wasn't yet fully cognizant of its yellow population, certainly not in the way it has been awakened to our presence during the coronavirus pandemic. It felt good to seamlessly meld my personal perspectives and my professional journalism to tell those stories in a publication as internationally important as the *Wall Street Journal*.

When I joined the San Francisco bureau, the journalists were all white men. Just before I got there, the bureau had a Black reporter, but he switched to the *Washington Post*. Starting in the mid-1970s, Janice Simpson, a bright and delightful Black woman from Harlem, New York City, joined our staff. Several other women, all white, came on board later, either replacing a white man or being added to staff. In all, we were a congenial and increasingly diversified bunch.

Politics were brewing in the *Journal*'s New York headquarters in the late 1970s. The managing editor, Frederick Taylor, an old-school ex-reporter, was promoted to executive editor. Who would replace him? Lawson, our bureau chief, was thought by some on staff to be a leading candidate to succeed Taylor. Larry O'Donnell, the Detroit bureau chief, however, was chosen. That signaled problems for our bureau because O'Donnell had been rumored as wanting to replace some bureau chiefs and shake up bureau assignments. Lawson quit shortly after O'Donnell's promotion, and O'Donnell named Ken Slocum, who had a reputation of being O'Donnell's hatchet man, to be our new bureau chief.

I decided to hedge my bets, even though I hadn't heard specifically that I was in jeopardy. Sometime before the shake-up, I had gotten a phone call out of the blue from Robert C. Maynard, a prominent *Washington Post* journalist who happened to be African American. He apparently had seen my byline in the *Journal*. He and his wife, Nancy Hicks Maynard, a *New York Times* reporter, had left their prestigious jobs to start an initiative to recruit and train Black, Latino, Asian American, and Native American journalists, to help the news industry become less overwhelmingly white.

Maynard wanted to gauge my interest in some day becoming an editor of some sort. I was flattered to be noticed by the highly regarded Maynard, who planted an idea that I had not yet thought about. At the time, my *Journal* job was shaky, as was the case with some white male colleagues. However, becoming an editor of some sort? It had never crossed my mind until Maynard suggested it.

25

ACTIVISM, SORT OF

Before I get to my journalism transition, I want to share my media-activism period, such as it was. In my day, American journalists were supposed to be "objective," arm's-length unbiased observers, not "activists" in the cultural and social politics that journalism covers. I easily maintained my "objectivity" as a *Wall Street Journal* reporter in San Francisco. One could argue, however, that I was subliminally an activist when I wrote occasional Asian American–themed features. Yet those met the *Journal*'s usual high journalistic standards.

In my own time, however, I plunged into activist waters, joining local yellow media workers to advocate for more and better job opportunities and more and better yellow stories in Bay Area news outlets. Ling-Chi Wang and his colleagues at Chinese for Affirmative Action (CAA) inspired us. We were in synch with CAA's Chinese Media Committee campaign calling for more news media jobs for Asian Americans and better coverage of community issues. In 1976, a bunch of us yellow media workers, almost all a decade or more younger than me, attended a Chinese Media Committee career day, where some of us reflected on our collective employment status and content flaws in our industry. We brainstormed forming an organization to address these issues. After a few meetings—attended at least once by Wayne Wang, who would later become a star movie director—we announced a general membership meeting for the spring of 1977. About eighty people attended. We ended up calling ourselves Asians in Mass Media (AMM).

I was among the most outspoken about our woeful place in the industry. You know what happens when one speaks up too loudly in a new group of largely reticent participants? You slide into a leadership role. That's what happened to loudmouth me. I became AMM's first chair, leading a steering committee of writers, aspiring TV news stars, and behind-the-scenes workers of mostly Chinese and Japanese ancestries, with a few Filipinos and Koreans. While we shared a general feeling that our industry was flawed, we didn't all think alike regarding how to improve it. Our views reflected inherent differences in the various media that employed us. Which was most important—print, TV, or radio? Personality and ego conflicts were inevitable. Some members thought that we talked too much and did too little.

As chair, I tried my best to keep us focused. I sensed, however, that some members had their own agendas or were motivated more by self-interests than by group interests. Nonetheless, the steering committee came up with ideas to attract more members and to raise money to sustain AMM. Our fundraising events included a showing of Bruce Lee's *Enter the Dragon* film; a forum on the coverage of Wendy Yoshimura, an associate of Patty Hearst, the newspaper heiress who was kidnapped and then became a participant in her captors' criminality; an Asians in Media class at the University of California at Santa Cruz; and commentaries on KPFA-FM, a Berkeley progressive radio station.

At our peak, AMM had about seventy members. Most worked in TV news in various capacities, none yet at the top, either on screen or as a boss. A smaller number were in print, radio, and advertising, most in low- to mid-level positions. We also had a few student and community members. Many members were early in their media lives. Many Asian American news media workers in the Bay Area didn't want to join an organization that had a political agenda, reflecting the professional mantra about "objectivity." They also didn't want to jeopardize their careers by implicitly or explicitly criticizing their employers.

AMM published a quarterly newsletter, of which I was editor and principal writer. Of the two major issues—representation and coverage—I took more seriously critiquing mainstream news coverage of our communities. I wrote to various publications, criticizing their coverage

Cover of first issue of Asians in Mass Media newsletter produced by author and his team. (Author's Collection)

of Asian American subjects. One of my most memorable was a letter to fabled *San Francisco Chronicle* columnist Herb Caen, who often used Asian names or subjects as the butts of jokes. I took him to task. His response? In a handwritten note to me, "Pathetic, Mr. Wong. Pathetic."

My writing critiques to established journalists and their publications were either ballsy of me or incredibly stupid since I, too, was a practicing print journalist who could get into professional trouble for openly deriding a colleague's work. Since the *Journal* wasn't part of the local news scene, however, I wasn't vulnerable to losing my job.

As woebegone of an organization as AMM was—no office, paid staff, or money—word got around we existed. That yielded speaking invitations, which I was happy to accept. College students were among those intrigued by what AMM was trying to do. In February 1978, a Stanford University student named Bill Sing invited me to talk about AMM and ethnic issues in journalism. Sing, a sharp Chinese American from Seattle, was interested in becoming a print journalist. After graduation, he joined the *Los Angeles Times* and eventually became its business editor. In 1981, he and other Los Angeles Asian American media workers organized what became the national Asian American Journalists Association (AAJA). In appearances promoting AAJA, Sing gave AMM and me credit for planting the seed.

AMM petered out in 1979 due to exhaustion, lack of funds, and my preoccupation with my tenuous status at the *Journal*. My final public act on behalf of AMM was in April 1979. AMM and the Chinese Media Committee, among others, were pressuring broadcast networks to create more shows with Asian American themes that were historically authentic. The ABC network happened to run a Western series called *How the West Was Won*, which aired for three seasons in the late 1970s. For the tenth episode of its third season, titled "China Girl," it invited Bay Area yellow media activists, including me, to a prescreening in San Francisco Chinatown. We watched in silence and disbelief. Muted grumbling could be heard among some of us as we got up to depart.

Something propelled me to say something. Rather than head for the door, I seized the microphone and started spouting my objections to what we had just seen. That outburst stopped many people from leaving. I asserted in no uncertain terms that the "China Girl" episode was more of the same old stereotyped portrayal of Chinese in the American West and that it did nothing to enlighten anyone about the truth of the yellow experiences in the nineteenth century. My fellow activists clapped or murmured agreement, while local network representatives stared at me in silence and, with one or two, ill-disguised contempt. Someone in the crowd was from the *San Francisco Chronicle*, which reported my little outburst in the paper's *Sunday Datebook* magazine. It was, I believed, a fitting—and spectacular—farewell to AMM's short life as a media activist organization.

The Los Angeles–based AAJA established regional chapters, one of which was in the Bay Area, a successor of sorts to AMM. I joined that chapter as one of the gang, no longer a leader. Privately, I felt envious that the Los Angeles folks were able to pull together a steadier organization than we in the Bay Area were able to. At the same time, I grew somewhat wary of the intentions of some AAJA members, who were either too young or disinterested in what AMM had tried to do. I noticed, for instance, a greater lean toward jobs and career advancement than better coverage of Asian American issues. Even with these doubts, I became more active in AAJA, even becoming its national vice president for print.

AAJA held splashy national conventions, starting in the late 1980s. There was always a large number of attractive, well-turned-out young people, seeking TV news reporter or anchor jobs. Fewer men or women wanted to get print jobs, or to improve yellow coverage. By the late 1980s and early 1990s, I was mid-career with management experience in newspapers and already writing columns in mainstream and community publications highlighting Asian American issues. My interest in career advancement was relatively muted compared with my younger colleagues.

The 1991 AAJA convention in New York City offered a perfect opportunity, I believed, for some of us to cover a hot issue involving Asian Americans and African Americans in greater depth than surface sensationalism. That issue was the Black boycott of Korean American–owned grocery stores in the Flatbush section of Brooklyn. The boycott, begun in January 1991, was still on when AAJA convened eight months later, but well beyond the duration needed for shock value.

Since the boycott had started making national news, I followed it as best I could from three thousand miles away. When I learned that the AAJA convention was going to be held in New York City, my anticipation grew. I looked forward to seeing for myself the site of the boycott and possibly writing about it, even if the hot action might be greatly muted by the time I was there. At the convention, I asked a few colleagues to accompany me to Flatbush. All declined, so I went via subway by myself.

I went into the first of two stores, whose bins were bereft of fresh fruits and vegetables. I approached the proprietor, the boycott target because of a disputed action by an employee against a Haitian woman customer. The proprietor said very little other than to vent against the city government led by David Dinkins, the city's first Black mayor. A more talkative employee said that his boss was determined to stay open with the help of other Korean American grocers and their community. If this store closed, boycott leaders would target other Korean American stores, he said. I crossed the street to the other store being boycotted. Its bins, too, were mostly empty. I talked with the brother of the proprietor, a man in his late twenties who had come to America seven years earlier. He had had a positive image of America then, but not now. He was angry and couldn't understand why his brother's store was being boycotted.

During the time I was there, several hours, only one Black protestor appeared, shouting, "Boycott! Boycott!" A few customers, Black and Latinx women, browsed the sparse merchandise; one bought a bottle of olive oil. Both stores had suffered huge sales plunges since the boycott began. I called the boycott leader twice. The first time, a man said that the leader wasn't available and told me not to make this protest about anything other than one possibly anti-Black incident. He said that not all Blacks hated all Koreans. The second time, a woman who answered criticized me as an individual "incidental" to the matter and stated that the Black community was the "victim."

I wrote a column for *Asian Week*, another San Francisco Chinatown–based newspaper, about the unresolved issue. This little episode epitomized a key difference in how I envisioned the role of Chinese American/Asian American journalists versus some of my yellow colleagues. Going to Flatbush was a highlight of my convention visit. I didn't understand why at least a few of my colleagues weren't interested in taking a fresh look at this widely reported interracial conflict. My intent here isn't to cloak myself in high moral glory. Rather, I believe that this incident illustrated different visions at the time of our role as yellow journalists in an industry that had too few of us in important positions. One vision was to be "professional" and apolitical. My preferred vision was to use our personal insights and professional skills to sort out messy and confusing political, social, and cultural crosscurrents of interracial conflicts and tell stories that would do justice to the facts and truth so all Americans could learn something that wouldn't further divide us.

Even though I had doubts about AAJA, I wanted to be its national president after finishing my vice presidency. I wanted to increase the organization's profile and illuminate the need for the mainstream news media to pay more attention to a growing yellow population and the many stories that could be told to better articulate fundamental demographic shifts in America. My candidacy, however, was undermined by a whisper campaign against me from some Bay Area TV news people. They didn't like my critiques of TV news in general and of Connie Chung, the most famous among our cohort. For the April 1989 national convention in San Francisco, I had written an *Oakland Tribune* column, headlined "Shame on you, Connie Chung," and distributed copies at the convention. Such an agent provocateur! At the time, Chung co-anchored a national broadcast TV news show. My basic criticism was that she held herself far apart from her ethnic community and didn't use her considerable influence to get her network to occasionally run Asian American–themed stories.

Beyond that, in Asian American publications, I criticized TV news in general for its superficiality, a common theme among us ink-stained wretches, who were perhaps jealous of our TV news colleagues for their fame and fortune. The price I paid for my curmudgeonly stance was losing the AAJA presidential election to a Bay Area TV news reporter, who was less mouthy than I was when it came to critiquing the industry.

I don't want to give the impression that I liked only print journalists. In fact, two people I've maintained lengthy friendships with are Felicia Lowe and Christopher Chow, both pioneering TV journalists. Lowe, a reporter at KGO-TV, the San Francisco station, interviewed Joyce and me about interracial marriages in 1973. We've been friends ever since. She went on to a successful career as a documentary filmmaker with several compelling films about Chinese America. Chow was the first Chinese American local TV reporter in the Bay Area and northern California when he began at KPIX-TV, the local CBS affiliate, in 1970. His TV journalism career was relatively brief, but he, too, became, among other things, a documentary producer and conscientious political and community activist.

In addition to AAJA were Black, Latino, and Native American journalists' organizations. The four organizations shared common goals of more jobs and better coverage, and all four sought funding support from their employers or umbrella groups that represented individual news outlets. In the early 1990s, the four organizations came together as UNITY: Journalists of Color to address common concerns with the white media establishment, a strength-in-numbers strategy.

In 1994, UNITY: Journalists of Color held its first convention in Atlanta. About six thousand non-white journalists attended, as did white news executives, who needed to show the flag and recruit talent. I was part of an Asian American contingent to help plan this convention. At one planning session, I sensed tension among the four organizations. Most of the time, we were professional and polite. However, there were discordant moments. As is my wont, I advocated for Asian American interests. An African American female print journalist with an outspoken national profile confronted me in blunt terms. In effect, she questioned the integrity of Asian American journalists by stating that in some circles, Asian Americans were considered "honorary whites." That zinger epitomized underlying issues that had to be overcome if the four groups were to act as one to influence the white-controlled news media.

The Atlanta convention itself was considered a success in that many non-white journalists met, mingled, talked, debated, learned, and partied together. No, it wasn't perfectly harmonious. Many attendees hung mostly with their own kind. But as a first effort, it worked to get the attention of major news companies, which helped fund the convention and the joint UNITY organization.

26

HOMETOWN PAPER

My *Wall Street Journal* journey ended in the autumn of 1979, nine years after it had begun. Knowing that the end was near, I didn't wait for the axe to fall. I pursued a safe passage, with the help of my old *Daily Cal* buddy, Ron Bergman. At one of our dinners out, he urged me to join him at the *Oakland Tribune* because of big changes going on there. "You'd be a star over here," he said. The changes Bergman spoke of involved—guess who?—Bob Maynard and Nancy Hicks.

Started in 1874, the *Tribune*'s golden era was under the Knowland family's ownership. Joseph R. Knowland, who had been in the House of Representatives for five terms, had bought the newspaper in 1915 and turned it into an influential Republican instrument. The Tribune Tower, built in the early 1920s a stone's throw from Chinatown, became a distinctive Oakland landmark. By the mid-1970s, however, the *Tribune* was in trouble. Joseph R. Knowland's son, William F. Knowland, had been in charge for more than a decade. Before that, he had been a powerful U.S. senator known as the "senator from Formosa," the former name of Taiwan, because he was stridently anti-Communist and pro-Kuomintang (Chinese Nationalist Party), which retreated to Taiwan after its defeat to the Communist Party. In 1958, Senator Knowland sought the California governorship, which he lost, ending his political career. A few years later, on the death of his father, he took control of the *Tribune*.

Once the dominant newspaper on the east side of San Francisco Bay, the *Tribune*'s business fortunes sank gradually through the 1970s. The William F. Knowland administration made some questionable business decisions. The *Tribune* had major operations in Contra Costa County, to the east of Alameda County, of which Oakland is the biggest city, and in southern Alameda County. Both areas had mostly been farmland and fruit orchards.

Oakland's strong economic status began to decline after World War II. White middle-class families started moving to the burgeoning suburbs to the east and south. Oakland's industrial base, once solid, began to crumble. Major interstate freeways, the MacArthur (Interstate 580) and the Nimitz (I-880), cut through Oakland like a sharp knife. Chinatown was hit hard by construction of the Nimitz, the Bay Area Rapid Transit (BART) system, Laney College, the Oakland Museum of California, and the Association of Bay Area Governments building. These public projects gobbled up some of Chinatown's housing.

Counterintuitively, the *Tribune* under William F. Knowland decided to greatly reduce its presence in these outlying areas at the very time they were growing with middle-class white families, housing, and businesses. Newspapers love that demographic profile because supermarkets, retailers, and car dealers buy newspaper ads to appeal to such households. For whatever reason, *Tribune* management under the former senator wanted or needed to cut costs. What it also cut was potential growth opportunities, a gift for smaller competing newspapers in these once-barren areas.

The senator's personal problems were a likely culprit in hurting the *Tribune*'s business fortunes. He had a bad gambling habit, and his marital life was shaky.[1] No longer a prestigious national political figure, now a big fish in a small pond but with a more troubled existence, he died by suicide in early 1974.[2]

Three years later, the Knowland family sold the *Tribune* to an Arizona-based communications company (local TV stations, outdoor advertising) that shortly thereafter sold it to the Gannett Corporation, a newspaper chain based on the East Coast. Gannett smartly hired Maynard to be the editor of the *Tribune*. It was almost unheard of in the 1970s for a Black man (or woman) to be the top editor of an American metropolitan newspaper. Given that Oakland's Black population was close to 50 percent in the late 1970s, Gannett wanted to make a statement by naming Maynard as the *Tribune*'s editor-in-chief.

Gannett also wanted to use the *Tribune* as a petri dish of sorts. Owning a struggling urban newspaper surrounded by the thriving whiter and wealthier suburbs wasn't really its mission. Gannett executives had much bigger national plans. It wanted to start a new national daily newspaper, and Oakland was the site of one of its prototypes. Maynard oversaw the creation of that prototype, *East Bay Today*, which had several distinguishing characteristics. One, it was available only at newsstands, not through home delivery. Second, it cost a dime, a bargain designed to attract readers, but a "loss leader" for the company. Third, its design—four orange-colored boxes above the front-page nameplate that served as "teases" for stories inside the paper, and all but one front-page story ending on the front page—was to stem the loss of readers attracted to the brevity of TV news reports. Its rollout in 1980 got lots of news coverage. Two years later, *USA Today* made its debut, a more sophisticated version of *East Bay Today*.

The Gannett-Maynard relationship was a business marriage of political, social, and cultural convenience, with hopes of overcoming powerful economic forces threatening the *Tribune*'s existence. Being a wealthy company with many suburban newspapers, Gannett could afford to pour money, at least in the short term, into the *Tribune/East Bay Today* experiment. For Maynard and Hicks, this golden opportunity would let them fulfill their dream of helping the news business become less white and male.

These forces converged to my benefit. The *Journal* gave me a severance package, saying that my dismissal wasn't personal. (Others in my bureau were also bought out.) I wrote Maynard for a job since he had previously shown interest in me. My request was exceedingly humble: I wanted to write about "my community" (i.e., Chinatown, Chinese America, Asian America). His rejoinder took me aback: "I want you to be the business editor." His offer reminded me of our phone call years earlier, when he had envisioned me being an editor of some sort.

Of course, I said yes, unsure of exactly what I was saying yes to. While I had been an editor in high school, college, and the Peace Corps, this level was entirely higher. Happy to be in the trenches as a bureau reporter, I had never had high ambitions at the *Wall Street Journal*. So, the transition to a leadership role at the *Tribune* was somewhat unnerving.

What makes a good leader? Who knows? I've never had any leadership training. Yet here I was in a fast-changing *Tribune* newsroom, the head of one of its smaller sections.

In a way, I was fortunate Maynard hired me at all. A year earlier, in 1978, I had mildly disrupted a conference he and Hicks had organized in Washington, D.C., commemorating the tenth anniversary of the Kerner Commission report that found in 1968, after fiery riots in urban Black neighborhoods, white racism underlay widespread racial unrest. By then, Maynard and Hicks had established their nonprofit organization to help integrate newsrooms. I was among the few non-Black conference participants, perhaps the only one of Asian descent. My moment came when, at a session where the time-honored Black-white racial narrative dominated, I declared that where I came from, California, civil rights issues weren't simply Black and white, but much more colorfully multicultural, including yellow, my color. Immediately after that session, Maynard and Hicks approached me. Both wore faint smiles and were cordial. Neither appeared visibly upset, but I could tell by their tone that they didn't want any other disruptions to their agenda. They said that they understood and appreciated my concerns.

A year later, all apparently was forgiven. I began at the *Tribune* in November 1979, when I was thirty-eight years old. Given the drive of Maynard and Hicks to help the news business hire and promote more non-white people, this time was the first that my race-ethnicity was a factor in me getting hired. I didn't mind in the least since the *Journal* didn't want me anymore and I was getting a job only a few blocks from my Chinatown. I never felt stigmatized by being a so-called affirmative-action hire.

Before my first official day of work, I visited the *Tribune*'s newsroom on the fourth floor of a six-story building attached to the famous Tribune Tower to formally meet Maynard and Roy Grimm, the managing editor. Grimm, a white man in his fifties who might have been even shorter and certainly slimmer than I was and who loved to smoke a pipe, had been with the *Tribune* for many decades, the most prominent holdover senior editor linking the Knowland years to the Gannett-Maynard era.

The atmospheric contrast between the two *Journal* newsrooms I knew and the *Tribune*'s was sharp. The *Journal* newsrooms were in relatively modern one- or two-story office buildings, with no more than a dozen people on the news side. The moment I stepped off the elevator into the *Tribune*'s newsroom, I felt a slight jolt of nostalgia for the eighteen months I had spent at two San Francisco newspapers in the early 1960s. Each of those newsrooms had an older, rickety feel, with a louder buzz and more chaos, yet also controlled. In the *Tribune*'s newsroom, I strolled on creaky, uneven wood floors past various clusters of messy and cluttered desks into the top editors' office suite.

To my surprise, Mary Ellen Rose Butler, a former *Daily Cal* colleague, happened to be there. The daughter of Oakland's first Black city council member, she had just finished meeting with Maynard and Grimm. That's when I learned that she was the new features editor. We hugged in mutual delight. Seeing her cheered me up immensely. We hadn't been in touch for many years. Both of us were members of the *Daily Cal* editorial board that had been fired. She went on to a successful journalism career, including the *Washington Star*, before working at the *Tribune*.

My first couple of days at the *Tribune* were, well, a wee bit embarrassing. In the corner section of the main newsroom where the business-news staff was situated, I immediately noticed the odd coupling of electric typewriters and boxy desktop computers, something alien to me. In my previous eleven years in various newsrooms, I had used only typewriters, the old-fashioned models with noisy keyboards and manual shift levers. I had never used a desktop computer before.

Hoping not to reveal my ignorance, I asked one of my new colleagues, a copy editor perhaps in his sixties, to show me how to use the computer. Following that minimal training, I shied away from using the computer immediately. Instead, I tapped out my first few stories on the typewriter. Hoping that no one would notice, I turned to the computer and keyed the story I had just typed on paper, using a "code" to enter the text. In other words, I was writing the same story twice! This technology transition stressed me no end, at least for a few days, until I gained confidence in using the computer only.

That mini-trauma aside, I was the new hotshot thanks to my *Wall Street Journal* credentials, and I came in with guns blazing. When Maynard offered me the job, he left out one essential detail—that I was the business editor of the new *East Bay Today* prototype, not the *Tribune*, which already had a business editor, a middle-aged, brusque, tough-talking woman.

Neither of us said anything openly about our murky shared editorship, and we each tried to not invade each other's jurisdiction. Awkward doesn't begin to describe our relationship, which, thankfully, didn't last long. She was transferred to another role elsewhere, and I assumed business editorship of the *Tribune* and *East Bay Today*.

My wise-guy assertiveness in wanting to impose *Journal* standards didn't go over all that smoothly. My early interactions with the three or four white men who were the business-news staff, all considerably older than I, were rocky. The business-news section was pretty much an afterthought at the *Tribune* (and at other metropolitan dailies) in the 1970s—small staff and very little space in the paper. The men assigned to that section were journeymen at best, not stars on the rise.

That mattered little to me. I was focused on trying to instill in them a harder edge, a more aggressive approach. A few of them nodded yes but carried on as they had before I got there, doing the thankless tasks of copyediting, writing headlines, and laying out the pages. None of them told me to my face that they didn't like what I was doing, but I could tell. Change is always hard. One, however, took to my leadership. He was Clifford Pletschet, an easy-going, tall, somewhat gangly man in his fifties. I made him a financial columnist, which he took to with enthusiasm, and, over time, developed a loyal readership.

Ironically, my gung-ho attitude imposing *Wall Street Journal* ways upset a non-business reporter the most. This reporter, a soft-spoken, middle-aged woman who had joined the *Tribune* from a community weekly, covered city hall. One of her stories was rerouted to the business section, which meant that I would oversee its editing. The version I read was adequate but lacked a liveliness that, in my estimation, would have lured more readers (a typical editor's judgment!). I rewrote its first few paragraphs, injecting more colorful language, in the manner that the *Journal*'s editors had done to my news features. When the city hall reporter read over my editing, she was mortified. She wanted her byline removed because she felt the story was no longer hers. Well, it was, and it wasn't, at least the first few paragraphs. I didn't relent, and her byline stayed. Over time, we developed a cordial relationship, but I learned a lesson: Be more judicious in my editing approach.

It soon became clear that as much as I wanted to uplift the *Tribune* business pages to *Journal* standards, that goal was laughably unrealistic.

The staff numbered fewer than ten. I had no idea what my section's budget was. Business news had only a page and a half for stories on most days, excluding the stock tables, and we didn't have a separate section but were in the back of the popular sports section. Soon, I got a couple of new reporters, although I had no say or foreknowledge; it was all Maynard's doing. At least for the business-news section, he and Grimm controlled the budget and hiring. The new reporters were welcome, helping me implement what Maynard wanted—more attention to local small businesses and increased coverage of the Pacific Rim. With his green light, I injected a more aggressive attitude in covering those topics.

One of the biggest stories to descend on the business-news section under my command was a fantastic plan of a Hong Kong developer named George Tan, who wowed Oakland city officials when he proposed in 1980 to build a skyscraper (seventy or eighty stories tall?) a few blocks from the Tribune Tower. I asked one of our new reporters to follow the case closely, including making a trip to Hong Kong. It turned out that Tan was a crook. His high-flying Hong Kong company, Carrian Investments Ltd., collapsed under a ton of debt, and he and associates were charged with fraud in a spectacular business failure.[3] The site where he wanted to build his skyscraper was turned into a much more modest six-story building called Trans Pacific Centre, without his involvement.

My early relationship with Maynard went swimmingly. We didn't really know one another outside a long-distance phone call or two (and that uncomfortable meeting at the conference he and Hicks had organized) before I joined him at the *Tribune*. He liked what I was doing with the business section. Early on, he beckoned me into his office and greeted me with his trademark incandescent smile and a high-five. A few times, he asked me to join him for lunch. His favorite place was in Chinatown, my 'hood! Except the restaurant he liked featured hot and spicy Sichuan cuisine, not the blander Cantonese cuisine I had grown up with.

Maynard was an affable yet arrogant man, brilliant, charismatic, effusive, and full of himself, yet charming. He dressed stylishly, in well-starched English-made dress shirts, colorful silk ties, and well-tailored dark suits. He spoke precisely in a deep, low cadence, punctuated by an occasional grin or sly smile. He got your attention. His weekly column was elegantly written, often with an uplifting moral message. He gained national recognition as a frequent guest commentator on ABC-TV's *This Week with David Brinkley* show. He was quite a contrast to my more introverted, much less fashionable, and decidedly uncharismatic persona. Sometimes, being in his presence could be intimidating and overwhelming.

I was mildly shocked the first time we had lunch together in Chinatown. He ordered in Mandarin, which I didn't speak. I hid my personal shame. Here I was, the Chinatown Chinese guy, who couldn't do what this outgoing, smart Black guy could, right there in my own Chinatown! Nonetheless, we had convivial conversations over delicious food, and I found him relaxed and personable.

As his status and power grew—from mere editor-in-chief to publisher to owner—our relationship became more distant, but still cordial. We never became buddy-buddy. When he came to Oakland, he already had an inner circle of friends and associates, built up over his years on the East Coast and through the creation of the Institute for Journalism Education, his and his wife's vehicle to further integrate American newsrooms.

My performance as business editor must have impressed him because in 1981, not quite two years from the time I began at the *Tribune*, he promoted me to be an assistant managing editor, one step away from the most important operational newsroom job of managing editor. That appointment boosted my sometimes-fragile ego. It also scared me. Heading up the small, somewhat inconsequential business-news section had given me some professional leadership experience. With this promotion, I acquired even more responsibility and more people under my command, directly and indirectly. Now, I supervised the entire hard-news operation. As such, I ran the daily meetings where section editors pitched their top stories, and I had the final say on the front-page content and order of importance. At first, I felt insecure asserting myself, but as time went on, I became more confident.

One small perquisite was a corner office in the main newsroom, not in the Maynard-Grimm suite. I held private court with other editors and reporters. It's almost unavoidable to feel powerful in this kind of setting, even if the *Tribune* universe was minuscule compared to that of the *New York Times*, the *Washington Post*, the *Wall Street Journal*, and even the San Francisco papers. The best thing that happened in that office was in the early spring of 1982, when I received a beautiful bouquet of flowers with a handwritten note from Joyce saying she was pregnant. I was meeting with two assistant city editors, and when the flowers and note came, I let out a yelp that almost echoed in the newsroom.

I've always seen myself as introverted in most professional and social situations, a subliminal (or subconscious) consequence of my first twenty years cocooned in a socially segregated Chinatown where we felt inferior to white people, especially men in power. Yet at times as assistant managing editor, I had to step out of my normally withdrawn self. My title and role meant that I was professionally in command of a lot of people, many of them white men and women, who in an earlier life would have intimidated me. Sometimes, I had to make tough decisions or firmly say no. The dynamics could be complicated by racial-ethnic implications.

On one occasion, the city of Oakland was sending a delegation to Hong Kong. As tight as the *Tribune*'s budget was, Maynard approved sending a reporter to cover the group. I suggested choosing our city hall beat reporter, an African American man in his twenties, skilled, but somewhat prickly. Maynard had someone else in mind, the business editor, a soft-spoken Chinese American man about my age. Maynard reasoned that his choice was better because the business editor spoke Cantonese, Hong Kong's dialect. That logic seemed reasonable to me, but the business editor didn't know the city hall officials. That, to me, argued against him going. Since Maynard was The Boss, he got his way. It was my job, however, to tell the city hall reporter, who wasn't at all happy. I braced for an emotional outburst from the rejected reporter, but he didn't erupt, at least not within my earshot.

Another time, the *Tribune* was invited to send a representative to attend a conference on the Monterey peninsula sponsored by a business-oriented nonprofit organization. I chose one of our business-desk editors, not a reporter. It was a good opportunity for him to expand his professional horizons. Attendees could bring a spouse or partner. Our guy happened to be gay, and he wanted to take his partner, which was fine with me. When the sponsor found out who we were sending, its representative wasn't explicitly homophobic, but was cool to our choice. I didn't back down. Later, we learned that the sponsor was severing its ties with the *Tribune*. I didn't regret my decision, and the editor we sent thanked me for standing up for the principle of equal rights.

During the three years I served as the hard-news assistant managing editor, Maynard aimed for a Pulitzer Prize, the highest journalism honor. His vehicle was a set of special reports on Oakland problems, such as education, crime, and a crack-cocaine epidemic. These reports placed a huge burden on our reporters, editors, and the graphics and photography teams. Over several months, our team produced impressively presented special Sunday sections with splashy graphics, photos, and in-depth reporting that won us local praise, even as some team members grumbled about the extra work. Alas, the local kudos were our prize, not the coveted Pulitzer.

At the time, I was naturally thought to be next in line to be the managing editor. Two years into my tenure, however, I noticed a subtle change in how Maynard and Roy Aarons, the new executive editor, treated me. A close friend of Maynard's from Washington, D.C., Aarons was brought in under the ruse of being the new features editor, when the end game was to be the top newsroom boss. To my eyes, the two appeared friendlier with two other editors, one at my level and one just below us in the hierarchy of newsroom leadership. My instincts proved correct, as the lower-level editor, a young, talented assistant on the city desk, eventually got the managing editor's job that some thought would be mine.

As the quality of my relationship with Maynard and Aarons eroded incrementally, I remained stoic. I wasn't at ease promoting myself to them. While I didn't openly covet the managing editor job, I did want it, but I kept that desire to myself, never explicitly expressing it. That reticence was part of my problem—I didn't kiss up to Maynard and Aarons. The most concrete sign I was no longer a Maynard favorite came one day in 1984. Maynard and managing editor Grimm told me that they had a new assignment for me: "How would you like to break some ground at the *Tribune* and become its first ombudsman?" Ombud . . . what? I had no idea what that meant, but their offer, couched ever so sweetly and even evoking Maynard's ombudsmanship at the *Washington Post*, was a sure sign I was being shoved aside.

A newspaper ombudsman is a senior staff member whom the reading public contacts directly with complaints about a story. We're talking not about typographical or grammatical errors but about ethical or fairness issues, major omissions, or perceived biases. In the 1980s, there were only about thirty ombudsmen among approximately 1,500 daily newspapers in the United States. Newspapers were seen as impenetrable institutional powers in their communities. Certainly, an aggrieved (or happy) reader could write a letter to the editor, which had a small chance of getting published. But its effect was minimal, at best. A reader complaint expressed in a letter to the editor was often ignored. Unlike powerful figures (politicians, business executives, celebrities), most ordinary readers don't have easy access to editors who count.

The *Tribune* ran a story introducing me as ombudsman and publishing a phone number and address so readers could contact me directly, which triggered letters and phone calls with reader concerns. I kept a log of such contacts, which could number a dozen or two a day, to decide which deserved my special attention and which I could refer to an editor or reporter. To fulfill my role as a "reader's representative"—another designation for ombudsman—I decided to write a weekly column, focusing on the most significant reader complaint or observation. This column gave the public a view of the process by which our news team wrote and edited stories. One column, for example, asked why the *Tribune* covered extensively the murder of a white suburban woman, while murders of Black and other minority women in Oakland got very little, if any, attention.

My relationship with Maynard, already growing more distant, got even more fraught as I delved into reader complaints. By that time, Maynard had become the publisher as well as editor. Publishers are more businesspeople than journalists, people especially sensitive to advertisers, whose financial support make up a sizeable chunk of any paper's budget.[4] The tensest confrontation I had with him was when I examined a reader's complaint about the hiring practices of a local men's clothing chain, a *Tribune* advertiser. As a matter of routine, I showed Maynard and Grimm my column in advance. After they read it, they called me into a meeting in Maynard's office.

The air was thick with tension in this heavily curtained, carpeted inner sanctum. No cordial salutations were exchanged. I sat down on the elegant leather couch, feeling vulnerable. First Maynard and then Grimm lit into me in no uncertain terms: They didn't like the column's tone or the fact I criticized the advertiser's hiring policies. I wasn't used to doublebarreled blasts of their verbal critique. Maynard's ombudsman hat had long been put away, replaced by a businessman-publisher hat. He didn't have to say it, but I knew that I had touched a sensitive nerve by criticizing a major *Tribune* advertiser. After all their bluster, neither man ordered me to kill the column. I stood my ground without being confrontational in return. The column ran as I had written it, and I never heard whether the clothier threatened to pull its ads.

If nothing else, the scolding confirmed for me that this ombudsman gig was a lonely island. How could I be buddies with my news colleagues if I might also side with a reader and not a reporter, an editor, or the powerful publisher himself? Whenever I approached an editor or a reporter with a substantial reader complaint, I did so professionally, without saying whether I agreed or disagreed. Such editors and reporters never raged at me directly, but it wouldn't be surprising if they berated me among themselves. The paper's leadership could take public pride in having someone high up on its news team—me—speak out on behalf of readers. I'm pretty sure that's not how the newsroom editors and reporters saw it, though. The role I played wasn't popular. It was like Us versus Them, with me now being at times with Them.

Some of my ombudsman columns weren't prompted by specific reader complaints. Instead, I meditated on a newspaper's role in a democratic society. Expressing big-picture thoughts was necessary, I believed, to declare journalism's value in a democracy. A few ombudsmen columns had Yellow American themes, my first attempt to use my unique Chinatown-based perspective in a newspaper a few blocks from where Pop and Mom had brought me up and that had been such a remote institution in my youth.

All good (or bad) things must come to an end. After two years of virtual isolation as ombudsmen, I was told that I'd again be an assistant managing editor, this time overseeing administrative and personnel matters. I wasn't told why the switch was being made. It was yet another sideways move, still far from actual newsroom power. I wasn't gleeful about the change, but at least I still had a job. This period, the mid-1980s, was a holding pattern for me. I had fancy titles but little impact other than possibly public relations (ombudsman) and bureaucratic. At least my ombudsman columns gave me a good, if limited, taste for writing again.

As I was getting shuffled around in the senior editor circles, the *Tribune* continued its financial slide, despite Gannett's infusion of untold millions when it first took over in 1979. Four years later, the company made newspaper history by selling the paper to Maynard, who got a loan from Gannett to buy it. That was the first time an African American owned a mainstream metropolitan newspaper. The hard truth is that ownership change was more historic symbolism than a wise business transaction. The *Tribune* was one of several news-and-advertising media properties obtained by Gannett and probably not the most attractive from an investment perspective. The optics looked good in that the company put in charge a highly regarded Black journalist. Its experimental prototype, *East Bay Today*, helped it create *USA Today*. But it wasn't in Gannett's long-term interest to hold on to the *Tribune*.

The paper's financial troubles were rooted in the reluctance of traditional advertisers (big retailers, car companies) to support a newspaper that had a thin middle-class and upper-middle-class readership who wasn't largely white. Its suburban competitors had that financially more desirable market now. After the initial high of joining the Gannett family, the excitement of Maynard's appointment, and the splashy *East Bay Today* debut, many of us worker bees became increasingly stressed as the paper was dangerously teetering. Rumors swirled about the paper's imminent demise. The union representing newsroom employees made concessions on wages and working conditions to help keep the paper afloat.

More than once, I sought newspaper jobs elsewhere. Colleagues did the same or simply quit. I went to Portland, Oregon, to interview for an editing job at the *Oregonian*. Nothing came of that. The *San Francisco Examiner* wanted me to be its business editor for a small kick up in pay and the promise of a parking space (a precious commodity!), but I decided to stay at the *Tribune*, for that position wasn't what I was looking for.

My administrative-personnel assistant managing editorship was hardly a personal morale boost. I did the job, but I wasn't the happiest camper. Then that mythical thought-bubble light bulb illuminated: Why not write a column full-time? Why not indeed? I approached Maynard and Aarons, and they agreed, with Aarons expressing reservations. When I told them that I wanted to include Chinese American and Asian American themes, Aarons questioned its sustainability.

My new column-writing gig didn't immediately replace my administrative duties. My early columns appeared once every other week on the editorial pages, with my name and photo prominently displayed. My first such column discussed the status of Asian Americans and why President Jimmy Carter had designated nine years earlier an Asian Pacific American Heritage Week. Two weeks later, my second column, headlined "The roots of Asian American crime," focused on a national conference in Oakland of public officials addressing a growing crime problem in Asian American communities. Those two columns were a good start to offer my thoughts on topics that were ignored by newspapers like the *Tribune* and that I was well positioned to address. They began to fulfill a long-term wish of mine to write about "my community" in a mainstream newspaper that had a readership much wider than Chinatown, Chinese America, and Asian America.

A few months later, by mid-September of 1988, my column went weekly. A month later, I made the full transition, with a new title, associate editor, lofty but largely meaningless. More important, my column began running three days a week. I was back to what had energized me about journalism—writing and telling stories. As a columnist, one has a luxury that reporters don't. You can express an opinion or a point of view. I saw this column as a perfect opportunity to deepen my racial-ethnic identity search and to highlight topics that were largely hidden from wide public consumption. At the same time, I knew not to write exclusively along racial-ethnic lines. That would be much too limiting and would pigeonhole me. Yet even when yellow ethnic themes formed only a fourth to a third of all my columns, I know that many folks thought of me as an "Asian American" columnist. That label has at least two interpretations: One is descriptive, and the other is limiting.

My mission was essentially twofold: Introduce *Tribune* readers to topics they had rarely read about but that were intricately interwoven with Oakland life and journalistically explore topics close to my soul. In my eight years of writing columns, I wrote about Oakland's Chinatown as well as Chinese American and Asian American matters of all sorts. Most of my *Tribune* columns, however, weren't devoted to those specialties. The subjects I addressed were eclectic, from local people and politics to regional, state, national, and international politics and culture, from the personal to perplexing social and cultural issues. For example, I opposed President George H. W. Bush's Gulf War. I favored sensible gun regulations. I wrote about parenting joys and challenges. I took on arts and cultural matters that intersected with race and class. I highlighted our society's growing multiculturalism.

Sometimes, I engaged a playful, satirical, humorous voice. A favorite column was published on January 30, 1989. A white Canadian psychologist had made a racially charged presentation at a San Francisco scientists' convention. His theory was that "Orientals" were superior to white or Black people in intelligence and social organization. His underlying message was that Black people were intellectually inferior. "Orientals" have bigger brains in cranial capacity and brain weight, he said. "That must be why I can't lose any weight," I wrote.

Before widespread use of the Internet and such social media platforms as Facebook, YouTube, Twitter, TikTok, and Instagram, being a newspaper columnist raised one's public profile. Shortly after my columns started running regularly, Nancy Hicks Maynard congratulated me on "beginning to find your voice," a high compliment from the boss's wife. A local Asian American activist power couple wrote to Maynard, thanking him for giving me a column. They liked that I wrote widely, not just about Asian American issues. General reader response was, as expected, good and bad. How readers communicated with a columnist was decidedly old-fashioned—calling on a landline phone or writing a letter on paper and mailing it in with a stamp. One reader hand-wrote me letters telling me that he hated my stuff, which led me to wonder: Why does this guy continue reading me when he doesn't like what I have to say?

After a column on Oakland political redistricting in which I highlighted the need to consolidate Asian American voters, one reader, "A concerned Black citizen," wrote, "If Chinese-Asians practiced birth control like everybody else there wouldn't be—so much population growth and burden on our City. And if the Chinese stayed off the boats and in China where they belong, they would NOT be here driving up my taxes and trying to take something that belongs to somebody else." Following a column about the Los Angeles mayoral race, in which Richard Riordan, a white man, had defeated Michael Woo, a Chinese American, a reader, signing his letter, "East Side White Pride, Oakland CA 94607," wrote, "You are an Asian racist. You are a hatemonger. You spew all of your poison sewage against whites eternally on the behalf of black activists."

Among *Tribune* colleagues, the response to my columns was more muted, nuanced, and indirect. Some told me directly that they liked what I was doing. One qualified his praise by saying that, in general, columnists don't hit the mark every time, but he believed that I did so often enough. One popular reporter, a white guy, liked to josh me about what he thought was my naïveté about a possible harmonious multicultural future that I sometimes conveyed in my columns about California's and America's browner demographic future. His edgy but good-natured skepticism was typical of the mind-set of others, I'm sure.

The oddest inside response came from a female reporter and desk editor, who had once worked under my business-editor command and, later, on the city desk. She was a quick, reliable, if opinionated colleague, one I wasn't particularly close to. After my column had been running a while, she came into my little office, told me that she liked what I had just written, and promptly walked out. Later, I heard the gossipy backstory on why she did that. Out of my earshot, she had earlier scoffed at my writing, so she wanted to show those she had complained to that she could, indeed, say something nice about me to my face.

My racially themed columns apparently upset at least one *Tribune* employee who worked in the basement where the papers were printed. A tall, muscular white man approached me one day, not in a threatening manner, but more in exasperation about what he believed was my antiwhite attitude. We chatted briefly without anger or resolution. At least he didn't choose to bop me. Others also didn't like what I was writing. I regularly parked my car in a lot across from our newsroom. One day, I found nails hammered into the two back tires of my car. That wasn't accidental.

27

WIN SOME, LOSE SOME

As for outsiders, my *Tribune* columns surprised—and delighted—many Chinese American and Asian American readers, most of whom didn't know of me or my work. Liking what I was writing, they started contacting me. Some were Chinatown leaders and activists in the wider Asian community who enjoyed the fact that someone at the hometown newspaper was paying attention to issues that were close to their hearts and minds. Some Black readers expressed their approval as well. A few Chinatown leaders invited me to lunch, providing updates on what was happening in their community and pitching me on column ideas. Asian American organizations invited me to speak, especially during May, which is Asian Pacific American Heritage Month. Aspiring and young Asian American journalists, noticing my new public status, sought me out for advice and counseling.

More broadly, I already had a following among Chinese Americans and Asian Americans who read me in *East/West* and *Asian Week*, which had tiny circulations, but an intense, nationwide readership. One Asian American activist called me the "icon of *Asian Week*" for my pieces that sometimes took up a full page. Others labeled me the "dean of Asian American journalism" for being one of the first yellow journalists to emerge during the post–civil rights era. Intrigued by what I wrote in

English, Chinese-language newspaper reporters interviewed me for stories about what I had to say. To them, I gave my Chinese surname, Gee, not the fake Wong surname that I used in my English-dominated life.

Asian American colleagues acknowledged my work. Phil Tajitsu Nash, who also had an *Asian Week* column, wrote, "William Wong is one of our community's national treasures, combining powerful writing skills with keen insights in a long career that has included a regular column at *Asian Week* as well as mainstream publications such as the *Oakland Tribune* and *Wall Street Journal*." He praised *Asian Week* for having "a journalist, historian, and humorist of Wong's stature." Serena Chen, one-time editor of *East/West*, said that my writings encapsulated what many Chinese Americans and Asian Americans thought, but weren't able or willing to articulate publicly. Another Asian American journalist, Ed Iwata, thought that my columns should be syndicated nationally, which was something I also wanted. I asked Bob Maynard for help, but nothing came of it.

I helped bring attention to issues favored by some activists, such as stopping a proposed closure of the San Bruno regional office of the National Archives and Records Administration (NARA), near San Francisco. This office holds thousands of original Chinese immigration records from the Angel Island Immigration Station, including those of Pop and Mom. NARA headquarters in Washington, D.C., wanted those files transferred to Kansas. That move would have made it difficult, if not impossible, for California descendants of Angel Island detainees to gain easy access to their ancestors' one-of-a-kind files. My *Asian Week* columns on this controversy helped activists lobby successfully to keep the San Bruno office open.

I can, of course, bathe in this small-bore, obscure glory, but I don't want to give the impression that all Asian American readers loved what I wrote. Some didn't. A few told me to my face or communicated their negative feelings directly. Through the grapevine, I heard that some Asian American women thought that I was sexist or wasn't sensitive to their concerns and causes. I also heard that some Chinese Americans thought that I was "pompous," apparently when I spoke publicly. Still others believed that my voice was too soft, tepid, or moderate when what was needed, they thought, was more fire and fury aimed at the racist white establishment.

As imbedded as I was in newspapers, a foundation of twentieth-century communications, I dipped a toe into the twenty-first century's powerhouse: writing on the Internet, or "blogging." I did some of that, gratis, for sfgate.com, a *San Francisco Chronicle* website, sporadically through the first dozen years of the new century, including a series celebrating Linsanity, the incredibly exhilarating performance of Jeremy Lin, the first Chinese American star in the National Basketball Association.[1]

In this foreign place, did I ever get an electronic jolt to my soft and sensitive self! Since I was a newbie in this Brave New (and sometimes Vicious) World of cyberspace, I decided to read reader comments that are much more easily communicated than the old-fashioned, twentieth-century letters to the editor. The modern way for a reader to comment on a writer's output is to tap in one's comments on a desktop computer, tablet, or smartphone and hit send; within seconds, a blogger like me can read what the reader had to say. Reading some such comments was a huge blow to my ego and self-confidence. While a few were neutral, even complimentary, most were scathing, ugly, and venomous. That's how I learned a new word or concept: *trolling* and *trolls*, mean readers (usually anonymous) who often used scatological language to let me know how worthless and despicable I was.[2]

I related my shock to friends and family. A few chuckled at my naïveté and told me that the Internet was crawling with hateful messages. Despite my trepidatious reaction, I was taken by one comment that described me as an "overripe banana." When used to describe a person of Asian descent, the term *banana* refers to someone who is "yellow on the outside, white on the inside," another way of saying "honorary white." As for the overripe part, I took that to mean "old," which happens to be true. This troll bashed Jean Quan and me as being two terrible examples of "leaders" who have emerged from Oakland's Chinese American community. Quan has been an activist and politician, having broken through the local yellow ceiling when she won an Oakland school board seat (along with the late Wilma Chan) in 1990 and becoming Oakland's first Asian American woman mayor (2011, serving one term). The troll said something to the effect that if Quan and I were the best that the Oakland Chinese community could produce, then our community was a joke. I suspect that the troll was a Chinatown person.

Back to a sunnier clime, my writing influenced prominent Asian

American political figures and activists. Two were Norman Mineta and Robert Matsui, pioneering Japanese American leaders and fixtures in California and national politics in the late twentieth and early twenty-first centuries.

Mineta's political career started in 1967 as a San Jose, California, city council member, then mayor in 1971. He became a U.S. representative (for twenty years) and a cabinet secretary under a Republican (transportation, George W. Bush) and a Democratic president (commerce, Bill Clinton). In 1992, California Asian American politicians and activists were excited because Clinton promised a new administration that "looked like America" (i.e., embracing racial-ethnic, gender, and cultural diversity). Invited by an Asian American organization, I was in Washington, D.C., to testify at a hearing and later met with Mineta in a group. He recognized me, knew my work, and, out of the blue, asked whether I'd be interested in a Clinton administration job.

His question wasn't the first time I'd heard that idea. Maeley Tom had asked me the same thing. Tom and I had been classmates at Lincoln School in Oakland in the 1950s (she was Maeley Lock then). We had been friendly, but not all that close. We had lost touch until I started writing about Yellow America and learned that she had become the top staff aide for leading Democrats in the California legislature (Willie Brown, David Roberti). A pioneer herself, she mentored many Asian American political staff members and deepened the party's reach in the Asian American community. As a member of the Democratic National Committee, she urged the new Clinton administration to hire Asian Americans. It was she who first wondered whether I might want to join the Clinton communications team.

The idea intrigued and flattered me, but I had doubts since I was a local journalist, a nobody to powerful national Democratic politicians. In the end, this was merely idle talk, and I didn't actively pursue potential political staffing opportunities. Even though the *Tribune* was in deep financial trouble, jeopardizing my job's future, a Washington political job wouldn't have been a good fit for me. For much of my professional life, I had watched, listened, and heard politicians do their thing and had analyzed their rhetoric, actions, and shenanigans. I knew the double-talk, hypocrisy, and complicity that are ingrained in the political game. The journalism game has these foibles, too, but I tried to avoid them or not be cloaked in them for extended periods. I don't want to come across as a pure-as-the-driven-snow kind of guy, but any sloppy political pigpen wasn't where I wanted to play.

Like Mineta, only ten years younger, Matsui was a Sacramento city council member before becoming a U.S. representative, serving thirteen terms. When one day in either 1991 or early 1992 he asked to meet with me at the *Tribune*, I was taken by surprise and, again, flattered. I didn't know exactly why Representative Matsui wanted to meet with me in person, but I readily agreed.

A slender, handsome man, he sat across from me at my cluttered desk and, of all things, sought my advice on whether he should run for the open California U.S. Senate seat in 1992, as though I were a wizened political consultant, which I wasn't. That year, 1992, saw a regular election for the U.S. Senate seat from California and, simultaneously, a special election for the other Senate seat. I chose not to directly advise him to run or not to run. Instead, I waxed philosophical, asking him to consider where he felt more comfortable and powerful—in the House or in the Senate. I really had no standing to tell him one way or another, but the fact he'd ask my advice indicated a perception of my influence through my written opinions since we weren't personal friends, nor was I in his political orbit. Ultimately, he decided to stay in the House. Dianne Feinstein and Barbara Boxer were elected to the Senate from California that year.

Then there's Elaine Chao, one of the best-known Chinese Americans. A Taiwan native who came to America when she was eight years old, she has been a cabinet officer for two Republican presidential administrations (labor and Peace Corps director under George W. Bush, transportation under Donald J. Trump). And she's married to the powerful Kentucky Republican senator Mitch McConnell.

Here is my slender connection to Chao: In the late 1980s or early 1990s, while freelancing for *Asian Week*, I was in Houston to cover the national convention of the Organization of Chinese Americans (OCA), formed in 1973 by well-educated, well-off Chinese American and Chinese immigrant activists. The keynote speaker was Chao, a rising Republican political star. Rather than accede to the stargazing mantra and salivate at the appearance of a nascent political celebrity, my *Asian Week* column criticized OCA for choosing Chao as its top speaker. Here, my political bias was front and center, as it should be for a columnist. I didn't like her politics or defense of George H. W. Bush's policies. OCA seemed more interested in star power than it did substantive policy.

My distanced interaction with Chao didn't end there. When she became Peace Corps director in 1991, she was in the Bay Area, and her handlers set up a meeting with the *Oakland Tribune* editorial board, of which I was a member. I was anxious and excited. I knew her and the Peace Corps and wondered what her demeanor would be when she saw me, given our little history. To say the least, the start of that meeting—Chao and her assistant on one side, me with the other editorial board members on the other—was unsettling. In a soft but business-like tone, with a gentle smile, Chao remarked on my political opposition to her. Stone-faced, I kept silent. My colleagues listened in silence as well, at which point Chao made a standard pitch for the Peace Corps.

The irony wasn't lost on me since the Peace Corps had been my life twenty-five years earlier. I also chose not to confront Chao, even though her appointment as the agency's director was transparently political. Nothing in her public or political background spoke to the kind of public service exemplified by the Peace Corps. In her private and public life, she'd been in the banking and financial services industries as well as maritime transportation, her father's business. Her appointment as director of the Peace Corps insulted those of us who had been part of that noble effort.

After her two years as Peace Corps director, Chao climbed the political ladder, serving in the cabinets of Republican presidents. She was once described by people who'd encountered her as "an unapologetically ambitious operator with an expansive network, a short fuse, and a seemingly inexhaustible drive to get to the top and stay there" and as a "tiger wife . . . made of titanium."[3] She's courted controversy, including news reports that she used her transportation cabinet office to help her family's shipping business, especially in China, as well as questions about funneling lucrative projects to Kentucky, her husband's political home base.[4]

Chao's political loyalty didn't protect her from the blatant animosity of the last president she served, Trump. Trump had disputes with Chao's husband, Senator McConnell, and took it out on her with his trademark bigotry, calling her "Coco Chow" and McConnell's "China-loving wife."[5] While I disagree with Chao's politics, I'm sympathetic to her feeling aggrieved about her former boss's white supremacy.

An interesting, if gossipy, sidebar for me was learning who had introduced Chao to McConnell: It was Stuart Bloch, a McConnell friend married to Julia Chang, a mentor to Chao and the ambassador to Nepal under George H. W. Bush.[6] Why was this of interest to me? Well, I happened to have gone on a date with Chang when both of us were at Cal. As attractive as she was, we didn't connect. I hadn't given her another thought until I learned many decades later of her relationship with Chao. Checking her background possibly illuminates why we didn't connect. She's a native of Shandong Province, China, way to the north of where Pop came from, and her father was the first Chinese graduate of Harvard Law School. Me? I'm a working-class Chinatown son of a lower-class Hoisan native, and I don't relish hanging out with the upper classes of any race or ethnicity.

A final irony in this Chao-related saga: In 2001, OCA, the group I had gently lambasted for featuring Chao at one of its conventions, honored me for my pioneering journalism work. I suspect that its leaders weren't pleased with what I had written a decade earlier, yet apparently, they or their successors forgave (or forgot) my critique and decided to honor me anyway. Life can be funny that way. By the way, I applaud OCA's advocacy on behalf of Chinese Americans and Asian Americans.

The Committee of 100, a New York–based organization of highbrow, influential Chinese Americans, also knew of my work. Founded in the late 1980s by the late famed architect I. M. Pei (with prodding from former Secretary of State Henry Kissinger), C-100, as the group is called, is, according to its website, a "nonpartisan leadership organization of prominent Chinese Americans in business, government, academia, and the arts." It seeks to promote Chinese American participation in American life and serve as a constructive bridge between the United States and China—noble goals, indeed, given that we're talking about the world's two greatest powers.

The most prominent Chinese Americans who have been or are members include the aforementioned Pei, famed cellist Yo-Yo Ma, conceptual artist Maya Lin, Yahoo! founder Jerry Yang, Olympic ice-skater Michelle Kwan, and former Washington State governor and ambassador to China Gary Locke. A friend or two of mine are members, too, but of a slightly lower public profile. It is by no means false humility for me to state that

I am nowhere near their superstardom. Two cursory brushes I had with C-100 in its earlier days illustrate the stark class differences between me and this group.

Our first encounter was at C-100's national conference, held in the San Francisco Bay Area in the early 1990s, when I was freelancing for *Asian Week*. At a press conference featuring a People's Republic of China official, I asked an innocuous, noncontroversial question. Before he could respond, a C-100 leader stepped forward and said that the China official had to be somewhere else. Huh? We had only been in session for a short time. Why such an abrupt ending? The organizer didn't elaborate, and we plebeian journalists were practically shoved out the door.

The overly protective C-100 leader was Shirley Young, who at the time was a high marketing executive with General Motors. Her intervention was puzzling. Why had she suddenly ended the session? It wasn't as though my question were so penetrating, so irritatingly invasive that the Chinese official would feel attacked. It was as though Young wanted to emulate what the Chinese government is famous for—its suppression of a free press. I wondered: Were we in America or China?

My second encounter was maybe ten years later, in September 2001, in New York City. I happened to be on my way home to the Bay Area after a trip to South Africa, where I had attended a United Nations Conference on Racism as part of a delegation (as a freelance writer) from a San Francisco civil rights organization, Project Change. Returning to America, I stopped in the New York metropolitan area to see my son, who had just begun college in upstate New York, and to visit Joyce's family in New Jersey. Prior to my South Africa trip, I had been in email contact with Henry S. Tang, the C-100 director, who knew my writings. He wondered whether I might do some writing for the organization on an unnamed project. I told Tang, an investment banker, that I'd be in his area in September. Pleased to hear that, he invited me to lunch at C-100's office on Fifth Avenue in Manhattan's upscale office and shopping district. As we ate high-quality Chinese takeout, we talked about the writing project in vague terms. I told him that I was interested and available, depending, of course, on a more precise plan for my services. I left without a firm resolution and headed back to New Jersey.

The memory of that day, September 10, 2001, is seared into my brain as being a glorious late summer day in New York City. Early the next morning, September 11, another bright, clear day, my brother-in-law Larry Fridkis drove me from the Princeton area to JFK International Airport in Queens, New York, about a ninety-minute drive. My United Airlines flight destined for San Francisco took off around eight o'clock. The plane was half empty. Happy to be headed home, I was relaxed, daydreaming about being with my family again and reflecting fondly on my South Africa trip, seeing my son, and meeting with Tang.

My carefree thoughts were quickly interrupted by a stunning announcement from the pilot, who said, in a numbing monotone, that we were being diverted to land in Indianapolis. Indianapolis? He didn't say why. No longer relaxed, fellow passengers and I reached for our cell phones to see whether we could glean any information about why our flight was being cut short, or to call loved ones. Alas, my cell phone's battery was dead. I borrowed someone's cell phone to tell Joyce of my plane's diversion. She told me about the horrifying World Trade Center disaster that occurred about forty-five minutes after my plane had taken off. My brother-in-law Larry, having learned of a plane crashing into one of the two towers, had awakened her in California to ask what my flight number was. He was concerned that the plane I was on might have been one of those hijacked. Still with no official announcement from our cockpit, we passengers didn't panic, but our anxiety levels rose as we faced grave uncertainty.

A side note on 9/11 and whatever higher being was looking after me: For many years, Joyce, hating flying, took a cross-country Amtrak train to visit her family, while I flew. For my return home, I'd normally fly out of Newark International Airport on a United flight that took off in the morning—that is, most likely the same flight, United #93, that was hijacked and crashed near Shanksville, Pennsylvania. Had my scheduled flight home from the New York area that fateful day not been part of a longer flight plan—Johannesburg, South Africa, to New York City to San Francisco—I probably would've been on United #93.

Upon landing in Indianapolis, we passengers scattered around the airport, unsure of what to do next. Over the intercom, we heard that Indianapolis Protestant churches were dispatching volunteers to help us— offering food, lodging, or whatever. That, I thought, was a most generous gesture. Tempted by that offer, I instead searched for a motel on my own and took a taxicab in what turned out to be a long trip that cost me about $50. No matter—at least I had a place to rest, get something to eat (at a Chinese restaurant!), and figure out how to get home.

My next call to Joyce yielded a rescue plan. My niece Allison, the oldest daughter of my sister Lai Wah, happened to be temporarily working for her insurance company employer in a Chicago suburb. Allison volunteered to drive to Indianapolis, a two-plus-hour trip, to get me, and I'd bunk with her in the company apartment until I could get a flight home. After days of searching for a flight during those maddening days, I finally got home four days later. And I never reconnected with C-100 on that proposed writing gig.

Not long after that, someone in the know told me that C-100 wanted the famous Public Broadcasting System (PBS) TV journalist and commentator Bill Moyers to do a documentary about the coming of age of Chinese America, for which C-100 would provide seed funds. So that was the unnamed project that Tang had been talking to me about! That happened to have been my best chance to be associated with Moyers's film, which generated a lot of buzz among Asian American activists and scholars.

Speaking of Moyers, before I put two and two together, and ignorant of the C-100 connection, I had sought out a chance to meet him and, frankly, hustle him to be part of that documentary. I've long admired his work. He and I even share the Peace Corps oeuvre, he having been a top administrator in the agency's earliest days, at about the same time as my service in the Philippines. The occasion of my blatant begging was some time in 2002, after my first book, *Yellow Journalist: Dispatches from Asian America*, had been published, and before his PBS documentary, *Becoming American: The Chinese Experience*, had aired in 2003. A friend who was an informal consultant on this project told me that he had suggested me to Moyers's producers as a possible interviewee. That caught my attention, of course, if for no other reason than to stroke my tender ego. I would've loved to have been part of a Moyers documentary. And I thought that I was more than "qualified" in the sense that I had been writing about Chinese America and Asian America for a long time.

Moyers and his people held a reception in San Francisco to meet Chinese Americans and to promote their future show. With a combination of hope and anxiety, I attended. I brought along a copy of *Yellow Journalist* that, if given the opportunity, I'd give to Moyers himself as a way of impressing him with my credentials. In your typical conference cocktail party setting, I wandered around, searching out the man. I saw him surrounded by supplicants like me. At the right moment, I approached him, introduced myself, and handed him my book. His demeanor wasn't unfriendly but stiff, rather formal, and unsmiling. He took the book and tucked it under one armpit. That face-to-face lasted barely a minute, as others sought the star journalist's attention too. Shortly thereafter, as I worked my way around the room, chatting with folks I knew, I noticed my book sitting on a chair lining a wall, nowhere near Moyers. I retrieved it with the intent of finding him again to give it back to him, which I did. Stiffly, he took it, again tucking it under his arm, and walked away without a word.

Really, what more could I expect? I was a nobody to him, and he was probably sick of getting solicited by unknowns seeking a piece of his reflected glory. He might have remembered that someone had mentioned me as a possibility for his documentary, but I never heard a word from him or his people.

Somewhere along the way, I'd heard the C-100 leader assert something honest but distressing—that it's best if a prominent white guy like Moyers front a documentary about Chinese Americans rather than a yellow person because it's easier to raise big bucks and catch more of majority-white America's attention. As sad as that is from a yellow perspective, I can't say that's untrue. By the way, his documentary did a fine job of telling the Chinese American story through many credible, strong, informed Chinese American voices. I merely had hurt feelings because mine wasn't included.

My disappointment says more about me than it does about Moyers, and it isn't necessarily flattering. Was I groveling for a wee bit of TV fame? In practically begging to gain Moyers's attention, was I exhibiting a psychological condition rooted in white supremacy, seeking the great white man's validation?

There's a bigger picture to consider here having to do with who tells our stories. It's a simple question without a simple answer. In old-school print journalism, your garden-variety reporter told all kinds of stories, many having nothing to do on the surface with race or ethnicity. When I started, white people, mostly men, were the reporters and editors, so they were the only ones, ipso facto, telling stories, even those that inherently had racial and ethnic implications. Now, many more non-white and female reporters and editors tell all sorts of stories, including ones with race and gender at their core.

Nonetheless, a strong argument can be made that we historically marginalized Americans have something important to say about ourselves, our communities, our otherness that should enlighten the white intellectual cognoscenti to help us find a place of belonging in America. Yet some of us (yes, myself included) somehow feel the need for validation from well-established white gatekeepers like Moyers, editors of elite news organizations, and academics, many of them white men with Ivy League credentials, ensconced in the Boston–New York–Washington, D.C., golden triangle.

Only in recent years, since I retired, are Chinese American and Asian American voices being heard more than ever in the broad cultural world, and a tiny—very tiny—bit in the political world. From the 1970s through the early twenty-first century, I was one of those voices in the San Francisco Bay Area, as well as a small voice nationally among Asian Americans. Still, it nags at me that I might have been blocked from greater opportunities by a combination of bad timing, institutional racism, and my own ineptitude at self-promotion.

28

LONELY DOWNSIZE

My *Tribune* columns caught the attention of someone at *NewsHour with Jim Lehrer* on the Public Broadcasting System (PBS) in 1995. Out of the blue, a producer at that well-respected TV news show invited me to be an occasional guest commentator. I, of course, was honored to be asked. My local profile would go national, a rarity for a Chinese American print journalist at that time. On an irregular basis, sometimes once every few weeks, sometimes monthly, I appeared with columnists or editorial-page editors from newspapers from other regions to talk about big issues of the day. I had appeared periodically on local TV and radio news shows, but PBS was the Major League of TV news. For my appearances, I drove to a San Francisco local TV news studio to connect with the Washington, D.C., area–based show that aired in the mid-afternoon, California time.

When it was my turn, a producer called a few days in advance to inform me of possible topics that Lehrer would ask us about. I can't honestly say that I was always fully prepared, as some topics weren't in areas I usually wrote about. That meant some last-minute research. At times, this unfamiliarity made me uncomfortable on air (a friend told me I should've been more relaxed), but I did my best to explicate on the spot. At other times, I felt quite at ease, such as when I informed Lehrer on a point I had earlier made to Bob Maynard and Nancy Hicks: that American civil rights issues were more colorful than Black-and-white, at least in California and other parts of the western United States.

This gig, which ended after a year, brought me attention I never got in the Bay Area alone. A few attendees at the 1996 Democratic National Convention in Chicago, when they saw me strolling around,[1] told me that they enjoyed seeing me on PBS. I even got marketing calls from financial planners, who apparently sought new clients by watching high-end TV news shows. I didn't respond. *Tribune* leaders, however, weren't impressed with me being on *NewsHour*. They never said a word to me about it. One would think that they'd feel good about one of their staff members talking news on a national newscast, with the name of their newspaper superimposed under his image. Their silence told me that I was in disfavor.

The one year I appeared on PBS, spanning parts of 1995 and 1996, happened to be my toughest time at the *Tribune*. Maynard's control of the *Tribune* had ended in 1992. He had become ill, and he had to sell his drowning paper. William Dean Singleton, who owned a Texas-based newspaper chain, MediaNews Group, was the buyer. His claim to newspaper fame was as a cost-cutter, not as a courageous journalistic giant. That reputation was ominous for us Maynard Tribbies, who enjoyed sympathetic, if embattled, leadership. The new ownership installed new top editors, among them C. David Burgin, a tough guy who had been editor (twice) of the *San Francisco Examiner* and other newspapers.

The new leaders did one symbolic thing that superficially assured *Tribune* readers that their interests would still be represented: In the first issue under new ownership, they published a full-page marketing photograph of Mary Ellen Butler, the editorial-page editor under Maynard; Brenda Payton, like me, a high-profile columnist whose piercing, funny, and satiric writings were must-reads; and me. The headline said something like "Nothing is changing," an unsubtle racial message to an Oakland that had a large non-white readership. That ad photo told these readers that the paper's editorial-page staff of two African American women and one Chinese American man was still in place as "representative" voices.

The new management moved the news and advertising teams out of the iconic Tribune Tower complex to a low-rise nondescript building in Jack London Square, a mile away. Print-shop workers stayed in the tower's basement. Granted, our new space was more modern, but it was bland in your typical white-collar office way, totally lacking in the lived-in, creaky-floor atmospherics of the old newsroom.

For the first two years of this new relationship, things didn't change all that much for me. I continued to write columns of my choice several times a week and an editorial, the unsigned views of the newspaper owners. Nonetheless, I was wary of the new editors, all of them white men who had no connection to Oakland. It was well known among the Maynard Tribbies the new editor-in-chief Burgin resented Maynard's reign. Grapevine gossip was that Burgin dismissively scoffed at the Maynard legacy of racial-ethnic diversity.

Shortly after these non-Oakland white guys took over, I wrote a column that drew syrupy, insincere attention from one of them. My column was about Henry "Hank" Aaron, the Black baseball star of my Chinatown youth, commenting on a *Sports Illustrated* piece recalling the racist hatred aimed at Aaron for surpassing the career home-run record of the great Babe Ruth. On the morning my column appeared, this white-guy editor gushed to me about how he loved Aaron, too, his way of telling me that he thought that I was okay. I thanked him, holding back any sign I thought that he was a phony.

About two years into the new regime, in early 1995, Payton and I were summoned to a meeting with Burgin and the editorial-page editor who had replaced Butler, who had left the paper the year earlier. Butler's departure had devastated me. She was my friend and my shield. Once she was gone, we had no protection. During our grim meeting, Burgin and the new editorial-page editor tried to assert control over Payton and me, telling us to write only about local issues and people, not national and world matters, as we occasionally did. Both of us protested. I argued that most of my columns were local. Payton did the same. She became so angry that she said she was quitting. Later, they talked her out of it. I didn't issue a similar threat, but the meeting told me in no uncertain terms that my job was in danger. A dark cloud began hovering over me.

So began a year of agony. They got into my head. I decided to try to conform to what I thought would satisfy them, while not compromising my writing integrity. My strategy: Write more about local figures who did newsworthy things that fit into a left-progressive ideological frame. That was a win-win approach, I thought: Satisfy Burgin with a focus on local people and myself from a political perspective. By doing this, I figured that I could save myself from the Burgin guillotine.

In an email I got in March 1996 from the editorial-page editor, who said that he wanted to come to Oakland to talk with me on Friday afternoon, March 22 (he was based in Pleasanton, thirty miles to the southeast),[2] he didn't say why he wanted to meet. I thought little of it, but I should've been a lot more suspicious. This editor, whom I shall not dignify with a name, a beefy, unkempt middle-aged guy about my age, came to our new Oakland office with another guy, tall, younger, more muscular, without a title. We met in an office near the newsroom. It was three o'clock in the afternoon.

Uh-oh, I said to myself as the three of us sat down, I facing the two of them. Without any small talk, the editorial-page editor told me that I was being let go.

"Oh, so I'm being fired," I said. No, he said, I was being "downsized."[3]

He handed me a check equaling two weeks' pay and a standardized personnel sheet. I grabbed the papers, glared at them, and stomped out, headed back to my desk. A few colleagues looked toward me. Now shaken up, I loudly announced, with an appropriate profanity, that I had just been fired. I reached my desk in the corner as though in a fog. By now, the volume in the newsroom was beginning to rachet up. My phone rang. Someone wanted to make an appointment to pitch a column idea. Not possible, I said, without telling the caller why. Still foggy, detached from reality, I thought of making a business call, not one to my wife, family, or friends.

Suddenly, I felt a presence looming over me. I glanced back and up. It was the big muscular guy, who leaned down and whispered that it was time for me to go. Ah, he was the bouncer. Without a word, I arose; picked up a photo of my wife and son, a few notebooks, and my Rolodex; stuffed them into my backpack; and started walking out of the newsroom, trailed by the bouncer. The buzz now was quite cacophonous. I got into the elevator without the bouncer and exited the building.

My advice: Don't take a spontaneously called meeting with your boss on a Friday afternoon.

As I walked to the parking lot a block away, Chauncey Bailey, a reporter, chased after me. Bailey and I weren't close friends, but we respected one another. He had joined the *Tribune* in 1993 and told me that he liked my work. He walked with me to my car and got into the passenger seat. He said that he was sorry and offered to help in any way he could. I thanked him, but I was at a loss as to what I was going to do next. We said goodbye, and I drove home to tell my wife and phone family and friends.

I never connected with Bailey again. Eleven years later, in 2007, he was murdered in broad daylight on an Oakland street as he was walking to work. He had left the *Tribune* to be editor of the *Oakland Post*, a weekly devoted to covering the African American community. He had been working on a story about possible financial wrongdoing at a Black-owned Oakland bakery.

My firing shocked many people who read me regularly. Many Chinese Americans and Asian Americans in Oakland and the Bay Area who knew of my work or my reputation rallied to my cause. Within days, some asked to meet me to strategize about how I could get my job back. This initial reaction surprised me in the sense that I hadn't fully realized the impact my writing had had on so many people. I knew that some readers either liked or hated my work, but the emotions expressed by a lot of people in the days immediately after I lost my job lifted my spirits and transported me to unknown territory. Several more spontaneous, loosely organized meetings took place at my house. The most energized among my supporters suggested a legal-defense fund. They also got a meeting with *Tribune* management to demand my reinstatement. As passionate as they were on my behalf, I didn't get my job back.

Meanwhile, as word continued to trickle out, local reporters, both print and TV from the English-language mainstream and Chinese dailies, asked me for interviews. I wanted to tell my story and was encouraged that my former colleagues believed that what had happened to me deserved attention from them. It's not often that a fired journalist gets this kind of media coverage.

One such piece carried the headline, "Writer's firing angers *Tribune* readers."[4] It said that "community outrage" over my firing "[wa]s still pouring into" the *Tribune*: "The Asian American community in particular is going to war with the *Tribune*—spearheading subscription cancellation and letter-writing campaigns to get Wong reinstated." One Chinese American activist called me "a treasure for Oakland." Another wrote to editor Burgin that "the dismissal of one of the nation's most prominent Asian American journalists is deeply troubling." Yet another called me "one of the few really important figures in the Asian American journalistic community." Even local political figures whom I had either critiqued or satirized said nice things about me. Saying that he was "frankly stunned" by my firing, Don Perata, a former Alameda County supervisor, said, "Bill had a real good feel for the community, and I think his work over time provided a corpus of real good civic criticism." Former Oakland City Council member Marge Gibson-Haskell said that I "frequently got into corners of the community that didn't get picked up by other people."

An item about my firing even appeared in the *Columbia Journalism Review*, which caught the attention of Norman Pearlstine, who at the time was editor-in-chief of Time Inc. I had met Pearlstine twenty-five years earlier, when both of us were *Wall Street Journal* reporters, he in Detroit, I in Cleveland. He occasionally came to Cleveland, and we played tennis with other *Journal* reporters. He was a friendly, congenial rising star who later became skilled in navigating the treacherous elite journalism leadership world. After he learned of my firing, he offered to introduce me to editors at any of the New York–based Time Inc. properties. I appreciated that gesture, but I wanted to stay in Bay Area journalism.

Approximately ten days after my firing, my fans of all racial and ethnic backgrounds rallied on my behalf in front of the *Tribune* office. About 150 protesters marched in a light rain, including someone in a wheelchair, demanding that the *Tribune* rehire me. Prominent Bay Area leaders spoke at the rally, including a San Francisco labor leader, and Jerry Brown, who at the time lived in Oakland but was between political offices.[5]

I was truly heartened by this vociferous public demonstration, confirming that my columns had touched a wide range of people. Like the news coverage, a public outpouring of support from readers was highly unusual for a booted-out local journalist. Although I had little direct contact with my suddenly former *Tribune* colleagues, I heard that the newsroom spontaneously chanted, "We want Bill" after my departure. Later, someone created and distributed "Where is Bill Wong?" desk tent signs, an act that warmed my soul.

In the weeks following, I inquired about opportunities at the four other local major newspapers: *San Francisco Chronicle, San Francisco Ex-*

aminer, *Contra Costa Times*, and the *San Jose Mercury News*. I either talked on the phone or met face-to-face with senior editors, all white men. I thought that my past performance and the fact I had many readers would persuade one of them to hire me. Being the first Chinese American/Asian American print journalist commentator in a region that was ground zero for Yellow America and that was increasingly multicultural was a bonus. How delusional of me. The editors were cordial, but none offered me a full-time gig. The best offer I got was a biweekly column for the *Examiner* at $150 per column, double what the *Examiner* usually paid a freelance writer. I guess that was a tribute, low ball as it was, to my reputation. Later, I freelanced an occasional column for the *Chronicle* for a little more money per piece.

Why couldn't I get a permanent, full-time writing job at those local papers? That remains a mystery. This unfortunate outcome was like a swift uppercut after my firing's painful gut punch. Maybe I was just too old, in my mid-fifties, a terrible time to resuscitate one's career. Another factor could have been the editors' insouciance to my selling point of being a pioneering Asian American voice when our region was becoming increasingly multicultural.

I managed to patch together other freelance writing gigs, mostly nonjournalistic, and one-shot "adjunct" journalism teaching. I was never able to earn what I did at the *Tribune*, which wasn't all that much to begin with. I was among the highest-paid writers, but *Tribune* salaries under MediaNews Group were embarrassingly low. I also worked for a year as a writer for Larry Tramutola, a well-known Oakland-based political consultant who had been one of my sources when I was at the *Tribune*. He was good enough to pay me approximately what I had been making at the *Tribune*, a financial lifeline when I really needed one.

Five years after my firing, I curated my Asian American writings into a book, *Yellow Journalist: Dispatches from Asian America*, published by Temple University Press. It won positive reviews from a few mainstream newspapers and Asian American publications. None of the Bay Area newspapers that didn't offer me a job reviewed *Yellow Journalist*, but two Washington State papers, the *Seattle Times* and *Seattle Post-Intelligencer*, did so in conjunction with a reading I gave at Elliott Bay Book Co. in Seattle in July 2001. The *Times* reviewer said, "More than a primer on recent issues, 'Yellow Journalist' is a distillation of what it means to be Asian American and should be required reading in classrooms and newsrooms across the country." *Post-Intelligencer* said, "And in 'Yellow Journalist,' he has given us a highly readable American archive that samples three decades of reporting from a man with an unpredictable, inquiring mind." *Asian Week*'s reviewers cited the lead essay in *Yellow Journalist*, about my growing up in Oakland's Chinatown, and called it "a classic of its kind—informative, funny, heart-rending and sad. It's a striking example of the kind of journalism Wong is capable of achieving. It's the kind of journalism he should have an opportunity to do more of in the future."

In 2004, I authored *Images of America: Oakland's Chinatown*, a photo history of my 'hood published by Arcadia Publishing Co. Three years later, I co-authored another Arcadia photo-history book, *Images of America: Angel Island*. The best contract writing job I got was with the Annie E. Casey Foundation, a well-regarded Baltimore-based progressive nonprofit organization with a mission to help low-income children and families. Some of my Casey writing was included in the foundation's publications distributed to its clients. In 2008, I slid happily into retirement.

My inability to get another full-time newspaper writing job irked me for the longest time. I wondered why Mike Barnicle had no problem getting a job when he got canned. A few years younger than I, Barnicle was a star *Boston Globe* columnist who was a colleague of sorts, since the two of us sometimes appeared on the same *NewsHour* segment, sharing a screen from studios thousands of miles apart. What I'm about to say isn't at all personal against Barnicle—from what I can tell, he's a smart, thoughtful commentator and a sharp, insightful writer, a good storyteller. What I'm about to describe exemplifies a subliminal institutional racism that afflicted me, not him.

In 1998, the *Globe* forced Barnicle to resign[6] for allegedly plagiarizing and making stuff up,[7] huge no-no's in journalism. A star columnist doing bad things generated much talk in elite journalism circles. Shortly thereafter, he became a columnist for the *New York Daily News* and *Boston Herald*. As if that weren't sufficient, he was a high-profile commentator on the *Morning Joe* show on MSNBC, the left-leaning cable news channel, exchanging pithy political sound bites, witty bon mots, and inside-baseball chatter with the host Joe Scarborough, a former Florida Republican congressional representative.

How was Barnicle able to land good journalism jobs after his bad behavior while I couldn't when I had done nothing remotely close to what he had? I believe that one reason is he's a white guy who's a better self-promoter than I am. The most important reason, however, is he's super well connected, a friend and chronicler of the late U.S. Senator Ted Kennedy of the famous Kennedy clan, America's political royal family, and a buddy of John Kerry, the former Vietnam War hero, U.S. senator, Democratic presidential candidate, and senior official with the Biden administration. Christopher J. Dodd, a former Democratic senator from Connecticut, is also a friend of Barnicle.[8] It's white-guy cronyism writ large. It doesn't seem to matter whether you've taken someone else's writings without crediting the original source or written fiction under the guise of facts, as long as you're chummy with powerful Massachusetts political royalty. It probably doesn't hurt if your wife, Anne Finucane, happens to have been the highest-ranking woman in Bank of America's executive suite.[9] Barnicle and his wife apparently have such an exalted social status that they were among the hundreds of elite guests at a Joe Biden presidential state dinner honoring French President Emmanuel Macron on December 1, 2022.[10]

I know, woe is me, but still, had I had Barnicle's network (and been a white guy), I probably would've landed a good newspaper job after my *Tribune* firing. When I didn't, I decided to sue the *Tribune* in 1997 for age and race discrimination. My case was tossed out before it got to first base, probably because I didn't have paper proof that the offending editors had fired me because they thought that I was too old or they didn't like me because of my race or political views. An interesting sidenote is the high-powered Oakland law firm representing the *Tribune* used a Black woman as its lead attorney in my case.

Did my racial identity and/or my frequent writing about Chinese America and Asian America help or hurt my career? That question is knotty, convoluted, and difficult to grasp logically and rationally. I don't really know. What I do know is that I have absolutely no regrets that I spent part of my journalism life writing about an aspect of American life—Yellow America—that few, if any, other mainstream journalists bothered to examine at the time I was doing it.

29

SUPPORTIVE HOMEFRONT

It's not as if I hadn't known I was in trouble with my *Tribune* editors. I just hadn't realized how much trouble I was in, or I feared confronting reality. The suddenness of my firing with a small last paycheck left me deeply concerned about our household's immediate financial future. This situation put a heavier burden on Joyce. We were in our twenty-sixth year of marriage with a young teenage son. Until that point, we had been each other's support system. Now, I was of no support, and we had no backup plan.

Since our marriage in 1968, both of us have either had jobs or been going to school. Her earnings, however, reflected her educational status, which had been slower developing than mine. When she joined the Peace Corps in 1966 at the age of twenty-one, she hadn't yet attended college. She began to rectify that educational shortfall when I was at Columbia. She took classes at Hunter College in New York and then at Cleveland State University when we moved to Ohio for my *Wall Street Journal* job. After my transfer to the *Journal*'s San Francisco bureau, Joyce enrolled at Cal Berkeley, my alma mater, where, in 1974, she got her B.A. degree, majoring in anthropology and joining Phi Beta Kappa too. She went on to graduate studies in education at Cal, San Francisco State University, and San Jose State University, eventually obtaining an M.A. degree in education. She then started a doctorate in education program but didn't continue.

Her work life has been eclectic—a job-skills instructor, a baker, executive director for several small Oakland arts organizations, and a city of Oakland employee on two different occasions, the last as director of the Oakland Public Library's adult-literacy program. She's also been on the boards of many arts and youth-serving nonprofit organizations. At the time of my firing, she wasn't quite on a full-time basis with the city of Oakland. Shortly thereafter, she gained full-time status, increasing her compensation and retirement benefits and thus stabilizing our household finances.

We had waited a while to have a child. I've joked that it was because we were slow learners about the sex thing. In truth, we were idealistically self-righteous in our early years together, and Joyce wanted a career beyond the secretarial realm. Recall that 1968, the year we married, was bizarrely explosive in terms of political, social, and cultural movements. We had just returned from Peace Corps service and were frankly forlorn about the country we were coming back to. We thought, "Do we really want to bring a child into this crazy world?"

Our idealistic arrogance faded, but when we actively sought to have a baby, Joyce discovered fertility problems. Five years of patient, caring treatment from Kaiser Permanente facilitated the birth in late 1982 of a boy we named Sam, after Pop. I was forty-one, Joyce thirty-eight. We, of course, thought of him as a miracle. Sam's mixed racial heritage was obvious, but not a big deal. Oakland and the urban Bay Area are somewhat accustomed to racial and cultural diversity. For our extended families, Sam being *hapa* (half white, half Asian) also wasn't an issue.

In early 1983, the East-West Center at the University of Hawaii granted me a three-month journalism fellowship. An honor, for sure, yet I was conflicted because Sam had been born only months earlier. Should I go alone or take Joyce and baby Sam with me? After checking with fellowship officials, I decided to take them with me for two months in Honolulu and one month in Asia (Japan, Taiwan, Hong Kong, the Philippines, Singapore), a total of about twenty thousand miles of travel that Sam has no memories of and a great passport as an infant.

Once back in Oakland, I started reading to him when he was six months old. He sat quietly and was attentive, soaking in the sound of my voice. At Joyce's direction, evoking her own New Jersey childhood, Sam learned how to ice-skate when he was three. This sport led to youth ice hockey. He also played soccer and T-ball and tried gymnastics. I tossed balls with him and showed him how to place-kick a small football. A big turning point came when, at age ten, he saw kids from Destiny Arts Center, a new Oakland youth martial-arts program, on stage at a big Oakland festival, for which Joyce was coordinator of the kids' program. He was intrigued, so Joyce took him to Destiny Arts Center, where he began training regularly. He met children of many racial and socioeconomic backgrounds, and he's grown friendships with them.

Joyce became so fascinated by his martial-arts training that she, at forty-nine, started the practice herself. Into her late seventies until she died of pancreatic cancer in early 2023, she practiced and taught Kajukenbo, a Hawaii-based form that blends Chinese, Korean, Japanese, and Filipino martial arts as well as self-defense. She and Sam have earned their black belts. Here's another little irony in my life: I'm the one from a culture that venerates the martial arts, but it's my wife of white European heritage and my half-Chinese half-white son who are or have been martial-arts practitioners, while I wouldn't know a horse stance from, well, a horse.

One more wonderful attribute of Joyce's: She was a bridge of sorts between my sisters and me. Not that I've been at odds with my sisters, but it's just that often, Joyce was much more socially convivial with them than I am, and that enriched our family relationships.

Epilogue

ARE WE THERE YET?

In Pop's sixty-five or so years on Earth, he traveled at least sixty-three thousand miles on nine voyages between China and Oakland. His American travels were limited to car, ferry, and train trips to places like San Francisco, Marysville, Stockton, Reno, and the like, a few thousand more miles. In my eight-plus decades of life, I've traveled close to a half million miles, throughout California to various states, and to Mexico, Asia, South Africa, Israel, and Europe.

The difference between the physical distances we each traveled reflects the circumstances of our lives, Pop's having been much more constricted than mine. The Chinese exclusion law, in effect for most of his life, limited his mobility. He couldn't work and live outside Chinatown until after World War II, when restrictions began to ease for us yellow folks. Chinatown provided for all his American needs—work, shelter, and social and family life. China filled similar needs and more—a childhood, some schooling, wives, children, and work.

Chinatown was my bubble, too, but only from birth to my early teens. Mobility, a very American thing, was a big factor in me growing culturally apart from Pop, who moved our housing arrangements out of Chinatown when I was seven years old but kept our Chinatown ties intact with our restaurant. Going to an almost all-white high school exposed me to life outside Chinatown in ways that Pop never experienced. By then, English was my lingua franca, not the *Hoisan-wa* that was native to both of us.

I straddled Chinatown and the outside white world during most of my teen years. After Pop died, when I had just turned twenty, and into adulthood, I was more often in the white world than in Chinatown. My chosen career, print journalism, was in the white world. Peace Corps service in the Philippines in my twenties was analogous to a puzzle wrapped in a mystery: a white Peace Corps culture inside a mixed up Asian-European-American culture that was partially anti-Chinese.

More than the wide gap in the physical distances we each traveled, our joint and then separate cultural journeys defined our father-son relationship as a kind of moveable feast (and occasional famine). He had China, off and on, for a third of his life and Chinatown for the other two-thirds. I had Chinatown for a quarter of my life and then mainstream America (white with a smidge of other colors and the Philippines) for the rest, with a para life in a Yellow America, a misty, tiny tributary to the roaring, mostly white mainstream.

Pop and I, of course, shared being ethnic Chinese, but our other identities were more distinct from one another. Pop never had the kind of cultural or national identity confusion that has animated most of my life. He was Chinese, period. During his years in Oakland, he never questioned his ethnic or national identity, Chinese, even though he spent more time in America than in China, presumably as a U.S. citizen since, when he first came, he was classified by U.S. immigration as a "son of a native," thus a legal entrant despite using partially fake papers. It was hardly his fault he didn't identify as an American. Thank you, Chinese Exclusion Act.

How would Pop feel about how China has evolved since his death in 1961, when it was still convulsing from the throes of the Communist revolution? The destructive Cultural Revolution hadn't happened yet. Since the late 1970s, however, China has taken off economically. Two decades and counting into the twenty-first century, it's the world's second-largest economy and could surpass America as number one if it can overcome a noticeable decline in the middle of the third decade of the current century. Politically, it remains tightly controlled by the Communist Party, but millions of Chinese have risen out of poverty into the middle and upper middle classes. There are now quite a few Chinese billionaires too. Is that a Communist thing?

These days, China's influence is felt all over the planet as it develops less robust countries while extracting valuable elemental resources to use in its world-class role as manufacturer of all manner of things for much of the planet's consumption. More than its economic resurgence, China's ascension since World War II signifies a huge reclamation from the international humiliation that began in the 1840s with its Opium War defeat by Great Britain. As much as Western democracies cringe at the Communist Party's control over the world's second most populous nation, the regime has restored China's pride and power that unsettle and threaten the so-called free world (principally, America and the European Union). China's renaissance is truly one of the Big Stories of our time.

I think that Pop would be proud of and perplexed by China today. He hated the Communists, but he loved his homeland, even in its squalor. He'd like that it's strong now, and he might not care its people don't have the kinds of freedoms (voting, speech, press, assembly, mobility) we Americans take for granted. Those concepts were never part of his China life and mostly unfulfilled ideas until much later in his Oakland life, if then.

Unlike Pop, I've had second—and third, and fourth, and on and on—thoughts about my identities. For most of my adult life, I have been searching for them, seeking an answer to which ones I truly am. To state the obvious, each of us human beings has multiple identities that we engage singularly or simultaneously and at different stages of our lives. A racial-ethnic identity has long been a high priority for so-called minorities in America. It has been for me. For my first dozen years, I thought that the universe was Chinatown. While it wasn't an exclusively Chinese enclave since people of other ethnicities and colors were always around in the first twenty years of my life, I felt warmly covered in a big yellow blanket, safe and secure with my family and other Chinatown denizens.

Does Chinatown translate to Chinese? Yes and no. Historically, American Chinatowns like Oakland's have been refuges for people of Chinese descent for two reasons: racism and culture. From the beginning of Chinese coming to America, there has been overt racism against my kind. Chinatowns were our refuge. Explicit racism has gradually eased to where some of us can feel that we finally belong, that we are "equal," sort of. During the coronavirus pandemic, however, our feeling of belonging was painfully shaken by many expressions of hate. Some of us have been forced to ask, "Do we really belong here in America? If not here, then where since so many of us know no other 'home'?"

I consider Chinatown to be a place *and* a state of mind. In the decades Pop and I were in Chinatown, it was like a Cantonese village transplanted on American soil. Different Cantonese clans from rural and urban settings lived, worked, and played together; competed against one another; and sometimes fought one another. It was a place of familiarity, comfort, and sharing, a true community. One difference prevented it from it being an exact China transplant: Chinatown was surrounded by dominant white America, which was officially hostile for almost a century after the first waves of Chinese immigrants and whose influence was inevitable on the generation after the immigrants, my generation and beyond.

Assimilation is a dirty word to some in non-white America. According to one perspective, if you are Black, brown, yellow, and shades in between, assimilation means that you've turned white. Recall the troll's description of me ("overripe banana," yellow outside, white inside) or the barb hurled at me by an African American female journalist ("honorary white"). There is irony here too: Many of those powerful white men debating in Congress on whether to pass a law banning Chinese laborers argued that Chinese people were "unassimilable." Well, guess what? I am one person of Chinese descent assimilated to America, and there are many more like me.

Some in my ethnic community might think less of me for having assimilated. Did I really have a choice? Should I have remained in Chinatown, inherited the restaurant, married a Chinese woman, had Chinese American children, and continued speaking *Hoisan-wa* as my primary language? If only. Taking to the English language wasn't a conscious decision of mine. I was only five years old. It happened, starting in kindergarten, as did my growing affinity for reading English-language publications, listening to English-language songs and radio shows, watching English-language TV and movies, and learning how to write English words to the extent that I made a living at it. My Chinatown bubble wasn't impenetrable; its walls were porously thin and couldn't block outside cultural forces.

I must again bring up the concepts of time and place. I was born in the vibrant San Francisco Bay Area a few months before the Japanese attack on Pearl Harbor. My formative teen years were during the somnambulant 1950s, and my college years in the late 1950s and early 1960s preceded the thunderously tumultuous mid- to late 1960s, when all sorts of political and cultural hell broke loose. That happened to be when I was far away in the Philippines, serving a peaceful mission while other American young men—many of them not of their own free will—were fighting and killing people who looked somewhat like me in countries just to the northwest.

It took me a while to catch up on what was happening in America after I returned from overseas in 1968. In the early 1970s, when I finally got back to the Bay Area, I learned about the young Asian American movement, which facilitated the search for my identities. Now, early in my ninth decade, have I found them? I thought that I might in the Philippines, Hong Kong, Taiwan, Pop's home in Hoisan, and such Chinese cities as Guangzhou, Shanghai, Hangzhou, Xi'an, and Beijing. If anything, after brief and long visits to all those places, I was as confused as I'd ever been.

In May 1998, the Overseas Chinese Office of the Guangzhou Municipal Government, via the Chinese consulate in San Francisco, invited me to join other Chinese American journalists for a two-week tour in late October and early November.[1] The tour's purpose was vague—to observe social and development trends in China over the twenty years (1978–1998) of Premier Deng Xiaoping's market-oriented economic reforms. After hearing nothing for months, I learned that the trip's timing and itinerary had changed because severe flooding along the Yangtze River had made the original plan undoable. Now, the trip would be in the first two weeks of December, and we'd visit Guangzhou, Xi'an, Hangzhou, and Shanghai.

Clueless as to why, I was nonetheless pleased to be invited. My guess is that someone in the Chinese consulate in San Francisco had been reading my Chinese American–themed columns. It turns out I was an outlier, the only American-born Chinese in the group. The seven others (five men, two women) had been born in China, Taiwan, or Hong Kong. They worked in New York, Australia, Singapore, and Canada. Their default spoken language was Mandarin or Cantonese; mine was English, which was secondary or tertiary to my traveling companions.

This language situation almost ruined this trip for me. Despite having a translator, I felt frustrated from the get-go. During our travels to various sites and at meals, my companions spoke Mandarin. Being left out of the social chatter, I was mostly mute. My translator, a nice young woman, tried to clue me in, but her English was limited, and she had other duties. For more than a week, I barely endured. At one point, I thought of bailing.

What saved the trip for me was Mr. Cheng (I never caught his first name). On the ninth day, as we were at the Xi'an airport headed for Hangzhou, Mr. Cheng approached me and chatted me up . . . in English! That surprised and pleased me. Finally, someone was engaging me in sustained conversation in a language I spoke! For the remaining five days, Mr. Cheng was my constant companion. He joked with the translator assigned to me that he was doing her job. My guess is that my travel mates, knowing my discomfort, chose among themselves someone to engage me in English, and Mr. Cheng drew the short straw. I didn't care how this happened; I was at last "included" (somewhat).

Five years older than I, Mr. Cheng had been born in Nanjing and moved to Hainan island, then to Taiwan, before coming to America in 1964, in his late twenties. He worked for a New York Chinese-language radio station and wrote for news outlets in Hong Kong and Taiwan. His accented English was excellent. I enjoyed talking with him about China, U.S.-China relations, Chinese and American literature and philosophy, New York Chinatown politics, the Dalai Lama, and human rights in China.

At trip's end, I was so happy to be back in America. If I had any doubts about my national identity, this little episode told me for certain that I am an American, whether I like it or not. Here was the starkest case of challenging my self-image about who I am—Chinese? American? Which parts of me are Chinese, and which American? What exactly is an American? Is one's identity fundamentally tied to one's language and culture? What role does one's birthright play?

During my other Asia visits—the Philippines in the 1960s, when I was in my twenties; Japan, Taiwan, Hong Kong, Singapore, and the Philippines in the early 1980s, when I was in my forties; twice to Pop's

China village, in 1994, when I was in my fifties and in 2014, when I was in my early seventies—I felt this weird insider-outsider phenomenon and ultimately came away knowing that I am an American by nationality and this indefinable cultural mix of Chinatown and American. Yet at the same time, I wasn't sure—and in some ways, still am not—whether my broad cohort (Chinese Americans and Asian Americans) and I truly belong here in America or in our ancestral lands—or, in truth, neither place, as though we are in a yellow purgatory. It is indeed an underlying weird feeling of belonging and yet not belonging.

I asked earlier how Pop might feel about China today. That's a fair question for me too. I've long been fascinated with China because it's where Pop and Mom were born and grew into adolescence or young adulthood, and, thus, it is my ancestral homeland, not my actual one. Through English-language sources only (newspapers, magazines, books, television, movies, and a few Cal classes), I've learned a little about its history and cultures, the vastness that wasn't part of my Chinatown life. That old bugaboo—lack of proficiency in spoken and written Chinese—limits my intellectual quest to know more about China. This limitation means that I'm unable to read and understand Chinese-language sources that tell China's history, culture, arts, and philosophy, a huge learning deficit.

The American me can't say that I very much like how the Chinese Communist Party limits the rights of its people in terms of access to ideas, information, and history; suppresses dissenting views; and ill-treats Tibetans, Uighurs, and even Han Chinese (the majority dominant ethnic group) who live in "semiautonomous" Hong Kong. At the same time, I mustn't forget that throughout its almost five thousand years of civilization, China has never been a democracy, as the concept is defined in America and Europe. In other words, should today's China be judged on "Western" standards of social organization, civil liberties, civil rights, and rule of law, or should it be judged on its own governing values as played out over many millennia in which autocratic imperial, not democratic, rule was the norm?

Honoring Pop and Mom, the sentimental me wishes China well, even while I'd like for it to grant its people more freedom, rights, and liberties. I'm not here to tell China how to govern its 1.4 billion people, for who am I, really, other than a son of a man of low status who was born and reared there oh so long ago, when it was still an imperial state, an elegant-sounding autocracy? Chinese leaders must figure that one out themselves. And is it wacky of me to hope that these leaders will seek the consent of the governed since, as noted earlier, China has never been a society in which leaders reached down to common people to ask what they wanted as a collective body?

A simple question about China won't vanish from my conscience, however. How were the high-moral teachings of Confucius and his disciples, like my clan mate Zhu Xi, compatible with the authoritarian imperial system that governed it for so long, and could a full-blown updated and modernized revival of Confucianism (including giving women true equal rights) nudge the Communist Party to allow dissenting voices to share governing power to make China a more equitable society? Whatever the case, as a Chinatown Chinese American, I admire China's monumental comeback from the century of weakness and dishonor visited on it by Western colonial powers, especially the arrogant, racist British Empire.

I often muse about the Big Picture today of America and China. Their giant economies are intertwined in so many intricate ways that mere mortals like me can't fully grasp. It is difficult, for example, to intricately parse the codependency of the economic relationship with an inherent competitiveness, envy, resentment, and cross-cultural dissonance. The two mighty countries are wary and suspicious of each other, in benign and aggressive ways. China's growing power scares many American officials, while Chinese officials seem to dismiss America as a nation in decline. Hyper-nationalism on both sides is worrisome, indeed. I hope that leaders of America and China, each with excessive arsenals of nuclear weapons and ethnocentric and nationalistic egos that won't quit, don't box each other into a corner out of which deadly force will be the only option.

Back to a smaller picture: My guess is that among the five million of us who are fully or partially ethnic Chinese living in America, feelings related to our ancestral roots and our current homeland are all over the place, from none to ones fraught with pride, respect, division, confusion, paranoia, and a wishy-washy transnationalism. Those of us who are a generation or more removed from immigrant elders may have little or no interest in the history, current state, or future of U.S.-China relations. Those of us who are relatively fresh newcomers to America may feel mentally and emotionally torn between where we came from and where we are now.

Speaking of my American ethnic cohort, I'm acutely aware of sharp yet subtle cleavages among us. The Chinatown Cantonese—Pop's and my crew—are in a distinct minority of ethnic Chinese in America, which itself is only a portion of Asian America. My generation, the tail end of the exclusion-era group, is way past its prime. Many of us have children, grandchildren, and beyond spread throughout America and globally, doing all sorts of things, mostly good, I hope, some bad maybe, that are American, wholly or partially. Our China and American roots are rural and working-class humble, but fortunes grew for some of us into American middle and upper-middle class.

I marvel at the tremendous growth and complexity of the much larger Chinese immigrant crew who came to America after 1965, when U.S. immigration laws changed to allow in greater numbers. Generally, these post-1965 ethnic Chinese generations are better educated, wealthier, and more fearless than Pop and I were. Many came for college or graduate studies. Their China roots aren't restricted to Pop's struggling Pearl River Delta region. They come from all over a now-ascendant China and even different parts of the vast diaspora, including a thriving, democratic Taiwan. They speak Mandarin, Shanghainese, Fujianese, and other dialects, with fewer Cantonese and *Hoisan-wa* speakers, and English too. Most settled not in Chinatowns but rather in American suburbs and places that heretofore had never met people like them. Many are white-collar professionals, technocrats, and upscale entrepreneurs, not blue-collar restaurateurs, laundry workers, and grocers. In this "new" Chinese immigrant group, a considerable number are outstanding in science, medicine, technology, academia, the law, business, finance, media, the arts, and, yes, even politics and social-justice activism and sports. Some are at the other end of the socioeconomic spectrum, insecure about basic needs like adequate housing, health care, food, and companionship.

This much larger group has one psychological advantage mine didn't—hearts, minds, and souls unsullied by the racist negative effects of exclusion. Sometimes, those of us who pride ourselves in the old, exclusion-era Chinatowns will whine that these newer Chinese immigrants don't know a thing about what our forebears had to go through—the rancid racism, the lost opportunities. We'll further bleat that they don't care to learn about the dastardly exclusion era and how it oppressed our elders.

I readily concede that some of us old-timers might be jealous of the chances these younger generations have gotten to "make it" in America and how so many of them are aggressive, assertive, ambitious, and able to successfully navigate the often-confounding shoals of the white establishment a lot better than Pop's and my generations did. It certainly soothes me to know that, in general, these newer Chinese Americans (and others of Asian descent) reflect the amazing ascendance of China and other parts of east and south Asia after World War II and America's reckoning of sorts to its systemically racist past (which really isn't over yet). At the same time, we exclusion-era Chinatown Chinese know little of the psychic scars of the younger generations from surviving wars and disasters that my group never experienced.

When I go to Silicon Valley or to the San Gabriel Valley east of Los Angeles, I feel oddly disconnected because many, if not most, of the Chinese folks in those two areas speak Mandarin (English too), and the restaurants and shops cater to them. Yes, we may all look alike, but we Chinatown Cantonese Chinese Americans may feel inferior to this newer version, compounding old-country ways of rural Cantonese being regarded as lowly by the haughty Beijing and Shanghai people. This class division is succinctly captured by one of the highbrow characters in Kevin Kwan's popular book *Crazy Rich Asians*: "'Everyone knows those ABCs [American-born Chinese] are descended from all the peasants that were too stupid to survive in China!' Nadine cackled."[2]

Something else nags at me, a feeling of belonging or not belonging. I feel that I "belong" in the urban San Francisco Bay Area. That shouldn't be—and isn't—an extraordinary feeling, since it's my home turf. But I've heard many stories about Chinese Americans who didn't feel that they belonged where they were born or grew up after migrating to America because they and their families were alone or in such small numbers that they stood out and were in many cases easy targets for racist taunting and bullying. They didn't have a Chinatown bubble to protect them and make them feel that they belonged like I did in my youth.

Both times I went to Pop's village, however, I didn't feel that I belonged. When in the Philippines, I didn't feel that I belonged, even though I enjoyed certain privileges as an American, albeit one who didn't "look" American. When I traveled to other parts of China, Hong Kong, and Taiwan, I didn't feel that I belonged in those overwhelmingly ethnic Chinese places either, even though, facially, I resembled almost all the people I encountered. In the America I have seen or lived in outside the urban Bay Area, I have experienced varying degrees of belonging, of feeling comfortable or uncomfortable.

One of those uncomfortable times was in New Orleans, a city I had wanted to visit because of its intriguing reputation, history, culture, and food. Overall, the five days I spent there in 2012 with Joyce were wonderful, except for the outrageous Bourbon Street chaos and a curious incident at a diner in the touristy French Quarter. Joyce and I passed by this diner several times as we strolled through the district. One morning, having seen its U-shaped counters and alluring food offerings, I said, "Let's try it." The place was almost full, mostly with white tourists. The staff was all Black. I enjoyed watching the cooks crack eggs, turn over hash browns, and fry up bacon and sausage links. The smells were intoxicating, the kind breakfast joints exude in volume. The place was buzzing, with customer chatter and a loquacious behind-the-counter staff who was in raucous performance mode.

One guy took the lead, cracking jokes and greeting new customers. He spotted me and another Asian male customer and specially welcomed the two of us as "Mr. Miyagi," the Pat Morita character in the *Karate Kid* movies. In a thunderous voice, he urged other customers to greet us with an exaggerated bow and pressed hands to the heart, the prayer pose. He did this routine several times. Suddenly, I felt funny. I never imagined that I'd be the center of attention, with all eyes staring my way, nor did I ever think that I'd be the butt of a racially tinged joke. All Joyce and I wanted was a good breakfast. As it became clear that the other Asian customer and I were the focus, my first response was reflexive: a wan smile and a soft chuckle, to play along and not cause a fuss. Inside, however, I was very queasy. Looking down at our plates, we ate our eggs and toast, drank our coffee in silence, and got up to pay and leave.

The lead guy behind the counter saw me and again greeted me as "Mr. Miyagi" to say goodbye, again with an exaggerated pressed-hand bow. By then, I was truly uncomfortable and wondered why this was happening. One explanation is easy: It was the diner staff's shtick to entertain customers. It just so happened that the staff was Black, and the customers were mostly white. The other Asian guy and I were two non-white customers (there were a few Black customers) who made a convenient vehicle for "entertainment" spun by the line cook–comedian. It just goes to show that mass-media images are pervasive and powerful. The Mr. Miyagi character is out there in the mass-media ether, easily snatchable as a stereotype to attach to Asian men. I'm surprised that the diner guy didn't conjure up Bruce Lee.

The power dynamics of this incident possess me, years later. A Black man was making fun of Asian men to entertain white folks. Why didn't I speak up in the moment? My lame excuse is I was too shocked to respond with either anger or reason, and I didn't want to confront the situation, especially when the offender was a Black man, who himself had likely been the target of racism in his lifetime. In the long history of personal and institutional racism, my New Orleans story is a teeny pellet in the endless sandy beach of humanity. It isn't even close to Pop's story of being victimized by the Chinese exclusion law and having to tell lies to live in America, in de facto segregation, the yellow Jim Crow.

Pop's story and mine exemplify, I believe, the Good America. At the same time, our stories are drenched in an invisible goo of race. This sticky substance represents the stubborn resilience of the Bad America.

The Good America is this: A rural Chinese teenager with no English skills comes to America to find some fabled gold pebbles to help his poor family. That America, however, doesn't want his kind to come at all. Yet he comes anyway, settling in a Chinatown, segregated from the dominant white world. He learns some English, earns a little money to send home, goes home to marry and have three daughters, starts a little business, and eventually, through the same "crooked path" he took two decades earlier, brings his young family to settle in Oakland and has four more children. His only son is nurtured in the Chinatown bubble, largely eschewing the possible threats of the monstrous white world right outside the thin bubble walls. But the sheltered son then begins to feel the sensuous allure of the outside white world seeping through those walls and steps outside to explore the seemingly limitless horizon when it becomes more possible to do so, something denied his father, and eventually achieves a degree of success in his chosen profession, quite a journey upward from his lowly beginnings.

Such a Good American Story, right? This American Story has been told many times, involving dreamers from all over the world for more than two centuries. Many did indeed find gold, if not literally in the streets, then at least metaphorically, much more than what they would have found in the troubled lands they left. Patriots and politicians love this American Story because it affirms what many of us would like to believe is the Exceptional America, the Good America, the one place on Earth where anyone can come to escape evil, persecution, and poverty to have a chance to survive, endure, and thrive, free of the treachery of the homeland, and to create brighter futures for our children and grandchildren, regardless of color, creed, or credentials.

Pop managed to find his way, despite roadblocks everywhere. As bumpy as his life was, he (and Mom) laid a solid foundation for my sisters and me. And he left a stellar legacy—seven children, thirteen grandchildren, thirteen great grandchildren, one great-great grandchild, and counting—of good Americans of full or partial Chinese descent. I was fortunate to come along when conditions were beginning to ease for Chinese and others of Asian descent in America. As much as I detest the systemic racism against my kind and other marginalized people in America, I like the freedoms and opportunities I've had in the land of my birth. Sure, there were times of raw and ugly racism against me personally, but there have been other times of generosity, friendship, and love from those not of my tribe. That's America's strength, an ability, despite itself, to offer freedom, opportunity, and a multicultural community.

In sharp contrast, here is the Bad America: I wish that both of our lives weren't so racially soaked, Pop's more than mine. But race has been a central American issue since the beginning of nationhood, and even before that. Yes, America has made racial and cultural progress since slavery; the genocide of Native peoples; Chinese exclusion; Japanese American internment; and the mistreatment of Latinx, Arab, and Islamic people, to say nothing of a troubling persistence of anti-Semitism, yet race persists as a major divider. After what some of us thought was a big racial step forward with the presidential election of Barack Hussein Obama, we regressed emphatically when Donald J. Trump shockingly won the presidency. Trump's victory emboldened white supremacists to act out openly, encouraged by his egomaniacal persona and racist rhetoric, actions, and politics. Trump gave white supremacy the most powerful platform, the White House, it's had in a very long time. It's not coincidental that Trump-inspired white backlash and anti-immigrant sentiments have blossomed when America is becoming less white.

The coronavirus pandemic hit the world with full force in Trump's last full year as president. True to form, he used his famous brand of racism to whip up the latest round of American anti-Asian bigotry, calling the pandemic the "Chinese virus" and "kung flu." Anti-Chinese, anti-Asian incidents ranging from taunts to murder cropped up like bad weeds, most troublingly in Chinatowns like Oakland's. Attackers were white, Black, and others.

If we were to address this matter logically, not emotionally, we must ask why Americans of Asian descent were targeted for racist attacks, when the deadly virus started in a Chinese city named Wuhan. What did Chinese Americans and Asian Americans have to do with a virus outbreak in China? Ah, we're back to old stereotypes, aren't we? We're back to "We all look alike, don't we?" Chinese Americans and Asian Americans had absolutely nothing to do with the virus jumping from, what, a bat or possibly another animal to a human being in some Chinese "wet" market.

There is irony here too. Some of us Yellow Americans have believed that other Americans never noticed we were here, a phenomenon others and I have labeled "visibly invisible" or "invisibly visible," you choose. Then, smartphone videos of elderly Asian Americans getting pushed, shoved, kicked, and killed began to alert ignorant Americans that we Yellow Americans do exist, right here as your neighbor, doctor, grocer, colleague. The Atlanta mass murders—a young white guy killing eight people, six of them women of Asian descent[3]—finally put Asian America on the map, so to speak. That realization, however, offends me and others because we've been here for close to two centuries, our parents and grandparents and great grandparents helping build America to be the "exception" that it has become. We also know that anti-Chinese, anti-Asian racism didn't just surface in 2020. It's been around since the Gold Rush, and certainly within my lifetime.

What was heartening during the pandemic bigotry was that many Yellow Americans fought back, continuing a tradition of our elders using the courts and what little political power they had with sympathetic and opportunistic assistance from white attorneys and Black activists to try to ameliorate discriminatory conditions. My way of fighting back has been to denounce in writing for many decades America's anti-Chinese, anti-Asian history. Many Americans of Asian descent spoke out against the latest outbreak of racist hate, and old and new media gave a few of us spotlights we'd never had before, showing the world that we were not passive victims. This phenomenon enhanced the "representation" rainbow now adding yellow more frequently, when it was missing most of my life. Heretofore, whenever America's racial issues got center stage in the public discourse, the quick reference was to *Black and white*. In recent years, *brown*, *Hispanic*, and *Latino* have been added in deference to the growth of the Latinx population. Will *yellow* stay visible in the American rainbow once the liberal white elite turns its attention to hotter, sexier contretemps?

America's racial issues are but one of a number that are potentially cancerous to our still evolving multiracial, multicultural democracy, a far cry from what our founding fathers—most, if not all, well-off, property-owning white guys—envisioned. For much of my adult life, the Republican Party has leaned far right in alarming ways, with Trump's election being the most glaring symbol of its white supremacist core. On a host of public issues—immigration, taxation, gun regulation, voting rights, women's rights, gender rights, health care, public education—Republican leaders and most of their followers have become rigidly radicalized and deeply intolerant of open-minded reforms that would benefit all Americans, not just those who swallow Trump's toxic Kool-Aid. I worry that the civil rights advances of the 1960s, a time that saw some ugly violence, for sure, but that began to equalize opportunities and liberties for more Americans, are being eroded to the degree that the Good America is veering its way from a truly just and fair society back to an era when straight white Christian men ruled over us powerless non-white folks.

This shorthand summary doesn't do justice to the complexities and cloudiness of the reality of America's wildly kaleidoscopic color palette. Within my constellation of universes, Yellow America, the label *Asian Americans* is overly simplistic and doesn't "represent" a true portrait that is much more layered, nuanced, and confusing than is frequently presented in public discussions that demand pithy sound bites because of short attention spans, an unwillingness to expend energy to learn more deeply, lazy ignorance, and, well, racism and xenophobia.

It was much simpler in Pop's time and in my youth, when the main Asian groups in America were Chinese, Japanese, Filipinos, and Koreans. Our collective numbers were barely detectable, and our all-but-mandatory enclaves were much more circumscribed by systemically racist policies. Even though I continue to engage it, the *Asian American* label is inadequate to describe Yellow America today. There are now Asian people in America who trace our roots to many more than four east and southeast Asian countries. We Asian-rooted Americans have some things in common, such as some philosophical and religious belief systems (Confucianism, Buddhism, among others), aspirations for a better life, being targets of bigotry, and a pan-ethnic strength-in-numbers political strategy, but many more that we don't, such as unique root-country dynamics and disputes, immigration histories, American experiences, cultural practices, differing core belief systems, acculturation and assimilation timelines, and identity issues.

And I haven't even mentioned the *PI* part of the AAPI acronym that's often used, standing for Pacific Islanders. Other than being of the same species, however distant from a region of the world that touches the Pacific Ocean, there's not that much that mainland Chinese have in common with, say, Samoans. Given the many variables, I don't have a new label that covers this ungainly collection of people whose ancestral links span from the vastness of Asia to Turkey, edging up to Europe.

Our most recent population number remains a relatively small portion of the American people (about 7 percent versus less than 1 percent in 1970), but it continues to climb. We are now everywhere, doing everything, from the wealthiest to the poorest, from law-abiding to law-breaking, from fitting in well to ill fitting, from speaking English all the time to not speaking it at all, from fully assimilating to clinging to home-country ways, to prioritizing race-ethnic identities to working nonracially on such world problems as climate change.

I need also to make clear that while we of Chinese and other Asian descent have been—and, sadly, still are—victims of prejudice, bigotry, and xenophobia, we aren't especially saintly or in any way morally superior. Among us are those with our own versions of prejudice, bigotry, xenophobia, and the entire panoply of strengths and weaknesses of the human species.

Another overarching question is "How important in the hierarchy of identities are race and ethnicity, and how much do they govern human behavior and interactions? Is race-ethnicity more 'important' than identities of, say, gender, socioeconomic status, geography, religious beliefs, cultural practices, or age?" If anyone has a plausible answer, please speak up.

America is no longer a place where only straight white Christian men are all powerful and preeminent. Make no mistake: Many still are, but an increasing number of "others" are making their marks, too—yes, including some of us yellow people. America's challenge now and into the foreseeable future is to find ways to fit its many disparate identities into a more cohesive whole (i.e., a More Perfect Union). In the third decade of the twenty-first century, that challenge appears to be enormous, as a white backlash epitomized by the forty-fifth president's unceasing Big Lies is strong and stubbornly resistant to America's attempts to achieve a more glorious, inclusive, and dignified democracy.

I'm not wise enough to know what the magic formula is for America to be a better, more open-minded society in which more of us can earn a decent living, feel welcome and less alienated, be better neighbors, and show more respect and understanding for others who are not like us. America's ongoing conundrums are, in my opinion, insoluble at an individual level, so I'll turn inward, first to my clan, and then to me and my son, the only child whom Joyce and I brought into this imperfect world.

Maintaining ongoing connections to my Oakland-birthed Gee Wong clan has been a dedicated mission of mine, a very Confucian thing, regardless of political and personal differences among my clan mates. Clan members have an array of political biases and personality quirks, a condition hardly unique to us. For the most part, we submerge political and personality differences when we get together. Like some other families, we tend to avoid direct confrontations and touchy subjects or only engage the latter in smaller circles with those with whom we agree. Not that our clan is absolutely "unified." One unit has broken off for reasons unknown, and the younger generations are less connected to one another than my generation, perhaps a natural organic development of families, again, not unique to us. As assiduous as Pop and Mom were in trying to create harmony among us, family "unity" is a conceptual ideal, not always a reality.

As for Sam, Joyce and I knew that his mixed race-ethnicity would be a "thing." By no means were we alone in this realization either, but the number of white-Asian children in America in the early 1980s wasn't overwhelming. There are more now. According to the *New York Times* analysis of the 2020 census, approximately 2.43 million Americans identified themselves as mixed white and Asian. That figure is derived from the following: In the latest census, 13.5 million Americans identified themselves as non-Hispanic and more than one race, more than doubling the number who did so in the previous census. Of that total, about 18 percent identified themselves as both white and Asian.[4]

Fortunately for Joyce and me, our respective extended families welcomed Sam unquestioningly. He's become a man of depth, dignity, empathy, warmth, compassion, and intelligence, and a loving, dedicated father to boot, now with two children of his own, even more racially mixed than he is. His lovely wife, Michelle, a first-generation American daughter of Filipino immigrants, is bright, dignified, and family-loving.

The first time I went to China, in 1994, I decided not to take Sam. He was about to turn thirteen. One lame excuse was that I didn't want him to miss school. Another was less concrete: I didn't think that he'd be ready to visit his paternal grandfather's village. Why did I think that? Was I feeling ashamed of him being only half Chinese, a status that might subject him to scrutiny and possible ridicule in a society known for its single-race clannishness? Or was I protecting myself from possible questions of why I didn't marry a Chinese woman and bring into this world a Chinese son?

Twenty years later, for a second visit to Pop's village, I took another tack, but only after being urged by Joyce and Sam himself. Initially, I had planned to go by myself because my mission was research for this book. I didn't want to bother Sam, who had just married and had a job. Joyce, however, was concerned about my age (seventy-three), energy, and stamina for solo travel. She insisted that Sam accompany me. In his early thirties, Sam endorsed that plan. I gave in and was glad I did. He was my technology sidekick (visual and video documentarian) and my protector, as I was no longer as supple as I had been twenty years earlier. He was most needed when we trekked up to the village gravesites of distant Gee relatives. There was no clear pathway, just a slog up through bushes and broken branches that could easily make one lose balance. Sam said, "I've got your back." That was literally the case.

More significant was the effect that the trip had on the two of us, individually and together. In the almost two decades Sam lived with us before leaving for college, I didn't aggressively promote aspects of our shared Chineseness, whatever it was. Growing up, he certainly was aware of my writing about identity issues and Chinese America and Asian America, but whatever he learned about that aspect of my life, he did through osmosis, not through any assertive "teaching" on my part. That is, I wasn't a "Tiger Father" (other than pressing him to keep up his high-school grades to qualify for entry to the University of California campuses). He also knew that I was still emotionally attached through a metaphorical umbilical cord to Chinatown, where I took him for meals and shopping. Cooking my versions of Chinatown cuisine forged one thin link to my own childhood.

Was I a "bad" Chinese father for not foisting on him a pure Chinese identity? I think not, because doing so would have disrespected the part of him that was his mother's side and because I was forever wrestling with whether I was "Chinese" or "American," or both. Instead, Joyce and I raised him to be as good a human being as possible, regardless of any specific racial-ethnic identity.

During that 2014 trip, I was curious about his feelings as we traveled around his paternal grandfather's home region. At one of our hotels, I decided to delve into how Sam viewed his own identity and what we were experiencing. Prior to that, we rarely, if ever, had talked about his racial mixture or racial identity issues. We were with my side of the family more than Joyce's, but Sam knew that both parents were integral parts of their extended families and that he belonged with both sides. During his teen years, rather than being a bookish academic grind, he spent a lot of time after school with peers of different racial-ethnic and socioeconomic backgrounds, particularly at the aforementioned Destiny Arts Center. He was rarely, if ever, in situations of all-white or all-Asian peers. His blended racial self was comfortable in multiracial, multicultural, and multiclass settings.

Author with his son, Sam, in author's father's village in 2014.
(Author's Collection)

Those experiences were why I was curious about how he felt being in an all-Chinese environment where English wasn't spoken and American ways were foreign. In our conversation, Sam acknowledged that Chinese was part of his heritage, but, as a person who's half-ethnic Chinese and half white-European, the Chinese part wasn't "at the forefront" of his identity: "I don't feel, like, a crushing, oppressive need to know and honor the legacy because, honestly, the legacy that I honor starts with you two [Joyce and me]. That is where I begin." He appreciated seeing where his paternal grandfather came from and seeing me interact with villagers. He enjoyed hearing me converse in my limited *Hoisan-wa* with a man about my age who drove us around the village area. But he said that he didn't feel "connected" to modern China.

I told him that there had been times when I felt ashamed or embarrassed by my parents' Chineseness. He said that that's a common feeling among the generation that follows immigrants to America. "Living in the Bay Area and having experiences with different ethnic groups and people who have first-generation parents, whether they be Filipino,

Ethiopian, Mexican, and seeing the children of these immigrants and their [desire] to fit into an American lifestyle that is different from their parents yet is different from the white ideal; that allows people to come together. I guess you can call it an identity crisis—I think that is too harsh of a label for it—that can actually be a unifier. Are we really that different when our struggles are the same?" He also made the wise observation that my never-ending identity search was like a "time capsule," a period that's long gone.

After digging more deeply and widely into Pop's life, I felt inspired to reclaim my true surname, Gee, by legally adding it as my middle name in 2014. When Sam and Michelle had their first child, they didn't tell Joyce and me anything in advance, including what they would name him or her. After the birth of a boy, Sam said that his first child (and, subsequently, his second, a girl) wouldn't take his surname but, to honor Pop and me, be surnamed Gee, as American a name as Smith, Jones, . . . and Wong.

Surname of author and his father. (Author's Collection)

ACKNOWLEDGMENTS

There are many to thank for helping me research, write, edit, and produce this book. First and foremost were my sisters Li Hong, Li Keng, Lai Wah, Nellie, Leslie, and Flo. The oral tradition has been alive and well through our many decades together, and their memories have greatly enriched the portrait of Pop (and Mom). Some also read earlier versions of this book and gave me valuable feedback. The next generation of the Gee-Wong clan was most helpful as well in relaying their memories—Vickie Lew, Melvin Lew, Julie Shiraishi, Stanton K. Wong, Karen Weller, Allison Chop, Alexandra Lieu, Felicia J. Wong, and Bradley J. Wong.

Two scholars were most generous with their expertise, advice, translating skills, and overall guidance. Ling-Chi Wang, of the University of California at Berkeley's Ethnic Studies Department, offered the full gamut of support, from broad theoretical framework to logistical details of my 2014 trip to my father's China village. In addition to tutoring me on the intimate history of Pearl River Delta migrants like my father, Selia Tan, of Wuyi University in Jiangmen, Guangdong Province, China, accompanied me and my son to Pop's village and translated stories told by two villagers that revealed aspects of Pop's life I had never heard before and that filled important gaps in what my sisters and I knew. I consulted other scholars of Chinese America, Asian America, and American immigration history and am grateful for their insights. They included the late Judy Yung, Erika Lee, Madeline Hsu, Sucheng Chan, Wendy Rouse Jorae, and Marian Smith. Patricia Holt and Fred Setterberg were early advisers with knowledge of the publishing world who gave me useful guidance.

In addition to Wang and Tan, those who translated Chinese-language documents were first and foremost Genevieve Leung and Sheau-yueh Janey Chao. Others were Roland Hui, Linda Lei, Jane Tang, Genong Yu, Liu Dan, and Wen Yee Chin Wong.

Friends and colleagues read earlier versions of a whole manuscript or key portions. I called on Carolyn Jackson the most, and she was extraordinarily generous with her time and expertise. Others who volunteered to do me this great favor were Lori Collier Chan, Nancy McKay, Leslie Rodd, Felicia Lowe, Jon Halperin, Pat Fewer, John Fleming, Mary Ellen Butler, Bradley J. Wong, Craig Whitaker, Judy Yung, Erika Lee, Roland Hui, Vincent Chinn, Kathy Staudt, Calvin Wong, Hao Zou, Marthine Satris, and Kathy O'Toole.

I was fortunate to hear stories and memories from people who either grew up in a Chinatown (Oakland's in particular) or who've spent considerable time in a Chinatown-related community environment or Oakland itself. They included Roy Chan, Victor Chinn, Richard Gee, George Ong, Manley Wu, Lily Gee Lee, Janet Chan Lem, Darlene Joe Lee, David Lei, Walter Lim, John Wong, Donald Yee Ong, Willard Fong, Ted Dang, Jeanie Lew, Doug Joe, Christine deVillier, Sherlyn Chew, Betty Chew, Harry Lim, Henry Tom, Tan Shi Cheng, Ed Sue, Christopher Chow, Russell Lowe, Russell Yee, Lisa Yee, Christina Ng, Mary Soo Hoo, Willy Wong, Jeanette Lee Gong, Leon Lee, Grant Din, Dara Tom, Liam O'Donoghue, and Eddie Wong.

Various institutional representatives played crucial roles in my research. They were Steve Lavoie and Dorothy Lazard, of the Oakland History Room of the Oakland Public Library; Betty Marvin and Gail Lombardi, of the Oakland Planning Department's Cultural Heritage Survey; Marisa Louie, William Greene, Neil Thomsen, and Daniel Nealand, of the National Archives and Records Administration's San Bruno, California, regional office; Gina Bardi, of the San Francisco Maritime Historical National Park Research Center; and Lincoln Cushing, a

Kaiser Permanente archivist and historian. The Authors Guild provided helpful legal advice.

Temple University Press personnel have been invaluable in bringing this volume to life, starting with my principal editor, Shaun Vigil, along with Will Forrest, Ashley Petrucci, Faith Ryan, Gary Kramer, and Irene Imperio. Heather Wilcox, the principal copy editor, did a splendid job improving the flow of my words and thoughts while making sure that the manuscript met the highest stylistic, grammatical, and punctuation standards. Bruce Gore's cover design was spot-on.

My son, Sam, and daughter-in-law, Michelle, were lovingly supportive in so many ways, from reading early versions to helping me technologically with a website, marketing, and outreach. Then, there was my dearly beloved Joyce, who pushed and prodded me to continue working on this book even when I no longer felt enthusiastic or focused. She's been my greatest cheerleader for more years than I can count. A very special thanks to my sister-in-law Karen Fridkis, Joyce's younger sister, who came to California from New Jersey to help me care for a terminally ill Joyce during her final months in early 2023. Karen's help gave me precious time to finish preparatory steps before this book went into full production.

GLOSSARY OF CHINESE NAMES

Gee Seow Hong 朱兆亨	*Author's father's immigration name*
Gee Ghee Gheng 朱箕鏡	*Author's father's inside-Chinatown name*
Gee Bing Fong 朱炳芳	*Author's father's paper father's name*
Gee Theo Quee 朱小桂	*Author's mother's immigration name*
Gee Suey Ting 朱瑞清	*Author's mother's real name*
William Gee Wong 朱華強	*Author's Chinese name*
The Great China 大中華	*Author's family's restaurant*
Jow Toon Goon Du Hahng 鄒村君子坑	*Author's father's China village name*
Long An Cun 龍安村	*New name of author's father's China village*
Hoisan/Toisan/Taishan 台山	*Guangdong Province county of author's father's village*
Guangzhou 廣州	*Capital of Guangdong Province, formerly called Canton*

Guangdong 廣東 — *Southeastern Chinese province, of which Guangzhou is the capital*

Pearl River Delta 珠三角 — *Southeastern Chinese region including Guangdong Province*

Zhu Xi 朱熹 — *Song dynasty Confucian scholar related to author*

NOTES

CHAPTER 1

1. I had previously visited Hong Kong three times when it was a British Crown Colony and thus technically not part of China until it reverted to Chinese rule in 1997.

2. The oldest sister, Li Hong, wasn't with us because she lived with disabilities that made it difficult for her to travel.

3. *Hoisan-wa* transliteration.

4. Decades later, Felicia J. Wong became president and chief executive officer of the Roosevelt Institute, a progressive think tank.

CHAPTER 2

1. *Zupu* or *Jiapu* in Mandarin, *jokpu* in Cantonese.

2. The author's spelling of *Hoisan-wa* transliteration. Jow Toon was a township that had several villages, Goon Du Hahng being one of them. Pop's village has since been renamed Long An Cun.

3. *Hoisan-wa* transliteration. Chu in Cantonese, Zhu in Mandarin.

4. A generic term meaning "wife." The absence of a woman's given name is another demonstration of Chinese patriarchy.

5. Author interview with Li Keng Wong.

6. By Genevieve Leung.

7. Thomas W. Chinn, H. Mark Lai, and Philip P. Choy, *A History of the Chinese in California: A Syllabus* (San Francisco: Chinese Historical Society of America, 1969), 2, 4.

8. In addition to Hoisan (Toisan, Taishan), they are Hoiping, Sunwui, Yanping, Namhoi, Punyu, Shuntak, and Chungshan (all Cantonese renderings).

9. Peter Kwong and Dusanka Miscevic, *Chinese America: The Untold Story of America's Oldest New Community* (New York: New Press, 2005), 19–20.

10. Madeline Y. Hsu, *Dreaming of Gold, Dreaming of Home: Transnationalism and Migration Between the United States and South China, 1882–1943* (Stanford, CA: Stanford University Press, 2000), 25–31.

11. Erika Lee, *At America's Gates: Chinese Immigration during the Exclusion Era, 1882–1943* (Chapel Hill: University of North Carolina Press, 2003), 120–121.

CHAPTER 3

1. With the help of the San Bruno, California, office of the National Archives and Records Administration, the author saw a copy of the SS *Manchuria*'s California-arriving passenger list that included Pop's name, Gee Seow Hong.

2. The SS *Manchuria*'s itinerary, according to the U.S. Customs Service and Immigration Service passenger list on ancestry.com, as searched by William Greene, an archivist at the San Bruno, California, office of the National Archives and Records Administration, August 25, 2015.

3. Stuart Creighton Miller, *The Unwelcome Immigrant: The American Image of the Chinese, 1785–1882* (Berkeley: University of California Press, 1969), 36.

4. Erika Lee, *At America's Gates: Chinese Immigration during the Exclusion Era, 1882–1943* (Chapel Hill: University of North Carolina Press, 2003), 24.

5. Him Mark Lai, *Becoming Chinese America: A History of Communities and Institutions* (Walnut Creek, CA: AltaMira Press, 2004), 20.

6. Martin B. Gold, *Forbidden Citizens: Chinese Exclusion and the U.S. Congress: A Legislative History* (Alexandria, VA: TheCapitol.Net, 2012), 338–339.

7. Ibid., 348.

8. Ibid., 362.

9. Lucy E. Salyer, "Laws Harsh as Tigers: Enforcement of the Chinese Exclusion Laws, 1891–1924," in *Entry Denied: Exclusion and the Chinese Community in America, 1882–1943*, ed. Sucheng Chan (Philadelphia: Temple University Press, 1991), 58.

10. Emma Woo Louie, *Chinese American Names: Traditions and Transition* (Jefferson, NC: McFarland, 1998), 114.

11. Madeline Y. Hsu, *Dreaming of Gold, Dreaming of Home: Transnationalism and Migration Between the United States and South China, 1882–1943* (Stanford, CA: Stanford University Press, 2000), 68.

12. Lee, *At America's Gates*, 213–215.

13. Gold, *Forbidden Citizens*, 305.

14. Erika Lee and Judy Yung, *Angel Island: Immigrant Gateway to America* (New York: Oxford University Press, 2010), 9–10.

15. Ibid., 57.

16. Robert Eric Barde, *Immigration at the Golden Gate: Passenger Ships, Exclusion, and Angel Island* (Westport, CT: Praeger, 2008), 13.

17. See http://www.libertyellisfoundation.org/ellis-island-history.

18. Barde, *Immigration at the Golden Gate*, 4–5.

19. Lee, *At America's Gates*, 75.

20. Lee and Yung, *Angel Island*, 57.

21. Immigration file of Gee Seow Hong, National Archives and Records Administration, San Bruno, California.

22. Immigration file of Gee Bing Fong, National Archives and Records Administration, San Bruno, California.

CHAPTER 4

1. *Uk Loon* in his *Hoisan-wa* dialect.
2. Sang Fat Chong was no longer in business by the time the author was a child.
3. The author obtained or saw photos of Pop in Lincoln School class photos of 1912, 1913, 1915, and 1918, collected by Janet Chan Lem, co-author with Darlene Joe Lee of *Memories of Growing Up in Oakland, California, Lincoln School Alumni* (self-published, 2011).
4. Ibid., 182–193.
5. Wendy Rouse Jorae, *The Children of Chinatown: Growing Up Chinese American in San Francisco, 1850–1920* (Chapel Hill: University of North Carolina Press, 2009), 137.
6. Telephone directories in the Oakland History Room, Oakland Public Library, Main Branch, Oakland, California.
7. From a review of Insurance Maps of Oakland, California, Volume Two, Sanborn Map Company, Broadway, New York, NY, 1903, at the Oakland History Room, Oakland Public Library, Main Branch, Oakland, California.
8. L. Eve Armentrout Ma, *Hometown Chinatown: The History of Oakland's Chinese Community* (New York: Garland Publishing, 2000), 74.
9. Lee and Lem, *Memories of Growing Up in Oakland*, 488.
10. Ibid., 446.
11. The author and his family called it *Mahng Sahng Waw* in Hoisan-wa.
12. *Waku* is a version of the Cantonese transliteration for "overseas Chinese," also rendered as *Wah Kue*.
13. Author interview with Arthur Tom.
14. Ma, *Hometown Chinatown*, 76.
15. *Moo* is a Cantonese honorific categorizing a woman as married or older.
16. Fong Get Moo's story came from the author's interviews with one of her sons, Clifton Fong, and from research in the 1970s by an Oakland Chinatown History Committee led by the late Frank Mar.
17. His surname was Joe (Zhou in Mandarin), but his American surname became Shoong, his given name, likely another example of how white immigration clerks used the Western standard of assuming that a person's second name was the family or surname.
18. Oakland's Chinatown has a building with the Kuomintang name on it that also displays the Republic of China (Taiwan) flag.
19. Mandarin pinyin transliteration. In Cantonese, it's *Quock Mun Dong*; in Hoisan-wa, it's *Quock Min Ong*.
20. Sunwui, Hoisan (Toisan, Taishan), Hoiping, Enping, contiguous counties west of Macao, Hong Kong, and the Pearl River Delta, *A History of the Chinese in California: A Syllabus*, Thomas W. Chinn, editor; H. Mark Lai, Philip P. Choy, associate editors, Chinese Historical Society of America, San Francisco, CA, 1969, p. 4. Informally called *Thlee yip* in Hoisan-wa and *say yup* in Cantonese, with *thlee* and *say* meaning "four."
21. Namhoi, Funyu, Shuntak counties close to Guangzhou (Canton) northeast of the Four Counties. Ibid., 2. Informally called *Thlom yip* in Hoisan-wa and *saam yup* in Cantonese, with *thlom* and *saam* meaning "three."
22. *Oakland Tribune*, March 13, 1912.

23. Elena B. Wong Viscovich, "The Story of the Ming Quong Homes," *Pacific Clinics*, https://upliftfs.org/who-we-are/history/the-story-of-the-ming-quong-homes/.
24. Author interview with Dorothy Eng.
25. From a review of Insurance Maps of Oakland, California, Volume Two, Sanborn Map Company, Broadway, New York, NY, 1903, at the Oakland History Room of the Oakland Public Library, Oakland, California.
26. Beth Bagwell, *Oakland: The Story of a City* (Oakland, CA: Oakland Heritage Alliance, 1982), 183–184.

CHAPTER 5

1. Hsiao-tung Fei, *China's Gentry: Essays on Rural-Urban Relations*, rev. and ed. Margaret Park Redfield (Chicago: Phoenix Books, 1953; first Phoenix ed., 1968), 32.
2. Immigration file of Gee Seow Hong at the National Archives and Records Administration regional office, San Bruno, California.
3. The Cantonese rendering. In *Hoisan-wa*, it's *Yee Thluey Ting*.
4. This background information was from U.S. Department of Justice/Immigration and Naturalization Service/Report of Investigation/Administrative Page, Yee Suey Ting aka Gee Theo Quee, Suey Ting Gee, Mrs. Sheng Wong, March 16, 1965, the government's so-called confession program.
5. *Hoisan-wa* transliteration.

CHAPTER 6

1. Li Keng Wong, *Good Fortune: My Journey to Gold Mountain* (Atlanta: Peachtree Publishers, 2006), 21–22.
2. Author interview with Lai Wah Chop Webster.
3. Obtained by the author from the National Archives and Administration regional office, San Bruno, California.
4. Wong, *Good Fortune*, 55–56.
5. Heading for Testimony, U.S. Department of Labor, Immigration Service, at a meeting of a Board of Special Inquiry held at Angel Island, California, November 28, 1933, p. 34, obtained by the author at the National Archives and Records Administration regional office, San Bruno, California.

CHAPTER 7

1. Author interview with Li Keng Wong.
2. Ibid.
3. Roland Hui, *Chinaman Tycoon: The Life and Times of Lew Hing (1858–1934)* (self-published, 2022), 232.
4. *Oakland Tribune*, September 13, 1908, "Daily Knave" column, quoting an unnamed San Francisco newspaper.
5. Gregory Y. Mark, "Gambling in Oakland Chinatown: A Case of Constructive Crime," in *Frontiers of Asian American Studies: Writing, Research, and Commentary*, ed. Gail M. Nomura, Russell Endo, Stephen H. Sumida, and Russell C. Leong (Pullman: Washington State University Press, 1989), 14–26.
6. Ibid.

7. Hui, *Chinaman Tycoon*, 231.
8. Mark, "Gambling in Oakland Chinatown," 18.
9. Author interview in 2011 with Manley Wu, who died a year later.
10. Author interview with Victor Chinn.
11. Author interview with Calvin Wong.
12. Author interview with Li Keng Wong.
13. "'COLLECTIONS' IN CHINATOWN GAMBLING TOLD," *Oakland Tribune*, May 1, 1919; "O'Neill Arrested; Nedderman Refuses to Quit; 'We Can't Sign Treaty,' Declares Rantzan," *Oakland Tribune*, May 15, 1919; "CAPTAIN BROWN DEMAND FOR PAY ALLEGED," *Oakland Tribune*, July 3, 1919.
14. "Lottery King Greets Friends at Feast," *Oakland Tribune*, December 18, 1901.
15. Earl Warren, *The Memoirs of Chief Justice Earl Warren* (Garden City, NY: Doubleday, 1977), 66–67.
16. "Application of the Federal Gambling Stamp Tax Law," *DePaul Law Review* 8, no. 2 (Spring–Summer 1959), 362.
17. "Strange Disappearance of Chin Bock Hing," *Oakland Tribune*, August 2, 1953; "Chin Bock Hing Found Living in Hong Kong," *Oakland Tribune*, November 4, 1954.
18. The Cantonese word *tong* literally means "hall," "large room," "club," or "organization."
19. *Boo how doy* in Hoisan-wa.
20. Jonathan D. Spence, *The Search for Modern China* (New York: Norton, 1990), 168–169.
21. Author interviews with Li Keng Wong and Nellie Wong.

CHAPTER 8

1. Flo Oy Wong, "West: Ai Joong Wah, Oakland, California," in *Sweet and Sour: Life in Chinese Family Restaurants*, ed. John Jang (Yin and Yang Press, 2010), 152.
2. *Guy dieu* in Hoisan-wa.

CHAPTER 9

1. This account is based on the sworn testimony of the author's father in the case of the *People of the State of California vs. Show Lee Gee*, Case #A_6057, the Police Court of the City of Oakland, County of Alameda, State of California, August 7, 1940, with some imagined scene setting by the author.
2. *The People of the State of California vs. Show Lee Gee*, the Police Court of the City of Oakland, County of Alameda, State of California, No. A_6057, August 7, 1940.
3. Ibid.
4. Flo Oy Wong interview with Lee Ming, mid-1980s.
5. Author interview with Lai Wah Chop Webster.
6. *The People of the State of California vs. Show Lee Gee*.

CHAPTER 10

1. Author interview with Li Keng Wong.
2. Author interview with Richard Gee.
3. Author interview with Betty Chew.

4. Author interview with Victor Chinn.

5. "Shooting Stirs Tong War Fear/Police Act to Prevent Vengeance After Chinese Wounds Kin," *Oakland Tribune*, April 25, 1940. The names were misspelled: Su Hung Gee should have been Seow Hong Gee, Pop's immigration name. Shon Lee Gee should have been Show Lee Gee, his immigration name.

6. "CHINESE SHOT BY BROTHER IN ROW," *Oakland Post Enquirer*, April 25, 1940.

7. "Attempted Killing of Oakland Chinese," *Chinese World*, April 25, 1940, translated by Ling-Chi Wang.

8. *Chinese World*, April 26, 1940, translated by Ling-Chi Wang.

9. The author heard elsewhere that the partnership was of six men.

10. *Hoisan-wa* transliteration.

11. Author interview with Li Keng Wong.

12. Author interview with Lai Wah Chop Webster.

13. Immigration and Naturalization Service Report of Investigation of Gee Hong Yin, aka Gee Chun Wing, for "Document Fraud," January 26, 1960.

14. Sworn statement of Gee Hong Yin to Immigration and Naturalization Service in New York, New York, January 26, 1960.

15. In truth, 1939.

16. *The People of the State of California vs. Show Lee Gee.*

17. "Shooting Stirs Tong War Fear/Police Act to Prevent Vengeance After Chinese Wounds Kin," *Oakland Tribune*, April 25, 1940.

18. Li Keng and Lai Wah weren't home at the time of the shooting.

19. Family oral history session in Oakland, May 28, 1977. Leslie died in 1985 at the age of forty-nine.

20. *The People of the State of California vs. Show Lee Gee.*

21. Alameda County's documentary file on microfilm of Pop's shooting case is missing a transcript of the trial itself but includes testimonies during the arraignment and preliminary hearing of the attempted murder charges.

22. Also known as Gee Seow Lee and Gee Bing Fook.

23. Affidavit of Gee Din Gai, also known as Gee Show Quon, "paper" brother of Pop and his shooter, Show Lee Gee, May 14, 1964.

24. *The People of the State of California vs. Show Lee Gee.*

25. Hand-written entry in an address book belonging to Pop. Author's collection.

26. He asked the author not to use his name.

27. $25 a month from Li Hong, $17 a month from Li Keng.

CHAPTER 11

1. *Hoisan-wa* rendering.

CHAPTER 12

1. *Goong* is an honorific for an elder man.
2. Author interview with Li Keng Wong.
3. *Aye Joong Wah* in *Hoisan-wa*.
4. A distortion of the *Hoisan-wa* phrase *Dop Thluey*, which, legend has it, Chinese

cooks in the Gold Rush days called cut-up bits of vegetables and perhaps meat they cooked for hungry non-Chinese miners.

5. Such combination restaurants are now a rare breed, if at all, in both Chinatowns.
6. Dollartimes.com.

CHAPTER 13

1. Author interview with Li Keng Wong.
2. Author interview with Lai Wah Chop Webster.
3. Author interview with Vickie Lew.
4. Li Keng and Lai Wah attended Oakland Technical High School. Oakland High honored Nellie with a new building named after her for her politically active poetry and community service.

CHAPTER 14

1. Cantonese transliteration, meaning "Overseas Chinese school."
2. Roy Terrell, "The Bandits of Baton Rouge," *Sports Illustrated*, November 17, 1958.
3. Michael Tiger went on to become a distinguished defense and human-rights attorney, with faculty appointments to Duke Law School, University of Texas School of Law, and American University's Washington College of Law.
4. Cal established a Graduate School of Journalism in 1967, five years after the author graduated.

CHAPTER 15

1. Chiang Monlin, *Tides from the West: A Chinese Autobiography* (New Haven, CT: Yale University Press, 1947), 8–9, 12.
2. Stephen R. Platt, *Imperial Twilight: The Opium War and the End of China's Last Golden Age* (New York: Knopf, 2018), 53.
3. *Chu Shi* in Cantonese and *Gee Hee* in Hoisan-wa.
4. See https://plato.stanford.edu/entries/zhu-xi/.
5. By Sheau-yueh Janey Chao, professor, Head of Cataloging, William & Anita Newman Library, Baruch College, City University of New York, whose expertise is Chinese genealogy.
6. Translated by Roland Hui.
7. *Hoisan-wa* rendering.

CHAPTER 16

1. Author interview with Flo Oy Wong.
2. Author interview with Lai Wah Chop Webster.
3. Ibid.
4. Cantonese rendering.
5. Author interview with Nellie Wong.

CHAPTER 18

1. The Peace Corps began service in China in 1993.
2. Tagalog, the principal Filipino dialect, originates in the northern island of Luzon, where Manila is.

CHAPTER 22

1. This was long before Rupert Murdoch bought the newspaper and its parent company, Dow Jones.
2. Far left and far right, respectively, on the front page.
3. *Qins*, pronounced "Chin."
4. Unpublished research by Christopher Chow and Suzanne Joe Kai.

CHAPTER 23

1. *Hoisan-wa* rendering.

CHAPTER 26

1. Gayle B. Montgomery and James W. Johnson, *One Step from the White House: The Rise and Fall of Senator William F. Knowland* (Berkeley: University of California Press, 1998), 283–288.
2. Wallace Turner, "Plans to Sell the Oakland Tribune Cause Split in Knowland Family," *New York Times*, December 7, 1976, https://www.nytimes.com/1976/12/07/archives/plans-to-sell-the-oakland-tribune-cause-split-in-knowland-family.html.
3. "Hong Kong Success Story Leads to Fraud Trial," UPI, February 24, 1986.
4. The other major chunk came from reader subscriptions and newsstand sales. This was before newspapers published on the Internet.

CHAPTER 27

1. sfgate.com, February 13, 2012, February 15, 2012, February 17, 2012, February 21, 2012, February 26, 2012.
2. The author didn't read any reader comments on his Linsanity series, for he had learned by then not to.
3. Jason Horowitz, "Girding for a Fight, McConnell Enlists His Wife," *New York Times*, May 13, 2014.
4. Tanya Snyder, "Chao Resigns from Transportation Department, Citing 'Traumatic,' 'Avoidable' Capitol Riot," Politico.com, January 7, 2021.
5. Meredith McGraw, "The Private Angst over Donald Trump's Racist Attacks on Elaine Chao Goes Public," Politico.com, January 25, 2023.
6. Horowitz, "Girding for a Fight."

CHAPTER 28

1. The author was at the convention on behalf of *Asian Week*. I also wrote convention columns for the *Oakland Tribune*, even though it had nothing to do with me being there.

2. The *Oakland Tribune* was one of several East Bay area newspapers owned by MediaNews Group, and, as such, the editorial-page editor oversaw the contents of editorials and opinion columns in all those papers, not just the *Tribune*.

3. The author was the only person "downsized" that day.

4. *San Francisco Examiner*, March 31, 1996.

5. A few years later, Jerry Brown became Oakland's mayor, after which he went on to his second go-round as California's governor.

6. Felicity Barringer, "Boston Globe Columnist Resigns over Authenticity of 1995 Story," *New York Times*, August 20, 1998.

7. Alison Bass, "Does Mike Barnicle Deserve a Second Chance as a MSNBC Contributor?" Medium, May 31, 2022, https://medium.com/@alisonbbass/does-mike-barnicle-deserve-a-second-chance-as-a-msnbc-contributor-38c9e988b10a.

8. "Two of Bank of America's Post-Crisis Leaders Will Retire," *New York Times*, August 27, 2021.

9. Ibid.

10. Aishvarya Kavi, "The Full Guest List for the State Dinner," nytimes.com, December 1, 2022.

EPILOGUE

1. Guangzhou is the capital of Guangdong Province, where the author's father's village is.

2. Kevin Kwan, *Crazy Rich Asians* (New York: Anchor Books, 2013), 106.

3. March 16, 2021.

4. Sabrina Tavernise, Tariro Mzezewa, and Giulia Heyward, "Behind the Surprising Jump in Multiracial Americans, Several Theories," *New York Times*, August 13, 2021.

INDEX

Aaron, Henry, 103, 242
Aarons, Roy, 220, 224
ABC-TV, 207, 219
affirmative action, 215
African Americans. *See* Black Americans
Alameda: city in California, 34, 40, 60, 91; county in California, 40, 56, 62, 63, 84–85, 110, 213
Angel Island, 25–26; Immigration Station, 20, 24, 25–26, 48, 50–53, 80, 229
Annie E. Casey Foundation, 247
Anspacher, Carolyn, 146
anti-Asian hate and racism, 201, 262–263, 265, 266
anti-Chinese hate and racism, 21, 201
Armstrong, Louis, 34
Asian America, 184, 214, 225, 237, 248, 260, 270
Asian American Journalists Association, 207–210
Asian American movement, 185, 198, 256
Asian Americans, 120, 129, 155, 185, 198, 204, 205, 209, 211, 225, 226, 228, 231, 234, 237, 239, 244, 246, 258, 262–263, 265, 266–267
Asians in Mass Media (AMM), 205–208
Asian Week, 209, 228, 229, 232, 235, 247

Attles, Al, 201
author. *See* Wong, William Gee

Bad America, 8, 263–265
Bailey, Chauncey, 243–244
Balch, James, 112, 116
"banana," 230, 255
Barnes, Dick and Bonnie, 183
Barnicle, Mike, 247–248
BART. *See* Bay Area Rapid Transit
Basie, Count, 34
Bay Area Rapid Transit (BART), 213
Becoming American: The Chinese Experience (documentary), 237
Berger, Mike, 126
Bergman, Ron, 125–126, 212
Black Americans, 33–34, 36, 60, 121, 146, 148, 155, 171, 185, 195, 202, 208–209, 210, 211, 213, 215, 216, 219, 220, 224, 226, 228, 241, 244, 248, 255, 262–263, 265, 266
Black Panther Party, 185, 195
Bloch, Julia Chang, 234
Bloch, Stuart, 234
Boxer, Barbara, 232
Briscoe, David, 171
Brown, Jerry, 200, 245
Brown, Willie, 231

Burgin, C. David, 241–243, 245
Bush, George H. W., 225, 233
Bush, George W., 231, 232, 234
Butler, Mary Ellen Rose, 216, 241–242

C-100. *See* Committee of 100
Caen, Herb, 206
Cal. *See* University of California, Berkeley
California Gold Rush, 17, 21, 56, 64, 265
Cameron, Donaldina, 39
Canton. *See* China
Cantonese, 3, 11, 25, 31, 37, 38, 54, 56, 65, 95–97, 99, 108, 117, 119, 122, 126, 132, 136, 173, 180, 218, 220, 255, 257, 260, 261
Carter, Jimmy, 225
Castain, Curtis, 148
Castro, Fidel, 145
Celeri, Bob, 102
Chan, Wilma, 230
Chang, Julia, 234
Chao, Elaine, 232–234
Chavez, Cesar, 199
Chel Goong (Gee Chew), 96, 98, 101
Chen, Serena, 229
Chew, Betty, 78
Chew, Effie Bailey, 32
Chiang Kai-shek. *See* China
Chickencoop Chinaman (play), 202
Chin Bok Hing (Chan Bock Hing), 64
Chin, Diane Lee, 33–34
Chin, Frank, 118, 121, 123, 202
Chin, Morris D., 34
China: Aye Leng in, 42; Beijing in, 1, 17, 188, 256, 261; Chiang Kai-shek in, 37; Chinese Communist Party in, 37, 55, 150, 154, 212, 253–254, 258, 259; Chinese Nationalist Party (Kuomintang) in, 37–38, 55, 212; Confucianism in, 55, 115, 119, 131–136, 142, 259, 267, 268; Confucius in, 132, 142, 259; Cultural Revolution in, 196, 253; Deng Xiaoping in, 256; Enping in, 38; Four Counties in, 38; Goon Du Hahng in, 3, 11, 15, 42–43, 48, 80–81; Guangdong Province in, 17, 44, 64, 65; Guangzhou (Canton) in, 1, 16–17, 38, 50, 256; Hainan in, 257; Hangzhou in, 256–257; Heaven and Earth Society in, 65; Hoiping in, 38; Hoisan (Taishan, Toisan) in, 4, 17, 19, 35, 42, 64, 70, 80–81, 99, 117, 119, 234, 256; Hoisan City (Taicheng) in, 18; Hong Kong in, 16–20, 38, 43, 45, 46, 50, 64, 176, 179, 180, 218, 220, 250, 256, 257, 258, 262; Japanese invasion of, 37, 55; Mao Zedong in, 17, 37, 126; May 4 movement in, 37; middle-class of, 4; Nanjing in, 257; Opium War in, 16, 254; Pearl River Delta in, 17, 29, 37–38, 50, 55, 260; during Pop's (author's father) childhood, 16; Qing dynasty of, 17, 37; Republic of, 37; Shandong Province in, 234; Shanghai in, 1, 17, 20, 50, 256; Sun Yat-sen in, 37; Sunwui in, 38; Taiwan versus, 38; Three Counties in, 38; Tibetans in, 258; Uighurs in, 258; Wuhan in, 265; Wuyi University in, 44; Xi'an in, 256–257; Yangtze River in, 256. *See also* Zhu Xi
Chinatown, Manhattan, 184–185
Chinatown, Oakland: after 1906 San Francisco earthquake, growth of, 30; bigotry, incidents of, 265; Bowen Liquor Store in, 33, 76; Broadway in, 29, 35, 36–37, 70; Buddhist temple in, 39; businesses in, 33–34; Chinese American Citizens Alliance (CACA) in, 35; Chinese Independent Baptist Church in, 113–114; Chinese Nationalist Party (Kuomintang) in, 37–38; Chinese Six Companies (Chinese Consolidated Benevolent Association) in, 23, 64–65; Chinese Young Women's Society in, 39; conflicts, jealousies, and resentments in, 82–84; Dorothy Eng in, 39; Episcopal church in, 38; Fong Get Moo (Lon Yoke Wong) in, 35–36; Franklin Street in, 35, 71, 82; gambling in, 33, 56, 61–65, 85; Gee Nom in, 62–63; Great China Restaurant in, 93–106, 129, 140, 142, 143, 193, 195; Hamburger Gus in, 33; Hamburger Joe in, 33; Harrison Railroad Park in, 70; Harrison Street in, 35, 69, 73, 76, 77, 82, 83, 88; immigrants v. American-born in, 118; Latin Quarters in, 34; Lew Hing in, 37; Lincoln School in, 30–32, 35, 90, 117; Lincoln Square in, 70, 118, 120; lottery

in, 33–34, 55–63, 64, 71–73, 75, 82–83, 85; Man Sing Wo in, 34; meditation on, 254–255; Methodist church in, 38; Ming Quong Home for Girls in, 39; Ng Poon Chew in, 32; Oakland Chinese Community Center in, 37; organizations in, 37, 64; Pekin Exchange in, 33; police corruption and raids in, 60–64; Posey Tube in, 34; post–World War II decline in, 195; Presbyterian church in, 38; Protestant churches in, 38–39, 118; revival of, in 1970s, 195–196; Sherman Hotel in, 33; Joe Shoong in, 37; shooting of Pop (author's father) in, 75–86; Simon Hardware in, 196; tongs in, 64–65, 69, 72, 75, 78–80, 83, 85, 141, 144, 201; Waku Auxiliary in, 34; Wa Sung baseball team in, 34; Webster Street in, 29, 34, 35, 54, 68, 69, 70, 71, 76, 77, 85, 93, 119; Wing On Teng in, 76; Wong Family Association in, 34; Young Chinese Athletic Club in, 34; Yuen Hop in, 76
Chinatown, San Francisco. *See* San Francisco Chinatown
Chinese America, 17, 201, 210, 214, 225, 237, 248, 270
Chinese Americans, 37, 56, 88–90, 120, 121, 122, 124, 125, 129, 130, 146, 149, 152, 155, 196, 198, 202–203, 205, 209, 220, 225, 228, 229, 230, 234, 237–239, 240–241, 244, 246, 258–261, 264, 265, 267; population of, in 1940s, 184–185
Chinese Communist Party. *See* China
Chinese Confession Program, 81, 150
Chinese Consolidated Benevolent Association. *See* Chinatown, Oakland
Chinese Exclusion Act, 7–8, 11, 17, 19, 20–23, 25, 27, 56, 88–89, 125, 184–185, 252, 253, 260–261, 263, 264
Chinese for Affirmative Action, 197–198, 201, 204
Chinese Nationalist Party (Kuomintang). *See* China
Chinese New Year, 10, 57, 119
Chinese Six Companies. *See* Chinatown, Oakland
Chinese World, 80
Ching, Frank, 188

Chinglish, 117, 150, 194
Chinn, Victor, 59–60, 78
Chinn, Yung-Chu, 59
Chop, Alexandra, 112
Chop, Allen, 111–112, 114
Chop, Allison, 108–109, 112, 237
Chop, Lai Wah. *See* Lai Wah
Chow, Christopher, 210
Chung, Connie, 210
CIA (Central Intelligence Agency), 157
Cleveland, Ohio, 186–188, 190, 191, 199, 202, 245, 249
Cleveland Cavaliers, 190
Clinton, Bill, 201, 231
coaching books (or papers), 19, 24–25, 48, 50
Cold War, 127, 130, 154, 157
Columbia Journalism Review, 245
Columbia University Graduate School of Journalism, 182–186
Committee of 100 (C-100), 234, 237–238
Confucianism. *See* China
Confucius. *See* China
Contra Costa County, California, 56, 213
Contra Costa Times, 246
Crazy Rich Asians (Kwan), 261
Cronin, A. J., 101

Daily Californian, 125–130, 144–145, 146, 152–153, 212, 216
Davis, Sammy, Jr., 34
Democratic National Committee, 231
Democratic National Convention (1968), 178
Der, Henry, 198
Dinkins, David, 209
Dodd, Christopher J., 248

East West Center, University of Hawaii, 250
East/West Chinese American Journal, 196–197, 228, 229
Eckstein, Billie, 34
Eisenhower, Dwight D., 153
Ellington, Duke, 34
Elliott Bay Book Co., 246
Ellis Island Immigration Station, 26
Emeryville, California, 58, 102
Enter the Dragon (film), 205

Fairbanks, Charles, 22
Fasi, Frank, 201
Feinstein, Dianne, 232
Fewer, Patricia, 175–181
Filipino Americans, 30–31, 33, 37, 56, 154, 185, 203, 205, 267, 269, 271
Fimrite, Ron, 146
Finucane, Anne, 248
Fitzgerald, Ella, 34
Florence (author's sister, also Flo Oy Wong), 3, 5, 66, 68–69, 74, 82, 94, 104, 108, 109, 113–114, 124, 133, 138–141, 143–144, 151
Fonda, Jane, 127
Fong-Torres, Ben, 65
Ford Foundation, 183
Formosa. *See* Taiwan
Four Counties. *See* China
Freedom Socialist Party, 112
free speech movement, 195
Fridkis, Larry, 236
Friendly, Fred W., 184

gambling. *See* Chinatown, Oakland
Gannett Corporation, 213–214, 223–224
Gartner, Michael, 186
Gee Bing Chew, 12
Gee Bing Fong, 27–28, 47–48, 51–53, 80
Gee Bing Fook (also Gee Seow Lee, Seow [Show] Lee Gee), 72–77, 81–84
Gee Cheng Woon, 12, 28
Gee Fook Ying, 44
Gee genealogy book, 11, 133
Gee Ghee Gheng. *See* Pop (author's father)
Gee Lai Wah. *See* Lai Wah
Gee Li Hong. *See* Li Hong
Gee Li Keng. *See* Li Keng
Gee Seow Hong. *See* Pop (author's father)
Gee Seow Lee. *See* Gee Bing Fook
Gee Suey Ting. *See* Mom (author's mother)
Gee Theo Quee. *See* Mom (author's mother)
Gee-Wong clan, 6, 9, 67, 98, 160, 268–269
Gee Yee Lo, 12
Gee Yuey Yung (also How Chooey Goong, Goong, Kim Gee), 97, 107–108, 193–194

German, Bill, 146, 148
Gibson-Haskell, Marge, 245
Golden Dragon Restaurant, 201
Golden State Warriors, 201
Gold Mountain (*Ghim Saan*), 15, 17, 70
Gold Mountain Guests (*Ghim Saan Haak*), 41, 44, 48
Good America, 8, 263–264, 266
Good Fortune: My Journey to Gold Mountain (Li Keng), 111
Goon Du Hahng. *See* China
Gould, William, IV, 200–201
Graham, Katherine, 178
Great China Restaurant. *See* Chinatown, Oakland; Mom (author's mother); Pop (author's father); Wong, William Gee
Grimm, Roy, 215, 216, 218, 219, 220, 222
Groseclose, Everett, 188, 191
Guangdong Province. *See* China
Guangzhou. *See* China

Hang Ah, 108
Hawaii, 20, 50, 155, 157–160, 161, 162, 165, 201
Hayden, Tom, 127
Hicks, Nancy, 203, 212, 214, 215, 218, 226, 240
Hinckle, Warren, 146
Hines, Earl, 34
Hoisan. *See* China
Hoisan-wa, 3, 7, 11, 15, 31, 38, 41, 51, 54, 65, 66, 74, 76, 88, 97, 117, 122, 132, 140, 154, 253, 255, 260, 271
Hokosawa, Bill, 188
Holmstrom, John, 161, 167–168
Hong Kong. *See* China
"honorary whites," 211, 230, 255
House Un-American Activities Committee (HUAC), 130
How the West Was Won (tv series): "China Girl" episode, 207
Hurd, Blanche, 121
Hyatt, Jim, 188

Images of America: Angel Island (Fanning and Wong), 247
Images of America: Oakland's Chinatown (Wong), 247
immigration policy, U.S., 8, 21–22

Independent Californian, 128
Indianapolis, 236
Institute for Journalism Education, 219
Iwata, Ed, 229

Jack London Square, 59, 241
Jackson, Joseph B., 77, 81
Jackson Café, 95
Japan, 55, 88, 160, 250, 257
Japanese Americans, 30, 33, 34, 37, 56, 88–90, 185, 203, 205, 264, 267
Jensen, Jackie, 102
Joe, Kenneth, 196
Johnson, Lyndon B., 171, 177
Johnson, Stephen, 122–123
Jow, Dennis, 113
Jow, Leslie. *See* Leslie
Joy Luck Club, 111
Judeo-Christian Western culture, 156

Kaiser, Henry J., 91–92, 104
Kaiser Permanente, 250
Kaiser shipyards, 91, 104
Kansas City Athletics, 103
Karate Kid (film), 262
Katzenbach, Larry, 171
Katzenbach, Nicholas deBelleville, 171
Kennedy, John F., 144–145, 152–153, 156
Kennedy, Robert F., 177
Kennedy, Ted, 248
keno, 56
Kent State University, 185
Kerner Commission (National Advisory Commission on Civil Disorders), 215
Kerry, John, 248
The Keys of the Kingdom (Cronin), 101
King, Martin Luther, Jr., 177
Kissinger, Henry, 234
Knowland, Joseph R., 212
Knowland, William F., 212–213
Korean Americans, 30, 185, 203, 205, 208–209, 267
Kuomintang (Chinese Nationalist Party). *See* China
Kwan, Kevin, 261
Kwan, Michelle, 234

Laine, Frankie, 34
Lai Wah (author's sister, also Gee Lai Wah, Lai Wah Chop, Lai Chop Webster), 5, 15, 48, 50, 52–54, 70, 82, 94, 99, 100, 102, 108, 109, 111–112, 114, 138–140, 179, 237
Lake Merritt, 34, 40, 105, 108, 196
Lal, Gobind Behari, 188
Larson, Louise Leung, 188
Last Hoisan Poets, 114
Lawson, Herb, 199, 202
Lee, Bruce, 205, 263
Lee, Charles, 34–35
Lee, Chol Soo, 188
Lee, Edwar (Lee Park Lim), 51
Lee, Kyung Won, 188
Lenton, Steven, 180
Leslie (author's sister, also Leslie Wong, Leslie Yee, Leslie Jow), 68–69, 74, 77, 83, 94, 109, 112–113, 115
Lew, Gordon, 196–197
Lew, Henry, 94, 104, 109
Lew Hing. *See* Chinatown, Oakland
Lew, Julie, 109
Lew, Li Hong. *See* Li Hong
Lew, Melvin, 109
Lew, Vickie, 109, 110
Li Hong (author's sister, also Gee Li Hong, Li Hong Lew), 5, 15, 42, 50, 52–54, 69, 74, 78, 86, 92, 94, 100, 104, 106, 109–111, 138
Li Keng (author's sister, also Gee Li Keng, Li Keng Wong), 2–5, 14–16, 43, 48, 50, 52–53, 54, 58–60, 69, 78, 80, 82, 86, 88, 93–94, 103–104, 105, 107, 109–111, 112, 113, 115, 133, 137, 138–139
Lim, Genny, 114
Lin, Jeremy, 230
Lin, Maya, 234
Lincoln School. *See* Oakland
Lincoln Square. *See* Oakland
Linsanity, 230
Lladoc, Jessie, 155
Lladoc, Letitia Morse. *See* Morse, Letitia
Lo Wong Bock, 101
Lock, Maeley. *See* Tom, Maeley
Locke, Gary, 234
Lodge, Henry Cabot, 22
Los Angeles, 226
Los Angeles Times, 207

lottery. *See* Chinatown, Oakland
lotto, 56
Lowe, Felicia, 210
Lum, Calvin, 118

Ma, Yo-Yo, 234
Macron, Emmanuel, 248
Madden, John, 201
Mandarin, 119, 219, 257, 260, 261
Manila. *See* Philippines, Republic of
Mao Zedong. *See* China
Mar, Patricia, 152
Marcos, Ferdinand, 68–69
Marcos, Imelda, 68–69
Marysville, California, 58, 65, 72–73, 79, 82, 252
Matsui, Robert, 231–232
Maynard, Nancy Hicks. *See* Hicks, Nancy
Maynard, Robert C., 203, 212–216, 218–224, 229, 240–242
McConnell, Mitch, 232–234
MediaNews Group, 241, 246
Mellinkoff, Abe, 146, 148
Mencher, Melvin, 184
Mende, Christine, 178
Mende, Herman, 178, 193
Mende, Joyce Ann: education of, at Katharine Gibbs School, 173; Gee-Wong clan, relationship with, 179; Mom (author's mother), relationship with, 179; New Jersey family and work of, 173, 175, 177–178, 180; in Peace Corps, 172–175; William Gee Wong, pre-marriage relationship with, 172–179. *See also* Wong, Joyce Mende
Mende, Karen, 178
Mende, Karl, 178, 180
Mende, Margaret, 178, 193
Meyer, Agnes Elizabeth Ernst, 178, 182
Meyer, Eugene, 178
Michelle (author's son's wife), 269, 272
Miller, Stuart Creighton, 21
Mills College, 39
Mineta, Norman, 231–232
Ming Quong Home for Girls. *See* Chinatown, Oakland
Miss Chinatown Pageant, 146–147
model minority, 33
Mom (author's mother, also Gee Suey Ting, Gee Theo Quee, Yee Suey Ting):
death of, 191, 194; early years of, in China, 42–43, 47, 50; family life of, 30, 66–70, 73–77, 82–84, 86; at Great China Restaurant, 93–106, 142; immigration of, 47–48, 50–53, 66–67; in Oakland's Chinatown, 54, 66–70, 73–77, 82–84, 86, 93–106; Pop (author's father), relationship with, 42–43, 48, 50, 56, 66–70, 73–77, 82–84, 86, 87–88, 107, 137–143; Joyce Mende Wong, relationship with, 192–194; William Gee Wong, relationship with, 88, 96, 148, 150, 153, 175, 179–180, 191
Morita, Pat, 262
Morse, Letitia, 155
Mott, Frank R., 40
Moyers, Bill, 237–239
Mr. Miyagi, 262–263

Nash, Phil Tajitsu, 229
National Archives and Records Administration, 229
National Association of Black Journalists, 210
National Association of Hispanic Journalists, 210
National Basketball Association (NBA), 230
National Committee for the Support of Public Schools, 178, 182
National Labor Relations Board, 200–201
Native American Journalists Association, 210
Nedderman, John F., 61
Nellie (author's sister, also Nellie Wong), 68, 74, 77, 82, 94, 109, 112, 113, 114, 116, 133, 141, 151, 179, 192
Newark International Airport, 236
New Jersey, 172–173, 175, 178, 186, 193, 235, 250
New Orleans, 262–263
NewsHour with Jim Lehrer, 240–241, 247
Newsweek, 170–171, 186
New York Times, 170, 188, 203, 219, 269
New York Yankees, 103
Northern Illinois University, 155

Oakland: Association of Bay Area Governments in, 213; Breuner's in, 105; Broadway in, 29, 35, 36–37, 70; Capwell Sullivan and Furth in, 40; China

INDEX 295

Hill in, 106, 148; Chinese and Japanese immigrants in, 30, 32–33, 88–90; City Hall in, 40; Destiny Arts Center in, 251, 270; *East Bay Today* in, 214, 216, 217, 224; First and Last Chance Saloon in, 59; Fox Oakland Theater in, 70; Harrison Railroad Park in, 70; Hotel Oakland in, 40; Housewives' Market in, 35, 98; I. Magnin store in, 113; Joseph Magnin store in, 113; Kasper's Hot Dogs in, 70; Laney College in, 213; Lincoln School in, 30–32, 35, 42, 90, 117–120, 231; Lincoln Square in, 70, 118, 120; MacArthur Freeway (Interstate 580) in, 213; Ming Quong Home for Girls in, 39; Nimitz Freeway (Interstate 880) in, 213; Oakland High School in, 112, 119–124, 139, 158; Oakland Oaks in, 102–103, 118; *Oakland Post* in, 244; *Oakland Post Enquirer* in, 78–79, 82; Oakland Public Library in, 250; Oakland Technical High School in, 42, 120; Paramount Theater in, 70; Peralta School in, 111; police corruption and raids in, 60–64; population in, in 1950s, 120; Posey Tube in, 34; post–World War II decline of, 195; Red Train in, 29, 34–35, 69; Roxie Theater in, 70; Swan's Market in, 35, 98; T&D Theater in, 70; Tooker Memorial House in, 39; Trans Pacific Centre in, 218; Washington Market in, 35, 106; white middle-class families, departure from, 195. *See also* Bay Area Rapid Transit; Chinatown, Oakland; Golden State Warriors; Jack London Square; Kaiser Permanente; Lake Merritt; Mills College; Oakland Athletics; Oakland Museum of California; Oakland Raiders; *Oakland Tribune*
Oakland Athletics, 125, 201
Oakland Museum of California, 213
Oakland Raiders, 115–116, 201
Oakland Tribune, 2, 62, 63, 78, 82, 95, 101, 103, 210, 212–227, 229, 231–233, 240–246, 248, 249
Obama, Barack Hussein, 264
OCA (Organization of Chinese Americans), 232, 234
O'Donnell, Larry, 202–203

Olszewski, Johnny, 102
Opium War. *See* China

Pacific Mail Steamship Company, 18, 20
Page Act of 1875, 21
paper daughters, 24, 47
paper sons, 20, 23–25, 27, 44
patriarchy, 1, 11, 48, 87–88, 90, 100, 115, 116, 135, 138
Payton, Brenda, 241–242
Peace Corps, 4, 153–175, 178, 180, 182, 186, 195, 214, 232–233, 237, 250, 253, 256
Pearl Harbor, 88, 89, 90, 256
Pearl River Delta. *See* China
Pearlstine, Norman, 245
Pei, I. M., 234
Perata, Don, 245
Petersen, Walter J., 61
Philippines, Republic of: Americans (including Peace Corps Volunteers), relationships with, 160–169; Benigno "Ninoy" Aquino Jr. in, 168–169; brief history of, 160; Cagayan de Oro in, 161; Cebuano dialect in, 156, 161, 162; Chinese, relationships with, 164–165; culture, as similar to Chinatown's, 156, 163; Davao in, 161; diaspora of, 160; hospitable culture of, 165; Iligan City in, 160–163, 165–166, 168–170; Leyte in, 155; Malacañang Palace in, 168; Manila in, 155, 162, 165–170, 173, 176; Marawi City in, 161; Mindanao in, 155, 160; Ormoc City in, 155; politics of, 167–169; San Miguel beer in, 162, 165, 174; Subic Bay in, 169; Sulu peninsula in, 161; Taboy's in, 174; Tarlac in, 169; Visayas in, 155; Zamboanga in, 161. *See also* Marcos, Ferdinand; Marcos, Imelda
Pi Alpha Phi, 130
Pletschet, Clifford, 217
Pop (author's father, also Gee Ghee Gheng, Gee Seow Hong, Seow Hong Gee): China, feelings about, 253–254; China, return trips to, 42–48, 50, 252; Confucian beliefs of, 115, 119, 131–136, 142; death of, 143–144; early years of, in China, 11–16, 252, 258; family life (including marriages) of, 14–15,

Pop *(continued)*
42, 47, 99–100, 105–109, 137–142; Great China Restaurant, relationship with, 93–106, 143; immigration (including Angel Island detention) of, 10, 17–20, 27–28, 51, 253, 264; legacy of, 264; lottery business of, 55–59, 71–72, 81–83, 85, 87; Mom (author's mother), relationship with, 14–15, 42–43, 47–48, 50, 51, 53–55, 57–58, 66–70, 73–77, 82–88, 93–94, 96–108, 115, 137–143; in Oakland's Chinatown (including Lincoln School), 29–31, 34–42, 49, 54–55, 93–106, 252; other work (including at a shipyard) of, 34, 68, 71, 87–88, 90–94; tong, relationship with, 65, 69, 72, 73, 74, 75, 83, 141, 144; as victim or target of shooting, 75–85, 87; William Gee Wong, cultural journeys associated with, 6–8, 120–124, 129–130, 131–134, 136, 144, 252–253, 263–264
Press, Harry, 14
Proposition 13, in California, 200
Pulitzer Prize, 220

Qing dynasty. *See* China
Quan, Jean, 230

Republican Party, 266
Richmond, California, 91, 104
Riordan, Richard, 226
Roberti, David, 231
Roosevelt, Franklin D., 89
Ruth, Babe, 242

Sam (author's son), 14, 44, 250, 268–272
San Francisco Chinatown, 7, 38, 56, 58, 79, 95, 108, 144, 147, 162, 196–198, 201, 207, 209
San Francisco Chronicle, 126, 145–147, 148, 149, 154, 206, 207–208, 230, 245–246
San Francisco earthquake (1906), 23, 30, 35
San Francisco Examiner, 188, 197, 224, 241, 245–246
San Francisco 49ers, 115
San Francisco News Call Bulletin, 148–151
San Francisco Seals, 103
San Francisco State University, 249
San Jose Mercury News, 246
San Jose State University, 249

San Leandro, California, 148
San Leandro Morning News, 147–148
Scarborough, Joe, 247
Seattle, 246
Seattle Post-Intelligencer, 246
Seattle Times, 246
Seow (Show) Lee Gee. *See* Gee Bing Fook
sfgate.com, 230
Shanksville, Pennsylvania, 236
Silicon Valley, 112, 261
Simpson, Janice, 202
Sing, Bill, 207
Singapore, 250, 256, 257
Singleton, William Dean, 241
Spindler, Paul, 148
Springer, Richard, 196–197
Stanford University, 114, 125, 145, 147, 161, 188, 200, 207
Stengel, Casey, 103
Stokes, George, 120–121
Sun Yat-sen. *See* China
Sunnyvale, California, 112, 114

Taishan. *See* China
Taiwan, 212, 232, 250, 256, 257, 260, 262. *See also* China
Tan, Amy, 111
Tan, George, 218
Tan, Selia, 44–45
Tang, Henry S., 235–237
Taylor, Frederick, 202
Teamsters Union, 199–200
This Week with David Brinkley, 219
Three Counties. *See* China
Tigar, Michael, 127
TIME, 170–171, 186
Time Inc., 245
Toisan. *See* China
Tom, Arthur, 35
Tom, Maeley, 231
tongs. *See* Chinatown, Oakland
Tramutola, Larry, 246
Trump, Donald J., 232, 233, 264–265, 266, 268
Tsai, Mark, 180
Turner, George, 22

United Airlines, 236
United Farm Workers, 199–200
United Nations Conference on Racism, 235

UNITY: Journalists of Color, 210
University of California, Berkeley, 93, 97, 102–104, 110, 113, 114, 124–130, 138–139, 144–145, 161, 180, 197, 249, 258
University of Southern California (USC), 126
USA Today, 214, 224
U.S.-China relations, 202, 234, 257, 259
U.S. News & World Report, 186

Vietnam War, 151, 153, 156, 169, 177, 184, 185, 195, 201–202, 248, 256
Voltaire (author's host in the Philippines), 161–162, 164, 167–168, 170

Wagner, Eileen, 180
Waldorf, Lynn "Pappy," 102
Waller, Fats, 34
Wall Street Journal, 186–191, 196–204, 207, 212, 214–217, 219, 229, 245, 249
Wang, Ling-chi, 197–198, 204
Wang, Wayne, 204
Warren, Earl, 62–63
Washington Post, 170, 178, 182, 202, 203, 219, 221
Watergate scandal, 178
Webster, Daniel, 112
Webster, Lai Chop. *See* Lai Wah
Weiss, Alexander, 26
white racism against Chinese, 21
white supremacy, 22, 115, 121, 174, 185, 234, 238, 264–266, 268
Winter, Ralph, 188
Wong, Bradley, 3, 6, 113
Wong, Calvin, 60
Wong, Edward K., 3, 6, 104, 113–114, 115–116, 143–144
Wong, Felicia, 5, 6, 113
Wong, Florence. *See* Florence
Wong, Joyce Mende: death of, 251; education of, at Cleveland State University, 249; education of, at Hunter College, 249; education of, at San Francisco State University, 249; education of, at San Jose State University, 249; education of, at University of California, Berkeley, 249; Gee-Wong clan, relationship with, 10, 195, 251; martial arts training of, 252; Mom (author's mother), relationship with, 193–194; New Jersey family of, 173, 178–180; parenting by, 250–251; William Gee Wong, post-marriage relationship with, 10, 181, 186, 190, 202, 220, 249–251, 268–272. *See also* Mende, Joyce Ann
Wong, Karen, 110
Wong, Ken, 196–197
Wong, Kirby, 110
Wong, Leslie. *See* Leslie
Wong, Li Keng. *See* Li Keng
Wong, Nellie. *See* Nellie
Wong, Roger, 2, 5, 110–111
Wong Sheng, 67
Wong, William Gee (author): Asian American issues, writing about, 197–198, 201–202, 204, 208–209, 223–235, 246–248; assimilation of, 117, 119–120, 122, 124, 129, 144, 151, 153–154, 190, 255–256; birth and early years of, 88–90, 92, 94, 100; China, feelings about, 258–259; China trips by, 1–7, 14, 44, 256–257, 269–272; Gee-Wong family life of, 1–9, 30, 35, 42–44, 47, 87–90, 94–104, 105–116, 131–136, 137–144, 151, 179–180, 191–195; identity, search for, 2, 6–8, 7–9, 10–14, 44–45, 119–122, 124, 130, 131–136, 147, 150–156, 158–159, 164–165, 175, 182, 184–185, 192, 197, 201–202, 237–239, 254, 256, 258–262, 268–272; Joyce Ann Mende, relationship with, 10, 172–181, 186, 190–191, 193–195, 202, 220, 236–237, 249–251, 268–272; in Oakland Chinatown, 2, 36, 65, 70, 87–90, 94–119, 195–196, 252–255, 260; in the Peace Corps, 4, 153–175, 186, 233; Pop (author's father), cultural journeys associated with, 6–8, 120–124, 129–130, 131–134, 136, 144, 252–253, 263–264. *See also* Wong, William Gee, education of; Wong, William Gee, journalism career of
Wong, William Gee, education of: Chinese lessons of, 119, 131–136; at Columbia University Graduate School of Journalism, 182–186; cultural-political-racial lessons of, 20–21, 117–119, 120–124, 127–130, 145–150, 153–156, 162–165, 167–169, 184–185, 191, 195–201, 237–239, 259–272; at Lincoln School, 117–119; at Oakland High School, 119–124; at University of California, Berkeley, 124–130, 234

Wong, William Gee, journalism career of: activism of, 204–211; at *Ang Boluntaryo* (Peace Corps/Philippines), 170–171; at the *Daily Californian*, 125–130, 144–145; freelance work (including *NewsHour with Jim Lehrer, East/West Chinese American Journal*, and *Asian Week*) of, 197, 208, 228–229, 230, 232, 235, 240–241; at Oakland High School, 120–121; at the *Oakland Tribune*, 2, 212–227, 240–245; at the *San Francisco Chronicle*, 145–147, 246; at the *San Francisco Examiner*, 246; at the *San Francisco News Call Bulletin*, 148–151; at the *San Leandro Morning News*, 147–148; at the *Wall Street Journal*, 186–191, 196–203
Woo, Henry B., 84–85
Woo, Michael, 226
Woo, William F., 188
Workingmen's Party, 21

World Trade Center, 236
World War II, 17, 59, 61, 88, 89, 94, 97, 105, 127, 184, 185, 188, 195, 213, 252–254, 261
Wu, Manley, 59

Yang, Jerry, 234
Yee, Dana, 113
Yee, Donald, 112–113
Yee, Erin, 113
Yee, Leslie. *See* Leslie
Yee, Noel, 113
Yee Suey Ting. *See* Mom (author's mother)
Yellow Journalist: Dispatches from Asian America (Wong), 237, 246–247
Yoshimura, Wendy, 205
Young, Shirley, 235

Zhu Xi, 132–136, 137, 142, 259

Writer and journalist **WILLIAM GEE WONG** has been a regional commentator for *The News Hour with Jim Lehrer*, a reporter for the *Wall Street Journal*, and a columnist for the *Oakland Tribune, San Francisco Chronicle, San Francisco Examiner,* and *Asian Week*, among other publications. He is the author of *Yellow Journalist: Dispatches from Asian America* (Temple). Visit him online at williamgeewong.com.